Transportation Service to Small Rural Communities
EFFECTS OF DEREGULATION

Transportation Service to Small Rural Communities

EFFECTS OF DEREGULATION

John F. Due
University of Illinois

Benjamin J. Allen
Iowa State University

Mary R. Kihl
Iowa State University

Michael R. Crum
Iowa State University

IOWA STATE UNIVERSITY PRESS / AMES

John F. Due is professor of economics, emeritus, at the University of Illinois, Champaign-Urbana.

Benjamin J. Allen is distinguished professor of business administration at Iowa State University, Ames, and is director of the Midwest Transportation Center.

Mary R. Kihl is professor of community and regional planning and associate director of the Design Research Institute at Iowa State University, Ames.

Michael R. Crum is associate professor of transportation and logistics at Iowa State University, Ames.

© 1990 Iowa State University Press, Ames, Iowa 50010

Manufactured in the United States of America

♾ This book is printed on acid-free paper.

First edition, 1990

Library of Congress Cataloging-in-Publication Data

Transportation service to small rural communities: effects of deregulation / John F. Due. . . [et al.]. – 1st ed.
    p.   cm.
    Bibliography: p.
    ISBN 0–8138–0315–2
    1. Rural transit – United States – Deregulation. 2. Rural transit – Government policy – United States. I. Due, John Fitzgerald.
HE316.U6T73   1990
388.3′0973′091734 – dc20   89–11151
                                         CIP

Contents

Preface

The purpose of this study is to provide a comprehensive examination of the transportation service to small rural communities in this period of changing transportation policies. Although the impacts of changes with respect to governmental policies are examined, the focus of the study is on the impacts on transportation service resulting from changes in the economic regulatory environment. To the degree possible the derivative impacts of the changes in the transportation service on rural communities themselves are examined and analyzed. Unlike previous studies that have focused on the effects of deregulation of a single mode, this study examines the impacts of regulatory reform in the airline, trucking, bus, and rail industries. (Throughout the book the terms "regulatory reform" and "deregulation" will be used more or less interchangeably.)

Most of the book is devoted to examining by mode the nature of these recent changes in regulatory policies, the nature of service provided to small rural communities, the impacts of deregulation on transportation service to these communities, and possible intermodal strategies to minimize the impact of deregulation. Chapters 2 to 5 attempt to examine these issues for the railroad, trucking, intercity bus, and airline industries. These chapters rely heavily upon previous studies in their presentation of the impacts of deregulation. Sufficient time has elapsed since the regulatory reform started — more than ten years for the rail and air industries and almost six years for the intercity bus industry — to allow more than transitory effects to be found. Chapter 6, departing from the rest by removing the modal straitjacket, develops global, intermodal policies and strategies for maintaining adequate transportation service for both passengers and freight to small rural communities in the era of deregulation. Both substitution strategies (e.g., trucking for rail) and complementary strategies (e.g., bus to air) for both freight and passenger transportation are presented. Additionally, potential linkages between freight and passenger transport service will be identified.

The study is the result of the joint effort of the four authors who conveyed their individual perspectives on deregulation vis-à-vis a specific mode and then merged their efforts in considering the impacts on intermodal transportation in nonmetropolitan areas. Chapter 2 on rail service was the work of John Due, professor emeritus of economics, University of Illinois, while Chapter 3 on the trucking industry was contributed by Benjamin Allen, distinguished professor of business administration, Iowa State University. Passenger transportation modes are discussed in Chapter 4 on intercity bus service by Mary Kihl, professor of community and regional planning and in Chapter 5 on air service by Michael Crum, associate professor of transportation and logistics. Chapters 1 and 6 reflect the work of all four authors and are the product of lively discussions held among them over the cause of writing the book. Benjamin Allen synthesized these ideas and committed them to writing.

The authors wish to thank all who helped make this work possible, especially graduate students and secretaries who provided yeoman service. They are greatly indebted to the Interstate Commerce Commission as well as to the U.S. Department of Transportation and the state departments of transportation for data and the other current information. They also wish to acknowledge financial support from the Department of Transportation and Logistics at Iowa State University and the Iowa State University Research Foundation. No such project would have been possible without the constant support and encouragement of their respective families.

Transportation Service to Small Rural Communities

EFFECTS OF DEREGULATION

Introduction

Changing National Transportation Policy and Rural Community Viability

During the brief period between 1976 and 1982, Congress substantially changed the economic regulatory environment for railroads, trucking firms, intercity bus operators, and airlines. The Railroad Revitalization and Regulatory Reform Act of 1976 (4-R Act),[1] though its impact was somewhat limited because of its content and its restrictive implementation by the Interstate Commerce Commission (ICC), was the inaugural regulatory reform legislation in the transportation area. Congress soon followed with more dramatic legislative changes in regulatory policy for the airline industry, the air freight sector in 1977,[2] and the passenger sector in 1978.[3] In 1980 Congress extended regulatory reform to the trucking industry[4] and made rail regulatory reform more substantive and less dependent upon ICC interpretation.[5] Congress eventually addressed regulatory reform for the intercity bus industry in 1982.[6]

A common concern that accompanied regulatory reform for all of these modes was the fear that rural communities would lose their transportation service, receive less service, or receive the same service at a higher cost. The perceived adverse impact of deregulation on the availability and cost of transportation service in rural areas generated questions about the relationship between deregulation and the viability of rural communities. The premises of this concern were that common carrier transportation is important to the viability of small towns in rural areas, that transportation to rural communities is inherently unprofitable or less profitable, and that regulation was the mechanism that forced or induced the carriers from redeploying their equipment and efforts to the more lucrative markets. The common carrier service obli-

3

gation that required the carriers to serve unprofitable markets and the entry and rate controls that limited competition on the more lucrative routes were argued to coerce and induce respectively the carriers to cross-subsidize their unprofitable or less profitable markets with excess profits earned on the more lucrative, protected routes.

The Nature of the Rural Transportation Problem

The contention that transportation to small towns in rural areas is inherently unprofitable or less profitable is based on the greater cost of providing transport service to such places. In general, both freight and passenger carriers exhibit economies of utilization (or economies of density in the transportation vernacular); that is, the cost per ton-mile or per passenger-mile for a given movement decreases as the volume of freight or passengers increases. The size of a community as measured by population and economic output (e.g., manufactured or agricultural products) thus affects transportation costs. Population influences not only passenger volume potential but also inbound freight transportation needs of a community. The level and nature of the economic output of a community affect the inbound (i.e., material input) as well as the outbound freight transportation needs, and also exert an influence on the community's demand for passenger transportation service (e.g., business travel). Additionally, smaller communities often suffer from imbalanced freight traffic flows, which create greater costs for the carriers. It should be noted that small is a relative measure — what is small to one mode may be relatively large to another as each mode has a different cost structure and cost behavior.

If small towns in general have transportation problems, small towns in rural areas are even more disadvantaged. The location of a small community with respect to distance from a large city or a major transportation artery (which links large cities) also affects its transportation cost and quality of service. Carriers often have an economic incentive to provide service to small communities located a short distance from their "normal" routes. The increase in traffic generated by the small communities permits economies of utilization on the carriers' longer hauls, which offset the cost of traveling the extra distance to the small communities. Many rural communities are located too far from the major transportation corridors to attract such service. They are served as origin or destination points rather than pickup or drop-off points, and thus incur greater transportation costs and less frequent service.

The federal Department of Transportation (DOT) in 1980 issued a study that provided several definitions relevant to the topic at hand. It defined a "rural area" as "any area outside of an urbanized area where the urbanized area boundaries have been designated by the Bureau of the Census."[7] It should be noted that some rural areas exist within the boundaries of the Standard Metropolitan Statistical Areas. A "rural place" was defined as any incorporated or unincorporated "place (as defined by the Bureau of the Census) located in a rural area." A large rural place has a population of 25,000 or more while a small rural place contains a population less than 5,000. A medium rural place falls in between these two categories. The study further defined small rural communities as those closely settled rural population centers that are not incorporated and that normally are not reported separately in census statistical populations. These communities usually have populations less than 1,000.[8]

Though these definitions are useful for census data reporting purposes, they have not been widely used in the research on deregulation's effects on rural transportation service. More often than not, previous research failed to distinguish between "small nonrural" and "small rural" communities. When such distinctions were made, the definitions of small and rural varied from study to study. Regardless of the definitions utilized, small communities and isolated communities are more likely to encounter transportation service problems than larger population centers. Federal transportation policymakers have long recognized the potential for such problems and have endeavored to prevent or alleviate them.

The Politics of Rural Community Transportation

National transportation policy in both the regulatory and promotional areas has long been argued to have favored rural areas. The restrictive regulations on rail abandonment and the congressional sanctioning of value-of-service ratemaking, which tended to lower rates on agricultural products, are examples of this policy or orientation in the regulatory area. Promotional policies, that is, federal investment and user charge policies, in the waterway and Interstate Highway System areas appear to have favored the rural and agricultural interests.[9]

Not surprisingly, certain members of Congress from rural areas and the trucking and airline industries, industries in which the overwhelming majority of firms opposed regulatory reform, used this long-standing political support of rural areas and the fear of what might happen to rural communities to oppose regulatory reform legislation. The claim that deregulation would do great harm to rural communities has been characterized as the most effective argument that the airline and trucking industries used in their battle against deregulation.[10] The federal DOT and other supporters of regulatory reform were forced to try to refute these claims by demonstrating through research that the common carrier obligation to protect unprofitable service had not been seriously enforced in either the airline or trucking industry. Other studies were conducted that demonstrated that rural community service was sufficiently profitable that adequate service would be provided in an unregulated environment. In the case of trucking deregulation, the DOT offered to survey shippers in any two communities in states of senators sitting on the Commerce, Science, and Transportation Committee, the lead committee in the Senate for transportation regulatory reform.

The congressional concern about the potential adverse impact of regulatory reform on transportation service to rural communities is reflected in the regulatory reform legislation. For example, the Airline Deregulation Act of 1978 established for the first time an explicit mandate that scheduled service for small communities in isolated areas be maintained, with federal assistance if appropriate. Furthermore, the act established a ten-year transition subsidy program to help small, isolated communities adjust to the new deregulated environment.

Two years later Congress established a similar policy statement for motor carriers of freight, again creating an explicit congressional mandate that trucking service should be provided and maintained to small communities. This new policy statement was later applied to the intercity bus industry in the Bus Regulatory Reform Act of 1982. Section 28 of the Motor Carrier Act of 1980 mandated that the ICC conduct a study to evaluate the effects of regulatory reform on trucking service to small communities. Section 14 of the act established the Motor Carrier Ratemaking Study Commission, which was given the charge to study, inter alia, the impact of the elimination of the antitrust immunity for collective ratemaking upon rural areas. Two years later in the Bus Regulatory Reform Act Congress required a similar study from the same commission but for the intercity bus industry.

Though less explicit, congressional concern about the impact of regulatory reform of the rail industry on rural communities is revealed, particularly in the 4-R Act. For example, the section 803 branch line subsidy program clearly revealed congressional concern, especially in the transition period, of the possible negative impact on rural communities of the increased abandonment activity that was predicted to result from changes to rail abandonment regulation.

This study indicates that these concerns may have been overstated. The experience of the last ten years has shown the impacts of deregulation on small communities to have been mixed. In fact, deregulation has not in itself caused major detriments to the viability of small communities. While it is true that bus and rail regulations have produced an exodus of carriers from rural communities, the legislative changes only accelerated trends that had been set in motion by the changing economic and social patterns at work in the country for at least the last twenty-five years. In fact, the loss of rail service cannot be shown to precipitate economic decline in small communities.

An overwhelming majority of the rural communities surveyed reported either neutral or positive effects as a result of trucking deregulation. Although not receiving the level of benefits experienced by their urban counterparts, rural shippers surveyed have not suffered from any major losses of service. Evidence does exist, however, that shipping costs in the least accessible areas are higher. The same can be said for air fares. Although airline deregulation has led to an aggregate increase in the quality and level of service to small communities, many of the smaller points have experienced substantial declines in passenger enplanements and cannot support nonsubsidized air service. This factor, much like continued declines in bus ridership, will in turn lead to further service reduction in a deregulated environment.

Good transportation is important to small communities, but government regulated transportation cannot assure even good transportation, let alone the economic vitality or the social viability of small towns. The search for an answer to the continued viability of small communities must encompass a much wider array of social and economic issues.

Notes

1. Public Law No. 94–210, The Railroad Revitalization and Regulatory Reform Act of 1976.

2. Public Law No. 95–163, The Federal Aviation Act of 1977.

3. Public Law No. 95–504, The Airline Deregulation Act of 1978.

4. Public Law No. 96–296, The Motor Carrier Act of 1980.

5. Public Law No. 96–448, The Staggers Rail Act of 1980.

6. Public Law No. 97–261, The Bus Regulatory Reform Act of 1982.

7. International Business Services, Inc., *Intercity Bus, Rail and Air Service for Residents of Rural Areas,* U.S. Department of Transportation, Report No. DOT-P-10–80–18, January 1980, pp. 2-1–2-2.

8. *Ibid.,* p. 2-2.

9. See Ann Friedlaender and Robert Simpson, *Alternative Scenarios for Federal Transportation Policy: Freight Policy Model, Volume 1* (Report for U.S. Department of Transportation) December 1978. See Chapter 2 for a discussion of this thesis and its supporting evidence.

10. Martha Derthick and Paul J. Quirk, *The Politics of Deregulation* (Washington, DC: The Brookings Institution, 1985), p. 125.

Small Community Rail Service

As the railroad network evolved in the nineteenth century, it replaced wagon transport and much of water transport as the major form of transportation for rural communities. The railroads become completely dominant, except to a limited extent where river transport was available. Wagon freighting simply could not survive, given cost and service considerations, except in transport to railheads. But the history of rural transport in the last seventy-five years has featured the rise of competitive forms. The result has been that while total rail traffic in ton-miles continued to rise, competition has resulted in reduced rail service to many areas, to the detriment of shippers and communities for traffic for which rail is superior. While the key concern of shippers and communities up to 1920 was to get a rail line, the concern in recent decades has been to retain rail service the communities have.

This chapter reviews changing policies by the railroads and regulatory agencies with emphasis on abandonment and rates, summarizes data on cost functions of light traffic railroads, reviews the experience with new railroad companies formed to take over lines abandoned or spun off by major companies, and indicates future trends and strategies.

The Coverage of Rail Service Prior to 1920

It is difficult in the 1980s to realize how extensive and dominant rail service was in the United States prior to the rise of the motor vehicle.

8

There are two major aspects: the extent to which rural communities were reached by rail lines, and the scope of the service provided.

The Extent of Coverage of Rail Lines

At the peak of the railroad mileage in the United States, there were very few rural communities with population over 500 that were not reached by rail lines. Location on a railroad line was most widespread in the area east of the Missouri River.[1] There were, of course, exceptions, small hamlets with a store or so, a tavern, a small restaurant, and later perhaps a gas station. The situation was in general the same in the states west of the Missouri, many parts of which were not settled until the railroads came.[2]

There were several reasons why few towns lacked rail service. Particularly in the West and Southwest, many communities came into existence on rail lines as the latter were extended. Where communities had developed previously, the rail lines were frequently built through them, and most bypassed by main lines received branches or local lines connecting with the main lines. Essentially it was profitable to build and operate a rail line into almost any community over a few hundred population, provided the town was not located at too great a distance from existing lines. The railroads typically regarded these branches as feeders to increase main line traffic, and gains from this were considered to offset any losses from operating the light traffic lines. There was very little careful calculation of whether particular lines were profitable or not.

Provision of service to many small communities was a product of competition among the railroads in the area, each seeking to pull in more traffic from communities not on the main line. One consequence was that many small communities received branches from more than one railroad; there were a number in Iowa, for example. When the larger roads would not provide a line to an existing community, commonly local interests would build a local railroad to the nearest point on the main line. Communities bypassed by a rail line and not receiving a branch or a local road were typically doomed to extinction if they were located within ten miles or so of a railroad. Some towns literally picked up and moved to get onto a rail line; others disintegrated, replaced as trading centers by nearby towns with rail service.

In a sense the very extensive rail network that was built in the last century led to the development of too many towns, compared to the number that would have been optimal by the middle of the present century, following the rise of motor transport. Economies of density of rail lines require concentration of traffic on a small network of lines, but accomplishing this today leaves many communities without rail service.

The Nature of Rail Service

The rail lines into rural communities provided virtually the sole transport connections with the outside world for carload freight, less-than-carload (LCL) merchandise freight, express service, mail, and passengers. The exact systems, nature, and frequence of service varied on the basis of the traffic volume, the length of the line, and railroad policies.

On the main lines with sufficient through traffic to warrant trains with limited numbers of stops, passenger, mail, and express service to small towns was provided by a local passenger train, usually one each way a day, making all the stops. Some of these trains ran through over long distances, a thousand miles or more. But commonly the main line would have a series of these trains, rather than one continuous run, for scheduling reasons. These trains typically averaged between fifteen and thirty miles an hour and were not luxurious; but they did provide service to the small towns at which the major trains did not stop. On secondary main lines, with limited traffic between major terminals, such a train was frequently the only service offered.

Freight service to intermediate points on the main lines was typically provided by local freights. These would handle the LCL traffic, loading and unloading at each stop or depositing an LCL car in the larger communities. These trains handled and switched the carload traffic as well. Service was frequently five or six times a week, though only two or three times on the very light traffic lines, with additional trains in the principal shipping periods.

Most of the larger railroads systems had numerous branch lines, and in addition there were hundreds of small local companies operating feeder lines to the major roads. All of these lines provided carload freight service, and the great majority provided passenger, mail, and express service as well. The nature of the branch systems varied. In some cases it involved an extensive system of fingerlike branches extending from the main line and not connecting with other lines, as for example the Great Northern's numerous branches extending north from the main line toward the Canadian border and the Union Pacific system's branch lines in Oregon and Idaho extending from its Portland line. Others such as the Burlington in southern Iowa and northern Missouri involved a network of intersecting lines.

The passenger train service was very extensive, as shown in Table 2.1. Of a sample of 488 branch lines in the early 1930s at least daily except Sunday service was provided on 410, or 84 percent, and service three times a week (twice in a few instances) on another 11 percent.[3] Two percent of the lines received service only once a week (primarily Milwau-

Table 2.1. Sample study of passenger train service on branch lines of selected railroads, early 1930s

Frequency of Service	Union Pacific	Rock Island	Santa Fe	Louisville & Nashville	Missouri Pacific	Great Northern	Milwaukee	Total	Percentage
Once daily	17	7	24	9	17	8	4	86	17
Once daily, except Sunday[a]	21	29	40	14	28	29	44	205	42
Twice or three times a week	7	7	5	6	0	7	20	52	11
Twice daily[b]	9	0	11	1	9	7	1	38	8
Twice daily except Sunday	11	4	7	4	9	5	9	49	10
Once daily Once daily, except Sunday	6	4	1	1	3	2	4	21	4
Once daily Once three times a week	1	0	1	0	0	0	1	3	1
Once daily, except Sunday, Once three times a week	1	0	2	0	0	1	4	8	2
One day a week[c]	1	0	3	0	3	4	1	12	2
None	6	0	0	0	0	3	5	14	3
Type of Train									
Passenger train	3	0	2	11	13	29	4	62	13
Motor train	12	2	17	1	2	2	3	39	9
Passenger and motor	1	0	5	0	2	0	3	11	2
Passenger and mixed	0	2	3	4	6	5	8	28	6
Motor and mixed	14	5	8	0	1	0	1	29	6
Motor and freight	2	0	3	0	2	0	3	10	2
Mixed only	34	39	54	20	39	27	50	263	57
Freight only	4	3	1	0	4	0	9	21	5

Source: Timetables of the respective roads, 1933–1934 period.
Data compiled by Suzanne Leever.
[a]In a very few instances, except Saturday or Monday.
[b]Two instances of service more than twice daily.
[c]Usually Saturday.

kee), and 3 percent received only freight service.[4] Of the total receiving at least weekday service, 86 received daily service; 205, daily except Sunday; 108, service at least twice daily (except Sunday on 70 lines).

On over half the lines (57 percent), the service was by mixed train, carrying passengers, mail, express, LCL freight, and carload freight. Some of these trains provided good quality service; in others, schedules were not maintained if there was substantial freight switching. But at least there was service. After the turn of the century, some railroads, particularly the Union Pacific and Santa Fe in the sample, operated branch line and some main line secondary service with gasoline (and later diesel) motor trains, some 19 percent in the sample. These allowed provision of regular passenger service with greater speed and comfort than the mixed trains, but the engines were notoriously unreliable, and breakdowns were frequent. On only 21 percent of the branch lines, regular passenger trains were operated (primarily on Great Northern lines).[5] Thus about 40 percent of the lines provided either regular passenger or motor train service. At the other extreme, on 5 percent of the lines service was provided by "freight trains carrying passengers" — service that attracted few users. These were primarily on the Milwaukee. Thus on the whole, service was very extensive — if by no means speedy — but communities did get regular service.

The frequence and nature of the rural area service remained largely unchanged from the time that the rail lines were placed in operation until the mid-1930s. But the development of the automobile and the building of passable roads in the 1920s and 1930s caused the loss of much of the passenger traffic, given the quality of the service and the short trips. The first major railroad to discontinue much of its local passenger service was the Southern Pacific, commencing on its Oregon lines in the 1920s. Others were slow to follow, and the state commissions frequently prevented discontinuance, even when, as was common, only two or three passengers a day were carried. Only the express and mail traffic made operation of the trains at all tolerable.

Following World War II, the railroads moved rapidly to eliminate both the branch line trains and the main line locals, and by the mid-1960s few were left. The shifting of all mail to trucks and buses, the decline and ending of LCL freight service, and the transfer of power over train discontinuance from the states to the ICC caused rapid disappearance. Carload freight service remained much the same but often less frequent as the mixed trains no longer operated with the ending of passenger service. Track maintenance standards were often allowed to decline. Some railroads replaced rail passenger service by bus service in the early years of discontinuance, but most withdrew from this service as well.

In general, the loss of the rail passenger, mail, and express service, while a source of inconvenience to some persons, was not a serious threat to economic survival of the rural economies. The effect was in fact largely psychological; the daily arrival of the passenger train was a major event in the life of the typical small community.

Changing Policies: Abandonment

The loss of carload freight service through abandonment of railway lines is a much more serious threat to rural communities than was loss of passenger train service. Abandonment is by no means new; some lines were abandoned well before the turn of the century including a long branch in south central Colorado in 1878. There was relatively little for a long period, but shifts in traffic patterns and changes in the attitudes of the railroads and federal legislation in recent decades have greatly increased the extent of abandonment and the concern of rural areas about it.[6]

The Policies of the Railroads

The policies of the railroads toward abandonment changed substantially in the mid-1970s.

Policies 1930–1975. In the period prior to the 1930s, the railroads gave little attention to possible abandonment of lines. Most of the early abandonments were of entire railroads, some of which were only partially completed when they ran out of capital and the completed segment was not viable. Others were lines that served mining or lumber areas that had been exhausted and no traffic remained. Absorption of one line by a parallel carrier led to removal of one of the lines. Either there were no protests to these, or if an entire railroad was to be abandoned, no way to prevent abandonment. And, as noted below, there were serious legal restrictions on partial abandonments, which discouraged the railroads from seeking to abandon.

Even from the 1930s down to the 1970s, most railroads gave little serious consideration to abandonment. The depression of the 1930s prompted some action, particularly in leading to abandonment of a number of independent railroads, but the major roads continued to neglect the desirability of abandonment. The view expressed to the author by the responsible official of a major and progressive railroad in 1973 was typical: "We have no system for regularly evaluating particular lines for abandonment; only when a major capital improvement is required on a line, as for example replacement of a bridge, do we consider whether or not we should retain the line." Apart from inertia, there were several influences deterring the railroads from seeking to abandon lines. One was the attitude of the Interstate Commerce Commission (ICC), noted below; the roads soon learned after 1920 that abandonment of lines carrying more than negligible traffic was not likely to be approved. Beyond this consideration was shipper goodwill; shippers on branch lines were sometimes major shippers on other lines. Ultimately, labor protection rules established by the ICC made abandonment much less attractive.

Changes in Attitude. From the early 1970s on, the attitudes of the railroads changed and federal action, discussed below, simplified abandonment and freed abandonment of substantial mileage from any control. There were several causes for the change. First, the continued low rate of return of many railroads caused them to become more conscious of the possible advantages of discontinuing lines. Second, with the elimination of passenger, express, and LCL traffic the protests against abandonment lessened; objections now were raised only by carload shippers and sometimes by community groups. Third, with the passenger train traffic gone and continued decline in carload traffic on many lines — particularly inbound traffic in the West and outbound traffic in the East — plus higher labor costs, continued operation became increasingly unprofitable on many lines. Fourth, the increased use of larger freight cars with heavier loading made more and more branch lines uneconomical, with large capital investment in heavier rail necessary to accommodate hundred-ton loads.

Finally, and perhaps of greatest importance, changes in regulatory policy (discussed in the next section) made abandonment much easier. Substantial mileage could be abandoned by Consolidated Rail Corporation (CONRAIL) without ICC approval under the Northeast Rail Services Act (NERSA); the government made no effort to prevent liquidation of the Rock Island system and partial dismemberment of the Milwaukee road. The Staggers Act encouraged the ICC to act quickly, and the commission itself liberalized its policies. The requirements for listing of lines for which abandonment is contemplated or considered stimulated railroad management to take action.

Government Restrictions on Abandonment Prior to 1980

Trends in abandonment have been greatly influenced by governmental policy, which has changed materially in the last decade.

State Control.   The earliest control rested with the state courts. Persons opposing abandonments had only the option of bringing suit in the courts. State courts, while varying somewhat, took the general position that the granting of charters to railroad companies, including the right of eminent domain, created responsibility for continued operation of a line. The courts generally held that (l) an entire railroad that was unprofitable could not be required to continue operation if, but only if, it could demonstrate the loss, and (2) a railroad could not abandon a portion of a line unless it could demonstrate that continued operation of a line endangered the ability of the company as a whole to continue operations.

As state regulation of the railroads by statute developed, particularly after the Civil War, the control of abandonment passed into the hands of the state commissions. The commissions, in the rare abandonment cases, followed the same policies as the courts. While these were slightly less restrictive on abandonment of money-losing parts of rail systems in general, rarely would they permit abandonment, stressing local interests over the railroad losses. But this was not a major issue, and there were not many cases.

The Interstate Commerce Commission Policies.   Not until the Transportation Act of 1920 did the Interstate Commerce Commission have power over abandonment. The power was given in the act somewhat incidentally, as a complement to the power over construction. But there was some concern about possible abandonments and even more concern about the very restrictive policies of the state commissions and courts and their difficulty in dealing with abandonments of an interstate nature. There were a number of initial disputes over the precise coverage of the power given the ICC, particularly the relevant powers of the states and the ICC. As interpreted by the Supreme Court, the ICC had power over abandonment for interstate commerce even though a line was located wholly within a state, but the state had the power to prevent abandonment for purely intrastate traffic. This power, however, was of little significance. Once the ICC approved abandonment of an entire intrastate line for interstate commerce, so little traffic was left that the states had no alternative but to approve abandonment of the entire line. With portions of interstate systems the courts held the power of the ICC to be complete, since forced continued operation for intrastate commerce would affect interstate commerce by leading to higher rates.[7]

Over the years the ICC developed procedures and general policy toward abandonment requests. The great majority of applications were not protested. In the 1921–1941 period only 28 percent of the applications granted had been contested, though these involved 58 percent of the mileage. Approval of the uncontested cases was almost automatic. When applications were protested, a hearing was held in the area served prior to action.

The general approach of the commission was to weigh the losses to the railroad from continued operation against the losses to the shippers from abandonment. There were problems in the determination of both of these, of course. But in general, if the losses were small relative to the shippers' losses from abandonment, the application would be denied. The higher the ratio of railroad losses to shipper losses, the greater the chance of approval. The more prosperous the railroad, the greater the chance of denial. At the other extreme, where the losses to the shippers would be minor, either because little traffic was moving or alternative transport was available at almost equal cost, the application would be granted. The borderline cases were more difficult to predict. But the railroads learned early that there was no point in seeking to abandon a line on which there was sufficient traffic that shippers would strongly protest abandonment.

Several other general rules came to be followed.

1. The commission would not and could not constitutionally deny permission to abandon an entire railroad if the railroad could demonstrate operating losses. This rule was clearly established by the U.S. Supreme Court in the Brooks-Scanlon decision in 1920.[8]

2. An application to eliminate a parallel line, the company to operate over the line of the other carrier, would universally be approved.

3. The objections raised by local governmental units over loss of tax revenues and by labor unions over loss of railroad jobs were not regarded as relevant, although the commission eventually came to require protection for employees who lost their jobs.

4. Demonstration that the railroad had deliberately tried to reduce traffic on the line to strengthen the case for abandonment would increase likelihood of rejection of the application, but mere failure to actively solicit traffic did not.

5. In some instances the commission would give shippers another chance—often for a year—to demonstrate that traffic would increase.

Approval of abandonment did not necessarily mean actual abandonment; there are rail lines in operation today whose abandonment was approved fifty years or more ago.

Table 2.2 shows the number of decisions on applications for abandonment from 1920 to 1988 and the commission action on them. As is evident, a very high percentage was approved. But this figure is somewhat misleading. Many of these applications were not protested, since

Table 2.2. Summary of ICC action on abandonment applications

Year	Number of Decisions	Mileage of Decisions	Percentage Approved		Percentage Denied	
			Applications	Mileage	Applications	Mileage
1920–1943	2,098	31,829	93	91	7[a]	9[a]
1946–1963	1,479	18,943	89	85	4[b]	7[b]
1966–1972	735	12,007	75	68	3[c]	5[c]
1973–1980	1,165	27,348	70[d]	58	3[e]	na
1981–1988	1,540	21,765	94[a]	87	6	13

Sources: 1920–1943: Interstate Commerce Commission, *Railroad Abandonments, 1920–1943* (Washington, DC: 1945); 1946–1963: Based on data in Michael Conant, *Railroad Mergers and Abandonments* (Berkeley, University of California Press, 1964); 1966–1972: Interstate Commerce Commission, *Annual Reports*; 1973–1980: Office of the Secretary, Interstate Commerce Commission, and Keith A. Klindworth, "Impact of the Staggers Rail Act on the Abandonment Process" (Washington, DC: U.S. Department of Agriculture, 1984); 1981–1988: Information provided by the Interstate Commerce Commission.

[a]Includes petitions dismissed.

[b]Seven percent of the applications, with 8 percent of the mileage, was dismissed without action.

[c]Six percent of the applications, with 9 percent of the mileage, was dismissed, and 16 percent of the applications, wtih 18 percent of the mileage, had not been acted on at the end of the period.

[d]Twenty-three percent withdrawn; 2 percent not acted on.

[e]Plus 2 percent denied in part.

they involved either parallel lines or lines no longer having any traffic. Another substantial segment consisted of entire railroads, which the commission could not compel to continue operations. But most importantly, the precedents set for rejection in earlier cases made very apparent to the railroads the type of situations in which abandonment would be denied, and thus they did not file applications in marginal instances.

Rather clearly the ICC policies restricted somewhat the amount of abandonment. Yet examination of the decisions suggests that the policy—unlike those of some state commissions earlier— was not irrational, even though it did involve continuation of cross subsidization of some lines by others. The commission faced a real dilemma. Where there were strong protests and obvious substantial economic losses from abandonment, the commission had no choice but to permit or deny abandonment; there was no other route such as subsidy available. But it is clear that the commission stressed the costs and benefits in terms of the individual lines under consideration rather than emphasizing national interest.

The commission for many years did not indicate a figure of minimum traffic it regarded as necessary for viability, although there was some suggestion that traffic under one thousand tons originated/terminated per mile was too low for viability. In the 1970s the commission developed its 34 car rule—that lines originating/terminating less than 34 cars per mile were not likely to be viable, while ones above presumably were. This rule, derived from experience with past cases, was not a binding figure. It meant, for example, that a twenty-mile line must originate and/or terminate 680 cars a year if it is likely to be viable; this would provide traffic of about forty thousand net ton-miles per mile. Clearly, however, there are many other influences relevant for viability, such as the relative cost of handling the particular traffic, the rates, and the length of haul on the branch and on the main line.

Rarely did the courts overturn the ICC's decisions in abandonment cases, the commission's conclusions based upon evidence being regarded as final.

The Change in Policy on Abandonment in the Last Two Decades

Legislation and ICC policy on abandonment had remained basically unchanged for over fifty years — 1920 to 1973. The somewhat restrictive policies had been under attack by persons arguing for deregulation and reorganization of the industry to allow increased concentration of traffic on fewer lines and elimination of light traffic lines. But the primary impetus to change arose from the collapse of the Penn Central. And for the first time since 1920, substantial abandonment occurred without the approval of the ICC.

The 3-R Act and Formation of CONRAIL.   With the collapse of the Penn Central and its obvious inability to reorganize, the most drastic federal legislation in many decades was enacted in the form of the 1973 Regional Rail Reorganization Act (3-R Act). All lines of the Penn Central and the other bankrupt eastern roads that were found to be unprofitable were excluded from CONRAIL. Profitability, not economic viability or importance to shippers, was the sole criterion for selection of the lines to be included in CONRAIL.[9] A total of 5,757 miles was excluded. Of this, about 3,600 miles were taken over by other roads, including a number of newly formed enterprises, and about 2,000 miles were abandoned without ICC jurisdiction. The surprising thing was that many of these lines had for years carried only negligible traffic — and the railroads involved had made no attempt to abandon most of them. The 3-R Act also provided for a subsidy program, which will be discussed in a subsequent section.

The 4-R Act.   The Railroad Revitalization and Regulatory Reform Act of 1976 (4-R Act), which was applied to the entire country, modified the abandonment procedure of the ICC in several respects, in addition to extending the subsidy program nationwide. The general aim of the abandonment provisions was to systematize the abandonment process, ensure that shippers had adequate notice, and at the same time lessen delays.

The major provisions were

1. Each railroad was required to file with the ICC and state authorities a list of lines in four categories: (1) those for which abandonment would be sought in the next three years, (2) those under study for possible future abandonment, (3) those for which an abandonment request is pending, and (4) those operated under subsidy.

2. A line a carrier wishes to abandon must be identified as being in category 1 at least four months prior to the abandonment application.

3. A time schedule for filing applications and ICC action was provided in order to lessen delays.[10] The schedule has been superceded by the Staggers Act.

4. An opportunity was given for any responsible person to offer financial assistance subsidy to keep the line in operation, either through payments to cover the deficit or for acquisition of the line. A time schedule was provided.

The act also required the Department of Transportation to classify all lines into four categories: main lines, secondary main lines, major branch lines, and secondary branch lines. This classification was designed to assist overall planning for rationalization of the rail system and possible abandonment.

Under the abandonment listing requirement (paragraph 1 above), the railroads indicated about 20,000 miles in the first three categories, somewhat less than DOT's figure of 25,500 miles or 10 percent of the rail network warranting consideration for abandonment.[11]

The next legislation affecting abandonment, the Rail Services Assistance Act of 1978, was not directly significant for abandonment authorization, but altered and sought to make permanent the federal subsidy for light density lines, thus lessening the likelihood of abandonment.

The Staggers Act: Present Policies.   The next major legislation relating to abandonment was the Staggers Rail Act of 1980. The changes were primarily in procedure rather than in substance relative to abandonment. There are three major provisions.

First, the ICC is no longer required to conduct an investigation if the abandonment is protested, which has been a slow process. The ICC has complete discretion with regard to an investigation. No longer do the hearings, if any, have to be held in the area served. A study by the U.S. Department of Agriculture of non-CONRAIL abandonment cases for the two years before Staggers and the two years after shows that 45 percent of the cases were investigated before Staggers and 30 percent after, with a substantial reduction in the average time before abandonment was permitted.

Second, the ICC policy has changed with regard to the granting of abandonments, even though the legislation has not. Data for 1981 and 1982 are not meaningful because of the large number of CONRAIL applications under NERSA noted below. Table 2.3 provides detailed information on the 1981–1988 action of the commission, for example.

In 1986 the commission rendered 132 decisions, totaling 1,840 miles. Of those, 117 totaling 1,417 miles, were granted; 4, totaling 148 miles, were denied; and 11, totaling 275 miles, were dismissed.[12] In 1987 the commission approved 59 applications; denied 2, with 32 miles; and dismissed 10. Thus only 3 percent was denied. This figure, however, is not directly comparable with those of earlier years because the carriers are well aware of the more lenient attitude of the commission and have been seeking to abandon lines that they would not have sought prior to recent years.

One new element that is now a consideration is the opportunity cost element, the specified rate of return on liquidation value that the railroad is forgoing by continuing to operate the line. The rate of return is determined periodically by the ICC; in 1988 it was 19.1 percent pretax, 11.7 percent after tax, the figure the ICC finds to be the cost of equity capital to the industry. This high figure is subject to substantial criticism on the grounds that it exceeds the overall rate of return in the industry.

A second new element is exemption from normal procedures and requirements. First, under a Notice of Exemption, any line that has been out of operation for two years or more can almost automatically be abandoned.[13] In the years 1985–1988 there were 173 instances, with 1,299 miles. Second, a railroad may apply for exemption (Petition for Exemption) from usual procedures; this is frequently granted if there is no opposition and there is reason for urgency. Exemption is usually granted if the line is to be transferred to a new small or regional railroad, as noted below. In the period 1985–1988 there were 199 cases, 1,830 miles, all granted (Table 2.3).

The commission now places the burden of proof of injury upon the protestants, not upon the railroad, although the latter has to present its case adequately and demonstrate losses. A number of applications are rejected because they are not complete. If the railroad can demonstrate avoidable loss from operations, abandonment is typically approved

Table 2.3. Abandonments since the Staggers Act

Fiscal Year	Applications							
	Filed		Granted		Denied		Dismissed	
	No.	Mi.	No.	Mi.	No.	Mi.	No.	Mi.
1981	161	3,219	81	1,342	1	12	11	25
1982	382	4,821	381	5,151	3	52	34	696
1983	178	3,702	123	2,454	2	28	7	91
1984	472	3,878	419	3,083	7	548	5	69
1985	138	2,877	148	2,343	3	109	32	674
1986	141	1,890	117	1,417	4	148	11	275
1987	60	1,208	59	818	2	32	10	155
1988c	8	170	13	242	2	17	2	9
Subtotal	1,540	21,765	1,341	16,850	24	946	112	1,994
Notice of exemption[a,b]								
1985	82	604	78	557	0	0	3	64
1986	30	221	43	346	0	0	6	53
1987	50	476	27	138	0	0	2	37
1988c	20	163	25	258	0	0	2	35
Subtotal	182	1,464	173	1,299	0	0	13	189
Petitions for exemption[a]								
1985	12	216	43	299	0	0	4	10
1986	93	861	56	324	0	0	4	6
1987	73	817	88	976	0	0	5	28
1988c	13	155	12	231	0	0	1	2
Subtotal	191	2,049	199	1,830	0	0	14	46
TOTAL	1,913	25,278	1,713	19,979	24	946	139	2,229

Source: Interstate Commerce Commission, information provided directly by ICC.

Note: Because of the lagtime in processing, all cases are not completed in the year filed.
There were some notices and petitions for exemption filed pre-1985. They total 100–150 cases. Computer records do not include them.
[a]Notices of exemption are the "out of service" line class exemptions.
[c]Through December 31, 1987.

without the need to consider opportunity cost, despite losses to shippers from higher freight costs, if there are no special circumstances as noted below.[14] Thus the delineation line between what will be approved and what will not has been moved substantially in the direction of approval.

Approval, however, is not automatic. The act requires that the commission consider whether the abandonment "will have a serious, adverse effect on rural and community development."[15] In 1984, for example, there were only seven denials, but these involved about 14 percent of the total mileage for which abandonment was requested. In the years 1985–1988 the mileage denied was small; 3 percent in 1986, 3 percent in 1987.

The case for denial is strengthened by several considerations.

1. The showing made by the shippers, communities, and other opponents. A strongly organized effort, with a number of participants, intense protests, and well-documented evidence, is almost imperative if there is any chance to obtain denial.

2. Evidence that the line is not suffering loss, or at least not an operating loss, even though opportunity cost is not covered. The commission does not insist that opportunity cost be covered for an application to be approved, but it does take it into consideration.[16]

3. Evidence of commitment to use of rail by the shippers such as a high percentage of traffic shipped by rail and willingness to contract to ship certain quantities. If shippers are using trucks for much of their traffic, as is common, approval of the application is almost certain.[17]

4. Conclusive evidence of increasing traffic. The ICC is wary of general statements about additional use of rail; strong evidence must be provided. Of recent denials, in a Burlington Northern case involving a thirty-three-mile line from Lookout to Hambone in California, strictly a bridge line, the application was denied because of the evidence of rising lumber traffic.[18] A similar decision was reached on a Seaboard case in Georgia.[19] Loss of traffic because of a railroad-imposed surcharge weakens the railroad's case, as shown in the ICG case noted previously.

5. Strong evidence of importance of the line to the shippers and communities in an area far removed from other rail service. In one major case, the commission denied abandonment of a 165-mile line of the Chicago and North Western in South Dakota, even though the line was suffering an operating loss, because of the strong case presented by the protestants and the fact that serious economic injury would be done to shippers who would be left far removed from other rail lines with substantially higher trucking costs.[20] Operation of the parallel line of the Milwaukee to Rapid City had already been discontinued.

A third provision of the Staggers Act places strict time limits on rail abandonment proceedings. Unprotested abandonments are permitted within 75 days after filing the application; protested but uninvestigated applications, 120 days. Final decision on investigated abandonments must be made within 225 days; the maximum overall time is 330 days.

The cumulative effect of abandonment shows up clearly in the data of total rail line mileage in the United States, despite the fact that some new construction has occurred, as shown in Table 2.4. Thus the total has declined by over one hundred thousand miles, or 40 percent, from 1920.

Table 2.4. Railroad line mileage, United States, selected years 1920–1986

| Year | Railroad Line Mileage | |
	Total	Class I only
1920	252,845	—a
1930	249,052	—
1940	233,670	—
1950	223,779	—
1960	217,552	—
1965	211,925	—
1970	206,265	196,479
1975	199,126	191,520
1976	192,396	185,395
1977	191,205	182,380
1978	190,555	175,912
1979	—a	169,927
1980	—	164,822
1981	—	162,160
1982	—	159,123
1983	—	155,879
1984	—	151,998
1985	—	145,764
1986	—	140,061

Source: Association of American Railroads, *Yearbook of Railroad Facts* (various years).
aData not readily available.

The question of ICC action on abandonment has been lessened in the last ten years by the extensive formation of new railroad companies taking over lines that the major carriers seek to abandon or spin off. Requests to transfer lines to the new carriers are typically handled by the commission under a presumptive exemption rule (Ex Parte 392), based on an exemption (Sec. 10901), allowing immediate transfer on the philosophy that such transfer is desirable in the interests of all concerned.[21] No labor requirements are attached to the exemption decisions, although in recent years the labor unions have been attempting, through legal action, strikes, and pressure on Congress, to require labor protection in these exemption decisions. The outcome remains uncertain even after U.S. Supreme Court action in the Pittsburgh and Lake Erie case.

NERSA (Northeast Rail Services Act, 1981).   In 1981 Congress enacted NERSA in a desperate attempt to make CONRAIL profitable, as a result of the fight between the administration, which wished to liquidate CONRAIL immediately, and Congress, which was determined to prevent it. CONRAIL was authorized to abandon any lines it wished, which the ICC could not deny unless an offer of financial assistance was forthcoming within ninety days from the time of the application. CONRAIL proceeded to abandon substantial mileage (4,600 miles, 1981– June 1985), including not only light traffic lines but some secondary main lines (e.g., Terre Haute–St. Louis line) to allow concentration of traffic on other lines. ICC policy is outlined in Ex Parte No. 149, November 25, 1981.

Finally, the government allowed liquidation of the Rock Island and partial liquidation of the Milwaukee, without ICC jurisdiction over the lines abandoned. About 3,500 miles of Rock Island and 5,000 miles of Milwaukee were abandoned and not acquired by anyone else.

The net effect of these changes has been to make abandonment easier, and the absence of local hearings makes the protesting of abandonments by local interests much more difficult.

The Impact of Abandonment

A number of studies have been made over the years on the effects of abandonment upon the areas served. The earlier studies were summarized in the ICC study *Railroad Abandonments, 1920–1943*[22] and later ones were summarized in the article by Benjamin Allen and John F. Due, "Railroad Abandonment: Effects upon the Communities Served,"[23] and the U.S. Department of Transportation study *Railroad Abandonments and Alternatives.*[24] There have been relatively few studies since the midseventies; one of the few is an unpublished study by the ICC in 1985. The general conclusion is that most past abandonments have had little overall effect upon shippers or communities served because of alternate forms of transport with comparable costs. But there have been some negative effects, especially upon agriculture, where the products are shipped in bulk; in fertilizer costs; and upon some manufacturing and wholesale plants, including a few forced to close or move.

The earlier abandonments in general were of submarginal lines, except for those cases where entire lines were abandoned. The slowness of the railroads to seek abandonment and the refusal of the ICC to approve abandonments except when there was very little traffic resulted almost inevitably in little economic harm when abandonment occurred. But the recent abandonments and some that are proposed are for the most part lines of substantially greater traffic. The various state rail plan volumes have analyzed in detail lines threatened with abandonment and for which assistance may be provided, and some of these show very high benefit/cost ratios.[25] A substantial number have ratios in excess of two, and some as high as fifty. The economic loss from abandonment of some of these lines would be very substantial. The extent of loss over the years, however, has been reduced by the lessening of the gap between rail and truck costs, largely because of higher weight and length limits for trucks and new lower cost truck operators.

The very strong efforts of various communities and shippers to preserve rail service by taking over the lines abandoned and to be abandoned, providing substantial money in the process, gives further evidence that current types of abandonment are likely to have substantial adverse effects upon the local areas and shippers.[26]

Governmental Assistance to Avoid Abandonment

Historically, while governments provided assistance in the last century to aid in the building of railroads, in general they did nothing positive to preserve lines that were being abandoned. The first action in recent decades began with a few states. Then the federal government entered the field in 1973 in the 3-R Act, ultimately expanded its role, but subsequently has largely withdrawn from assistance. Many states and local governments have played an active role, and some continue to do so.[27]

The first state action to ensure continued operation on a line serving rural areas was the purchase by Vermont of the north-south line of the Rutland Railroad when that road liquidated in 1964. The state contracted with two private companies to operate the line.

The significant action of various levels of government to preserve rail lines from abandonment came with the 3-R Act of 1973 and the formation of CONRAIL. The 3-R Act provided federal subsidy for a three-year period on lines not included in CONRAIL equal to 70 percent of the amount necessary to keep the line operating, provided states, local governments, or shippers would provide the rest of the funds. Under this program, about 2,700 miles of the 5,757 miles of the bankrupt roads not included in CONRAIL were kept in operation. But funds were available for only a two-year period, and were not available except in the Northeast.

The 4-R Act of 1976 extended the subsidy program to the entire country, with allocation of federal funds by state on the basis of eligible mileage. The federal share was 100 percent for the year ending in June 30, 1977; 70 percent for the next two years; and then it terminated. The funds could be used for rehabilitation, purchase of lines, operating subsidies, and some other purposes. The initiative for each line had to be taken by the states in conjunction with preparation of state rail plans, with the nonfederal portion of the subsidy to be made up from state, local, or shipper sources. A basic defect was that funds could be available on a line only after abandonment had been approved. The Local Rail Services Assistance Act of 1978 removed this provision and extended the program indefinitely, providing federal share of an operating subsidy on any line only for three years, with 100, 80, and 70 percent shares in the successive years. Funds were available on an indefinite basis for rehabilitation or acquisition of lines.

While the program was intended to be permanent when the legislation was passed in 1980, the Reagan administration was extremely hostile to it and sought as soon as it took office to eliminate the program completely. Congress was not willing to go as far, but the funds have been cut back drastically until only very limited funds have remained.

The nonfederal share has been provided from a variety of sources: the states, local governments, shippers, and regional organizations in the Northeast. Several states have gone well beyond providing their matching share of federal funds: New York, Massachusetts, Pennsylvania, and Michigan, for example. Others—including Indiana, Illinois, and Iowa—have established state loan funds to assist in rehabilitation.

These programs have been responsible for preserving a very substantial mileage of lines that would have been abandoned. By 1987 at least 7,400 miles had been aided, and about 6,000 miles were still in operation. These range from sections of former main lines, such as the Rock Island's line across Iowa, to small segments a few miles in length. None of these programs has been intended to continue indefinitely on any one line, but they have been designed to allow rehabilitation, purchase, and continued operation.

Apart from the primary federal funds through the Department of Transportation, limited amounts of money have been made available through various federal programs and agencies.[28] These include two agencies of the U.S. Department of Agriculture; the community facilities division, which has had available loan funds for acquisition of lines; and the business and industry division, which has a loan guarantee program. In addition, the Economic Development Administration and the Small Business Administration have had loan funds available. Funding of these programs, however, has been drastically reduced.

One of the most important roles the state and local governments have played in preserving rail service in rural areas is through the purchase of rail lines.[29] As of October 1987, states had purchased about 3,800 miles of line in sixteen states, primarily in the East, although the largest single purchase was South Dakota's acquisition of 820 miles of

Milwaukee track. With the sole exception of one line in West Virginia, all of the lines are operated under contract by private firms or, in New Hampshire, with private management acting for the state. As of October 1987, local governments had acquired some forty rail lines with a total of 3,133 miles. Purchases were made by cities, counties, transit districts, and a number by port authorities (even though no port is involved). The largest segment is a 389-mile portion of Rock Island main line across Kansas. Only a few are operated directly by the local government units, the others by private firms under contract.

Despite these activities of various levels of government, shippers on relatively light traffic lines face a major threat of abandonment. There is as of 1988–1989 little assurance of continued rail service on any line that does not provide a substantial volume of bulk traffic or a somewhat smaller volume of higher-rate manufactured goods, the latter, however, being particularly vulnerable to truck competition. It is impossible to define the necessary minimum at all precisely, but the old ICC rule of thirty-four cars originated and/or terminated, unscientific as it was, remains as a rough guideline. But even on lines that have substantial traffic, continuation of operation is questionable if the track is inadequate to handle modern high-tonnage hopper cars. There are many miles of line in the grain-producing areas that yield substantial traffic, but the rail will not support loaded hopper cars, and the traffic does not warrant replacement of the rail. Heavy cars can be operated short distances at very slow speed on light rail but not economically for any distance. The most vulnerable lines are the relatively long-distance light traffic lines laid with rail under eighty pounds. Another threat is posed by the possible abandonment of the connecting line.

Cost Functions of Light Traffic Density Rail Lines

A high percentage of the rail lines serving rural areas consists of relatively light traffic lines, and the provision of local freight service on the main lines has many of the characteristics of light traffic lines, except for track maintenance, which is independent of the provision of the local freight service. The ability of these light traffic lines to survive and the desirability of attempting to retain them by subsidy is dependent upon the cost of providing service on these lines. It is very difficult to get satisfactory information on the costs of service on branches of main lines, and thus studies were undertaken over a decade ago of the cost functions of Class II railroads, then defined as railroads with annual operating revenues under $5 million. These studies cannot be updated because the railroads involved are no longer required to file reports. But there is no reason to believe that the relationships would be different with current data.

Long-run Cost Functions

The first of the studies sought to determine long-run cost functions of a sample of Class II railroads (as then classified), most, but not all, of which are light traffic lines.[30] The assumption was made that the roads had all completed long-run adjustments — a not unrealistic assumption for these lines as they cannot vary trackage as long as they serve the same points, they adjust maintenance expenditures from year to year, and they can adjust their equipment ownership easily (they typically own only diesels and acquire them secondhand). The cross section analysis utilized two sets of data, one for 209 Class II railroads for 1968, and one for 44 such lines for 1973 with much more detailed information. Several long-run average cost functions were estimated, with two measures of output, net ton miles per mile of line, and distance of haul.

The major conclusions of the study are as follows:

1. There is strong evidence of substantial economies relative to traffic density, reflecting indivisibilities and economies of scale for light traffic lines, relatively far greater than those for the heavier main traffic lines.

2. Most of these economies are exhausted at a relatively low volume of traffic — many by 50,000 annual net ton-miles per mile of line, most by 250,000. These are very low volumes by main line standards.

3. Long-run marginal cost, therefore, is well below average cost. This is not an indication of "excess capacity" in the sense of unnecessary fixed plant, since for these single track lines to eliminate trackage would require their demise, and much or all of the traffic is from one end to the other. Rather, these roads adjust plant capacity by reducing maintenance and adjusting amounts of other types of equipment. Still, marginal cost remains below average cost.

4. The two largest components of cost — maintenance of way and transportation-rail line — are substantially influenced by volume but not by average length of haul. Only equipment maintenance, equipment rentals (mostly per diem charges for freight cars), and general traffic and administrative expenses are influenced to any significant extent by the length of haul as well as by volume.

5. Overall costs per ton-mile are, therefore, not influenced as much as might be expected by length of haul. The economies for short lines from increased length of haul, though not negligible, are not as great as might be expected.

6. In the lower-volume categories, there is a substantial range of observed average costs at given traffic volumes, depending upon frequency of operation required, wage rates, conditions affecting maintenance, and management effectiveness.

7. The declining nature of the average cost curve suggests that if traffic is relatively low and volume continues to fall, costs per ton-mile will rise to a point at which the line ceases to be economically justifiable.

8. The economic justifiability of a line is a function of the traffic density on the line, the length of haul on the line, the length of haul on the main line, alternative costs of hauling by truck (or water), and the costs of transference between rail and truck, as well as other influences on cost per ton-mile. A few generalizations can be made in this area.

    a. Lines with traffic less than fifty thousand miles per mile typically have costs over twenty-five cents per ton mile and are likely to be justifiable only if the line is very short — under ten miles — or special conditions allow very infrequent service, make truck costs or transfer-to-truck costs unusually high, or from a profit standpoint, allow an unusually high freight rate.

    b. Roads with traffic between fifty thousand and two hundred thousand ton-miles per mile may be justifiable, depending on the main line haul, length of the line, and the ability to hold costs down.

    c. Roads with traffic between two hundred thousand and eight hundred thousand ton-miles per mile and under twenty-five miles in length of haul are almost certain to be economically justifiable unless cost of transference from truck to rail is very low or main line haul is very short.

    d. Roads with traffic over eight hundred thousand ton-miles per mile are likely to be economically justifiable even without a main line haul.

9. Since long-run marginal cost is less than average cost, optimal rates for traffic on economically justifiable traffic lines should be below average cost, with difference subsidized out of government revenues (assuming that the economic distortions caused by the revenue source for the subsidy are less than those that would result from excessively high rates or loss of the road). In the past, this subsidy has often been provided by the connecting main line road through liberal rate division, in excess of the short line's contribution to the main line's net revenue, contrary to the basic economic objection to any form of cross subsidization. There is, therefore, strong justification for subsidization of those lighter traffic roads that are economically justifiable on the criteria already noted in addition to subsidization justified by externalities. With

the heavier density lines (over one million ton-miles per mile), marginal cost approaches average cost and subsidy is less necessary.

Short-run Cost Functions

The second study sought to determine the short-run responsiveness of total costs and various categories of cost to changes in traffic density, measured by net ton-miles per mile of road.[31] A sample of ten Class II railroads regarded as more or less typical were selected and data were obtained for the period 1963–1973. The short-run cost functions were estimated, and then elasticities were determined to indicate the magnitude of the reduction in average cost in the short run resulting from an increase in traffic density.

The results of the study show clearly that marginal cost is substantially below average cost, and thus an increase in traffic will reduce average cost in the short run. The roads fall into two distinct groups. The first group of six showed extremely low elasticity in the short run and thus drastic reduction in average cost as traffic increases. The primary determinants of the low elasticity are the two principal elements of cost: transportation rail-line costs and maintenance-of-way costs. For the second group of four lines the decline in average cost was substantial but much less than in the former group. The major differences between the two sets were in track maintenance, locomotive repairs, compensation of train crews, and traffic costs. The high elasticity of track maintenance for the second group probably reflects the effort to catch up on the deferred maintenance as traffic increases. The increase makes track repair more essential and also aids in financing it. Thus, on the whole, higher traffic volume will lower average cost in the short run but with different patterns for different roads.

The Significance of the Studies

The results of these studies make very clear the importance of density of traffic for average cost per ton-mile and the consequent difficulty of lines with very light traffic to survive. Of the ten lightest traffic lines included in the 1973 long-run study, in 1989—sixteen years later—only four were still operating, and the future of some of these was in doubt. Of the top ten in density, only one had ceased operations. By far the major cost items of the light density roads are track maintenance, which cannot be reduced below certain levels if trains are to be kept on the track, and costs of train operation—both involving true indivisibilities. The longer the light traffic line, in general, the less viable it is with a given volume of traffic; economies of distance are overwhelmed by the fact that a higher percentage of the total haul occurs on the light traffic line. There are exceptions, however, in which additional mileage will offer sufficient economies to offset the smaller percentage of the total haul on the light traffic line. This is particularly true when separate short lines are merged under common management.

The implications of this are very clear for any attempt to preserve service on light traffic lines. Below a certain level—the figure varying with circumstances—costs will be so high that attempts of the shippers or communities to preserve the line by subsidy will be unwarranted. Shippers then have the choice of shifting to trucks or relocating. A community, as distinct from individual shippers, can preserve a line indefinitely if it wishes—and doing so may be regarded as justifiable either in terms of externalities, such as avoiding the cost of rebuilding roads, or for future development. Another implication is the importance for shippers to use the rail lines as much as possible, perhaps paying somewhat more for freight on inbound commodities in order to increase the chances of retaining the line for lower cost on outbound products. Short-run minimization of transport costs may not result in minimization of costs over a longer period.

Future Trends and Strategies

It is very difficult to predict trends in service to rural communities with any degree of precision. The continued effects of deregulation, trends in petroleum prices and the state of the economy—including interest rates—are all important variables that cannot be predicted at all accurately. But some generalizations can be made about likely trends, and suggestions for strategy can be offered.

The Private Sector—Abandonment and Approaches

So far as the major railroads are concerned, it is most likely that they will seek to abandon additional light traffic lines. As of May 1, 1987, the railroads listed 5,365 miles in category 1 (seek to abandon in three years), 82 in category 2 (under study for future abandonment), and 2,067 in category 3 (abandonment application pending before the ICC). Thirty-five percent of the mileage in these categories is in six states: Illinois, Kansas, Minnesota, Ohio, Pennsylvania, and Texas. In the nine months ending June 1988, applications to abandon 1,508 miles had been filed. More and more, the large railroads are coming to regard themselves as wholesalers of rail service, serving only major points and leaving other service to small local roads or to truck connections. Shippers and communities, therefore, will increasingly face the issue of potential abandonment and optimal strategy.

Should Effort Be Made to Retain the Line?   A key question to be answered initially is: is it worthwhile to seek to retain the line? What effect will the loss of the line have on transport costs? From the community standpoint, what will be the effect upon expansion of existing activity and the ability to lure new economic activity to the area? What will be the cost to retain the line? This requires careful benefit/cost analysis, as provided in many state rail plans.

If the answer is in the affirmative, the next question is, what should be done to retain the line? One obvious answer for shippers is: use the line as much as possible. As suggested above, for a substantial amount of transport, rail and truck costs, all things considered, do not differ greatly. Saving a small sum currently by shipping by truck may result over time in higher transport costs if the rail line is discontinued. To the extent shippers will keep the marginal traffic on the rail line, the greater the chances of retaining the line — given the rapidly declining average cost as traffic increases on light traffic lines.

Opposition to Abandonment.   If the railroad lists the line as a potential candidate for abandonment or actually applies to abandon, there are several options. One is to oppose the abandonment request. This is not likely to succeed, but at least there is a chance. As noted in earlier sections, the commission approves most requests — but this is not automatic. As noted above, if the shippers and communities can present a strong case for retention of the line, there is a chance that they may succeed. But there must be considerable traffic and strong evidence of use of rail and commitment of continuing to do so, plus a well-presented case. The ICC has available a document entitled *A Guide for Public Participation in Rail Abandonment Cases Under the Interstate Commerce Act*[32] that outlines the steps protestants can take and indicates commission policy in substantial detail.

Acquisition of the Line.   A second alternative is to acquire or sponsor acquisition of the line. Under the Staggers Act, a line for which abandonment is authorized must be sold to any responsible person or group seeking to acquire the line and operate it.[33] The mandatory waiting period is only ninety days from the time of the approval of the request — a very short period in which to organize acquisition unless substantial effort has been undertaken prior to the abandonment request. In practice, a railroad will often wait a longer period if there are serious negotiations under way — especially if the road wishes to see the line in continued operation.

There are several alternative routes if an effort is to be made to retain the line. One of the best sources of information on doing so is the volume by R. Lawrence McCaffrey, Jr., and Peter A. Gilbertson, *Starting a Short Line;*[34] the ICC issued in September 1988 a pamphlet entitled *Before You Start a Small Railroad, A Brief Overview of Things to Consider.*[35] First, if there is one major shipper, the shipper may simply purchase the line and operate it in effect as an industrial siding. This has been done by several grain elevators in central Illinois, for example. This is not normally feasible, except for a very large shipper, on lines of substantial length because of the amount of capital required. Such a line, privately operated, cannot obtain a share of the joint rate but may receive a switching allowance. If such a line has potential traffic from another shipper, it may obtain ICC permission to handle this traffic without assuming common carrier obligations.

Second, a local company may be organized to acquire the line and operate it as a common carrier along the patterns explained in the section below on new carriers. Shippers and other local interests may participate.

Third, efforts may be made to interest outside enterprises to take over the line.

Development of such a line encounters a number of problems.[36] Some of the key issues include negotiation of a purchase price (for light rail, twenty-five thousand dollars a mile is a typical figure, but the figure can approach one hundred thousand dollars on high-grade track), raising of necessary capital, selection of a manager, negotiation of joint rates with the connecting carrier if at all possible, acquisition of equipment, and rehabilitation of track (which may cost more than the purchase price). The decision to start the enterprise requires careful estimate of costs and revenues — and the latter is particularly difficult to predict accurately.[37]

As in the period in which an attempt is being made to retain a branch line in operation, often the greatest contribution the shippers can make is to provide the line with as much traffic as is economically feasible. If the new railroad can obtain contracts from the shippers whereby they will agree to ship certain amounts or pay when shipments are less than the agreed on figures, it has much greater chances of success. But shippers may not be willing to make commitments, and under depressed economic conditions, they may not be able to continue to make the payments.

Quite apart from shipper involvement in the new railroads, local community groups such as the Chamber of Commerce or a citizens group organized for the purpose can play a major role assisting the development of the new line, seeking funding, state and federal assistance, and the like.

As noted above, the trend toward formation of new railroad companies has been facilitated by the exemption of such applications by the ICC and the refusal of the ICC to attach labor requirements.

The labor unions have become increasingly concerned about the shift of lines to new companies, especially the new large regional carriers.[38] They have attempted by legal action to force the ICC to attach labor protection and require the railroads to bargain over the changes in conformity with the Railway Labor Act, including strikes against the major carrier and are seeking legislation to require labor protection. In 1987 a district court upheld the right of the unions to strike the Pittsburgh and Lake Erie Railroad over its attempt to sell the railroad. In 1989 the U.S. Supreme Court ruled in favor of the Pittsburgh and Lake Erie Railroad. The 5-to-4 ruling did not cover the issue of branchline sales, and thus the labor protection question regarding the transference of lines to local and regional carriers remains unanswered. Meanwhile, the sale of lines by the major carriers has fallen sharply.

Section 10910 of the Staggers Act provides for the so-called feeder line acquisition, whereby the ICC can require the sale of a line threatened with abandonment to a responsible purchaser, even though application for abandonment has not been filed. Only one line was thus acquired by May 1988, a 56-mile line purchased by Indiana Hi Rail in 1981. In May 1988 one other case was pending on a 1.6-mile CSX line, for which there are two competing buyers (ICC Finance Dockets 31012 and 31013 Sub #1).

The Private Sector—Experience with New Enterprises

By now, there has been substantial experience with new companies formed to take over lines abandoned by or spun off from major companies.[39] In brief summary: between 1970 and June 1989, 289 new railroad companies (257 if those replacing other new small railroads are eliminated) were formed to take over abandoned or spun-off lines, totaling 13,927 miles. By 1989, 37 of these had been abandoned, and 28 were transferred to other small companies; 224 were still operating. In addition, 13 large regional carriers with 8,489 miles of line had taken over lighter traffic lines from major companies. Some of the new lines have purchased track; some operate on track owned by government units, some on leased track from the previous owners. They vary widely in length, traffic density, and type of traffic, though many are bulk commodity carriers. Some are owned by shippers; some by local entrepreneurs alone or in combination with shippers; some by outside entrepreneurs, several of whom run several lines. Failure has resulted from several major causes: inadequate traffic, physical problems such as poor track, management problems, lack of capital, lack of shipper support, lack of rate divisions. Several could operate only with subsidy, which has largely been phased out.

Those cases of failure and the experience of the successful lines suggest several requirements for success.

1. Competent, experienced management. This is often difficult for a small railroad to obtain.

2. Shipper support. Without strong support of the shippers, obviously a line is almost certain to fail.

3. Adequate quality of track. If the track initially is in poor shape, funds must be available to improve it. Rehabilitation is often more costly than purchase of the line.

4. Adequate traffic. It is impossible to provide any precise figure, which depends in part on the length of the line, the type of traffic, the rates that can be obtained, etc. But survival is almost impossible on less than twenty cars originated/terminated per mile per year, and even traffic between twenty and forty is marginal.

5. Other factors. Access to more than one carrier, cooperation of the connecting carriers, adequate capital, and state-local assistance are highly desirable. Even so, there are many hazards.

Despite the problems, a number of these new companies are operating successfully; they can operate much more cheaply than the major companies subject to standard union rules, and they can adapt their services much more adequately to the interests of the shippers.

State and Local Governments

As noted, some states and local governments have played a major role in assisting the development of the new enterprises. Other states have done little. There are several roles that these units can play.

1. Continuation of state rail planning.

2. Provision of technical advice and assistance to shippers and communities that seek to retain a line and to entrepreneurs who seek to take over lines.

3. Purchase of track, typically with operation contracted for by

private firms. Very little risk is involved from purchase, per se, as normally only salvage value must be paid, and thus if operations do not succeed, the line can simply be scrapped. Purchase of the line is often the major stumbling block to a private firm when getting a new line underway; little capital is required to purchase used equipment.

In lieu of purchase, states may provide loan funds, as several midwestern states do, to operators who wish to take over the lines. The governmental units have less control over the future of the line, which can be hazardous if the first operator does not succeed.

4. Provision of rehabilitation funds. As noted, the cost of rehabilitating a line may exceed the purchase price. The provision of loans or grants for rehabilitation purposes by state or local government can make a substantial contribution to the success of a new line. The risk is somewhat greater than with purchase, since it may be difficult for the governmental unit to recover this money if the line does not succeed. But this is not a controlling argument against providing the funds. If the government unit owns the track, the operating firm may be reluctant to place its own funds into rehabilitation.

5. Operating subsidy. A final possibility for the governmental units is to provide an operating subsidy, particularly during the initial years when the new firm is getting underway. There is strong justification for such a subsidy if there are significant externalities from continued operation of the rail line, and/or if there is a good chance of profitability in a few years. Such subsidies were initially provided under the federal 3-R and subsequent acts, and a few states have continued to subsidize. But there is substantial popular dislike of operating subsidies, and they always involve the danger of failure to maximize efficiency of operation and to resist unwarranted wage increases. If the subsidies are state (or federally) supplied, local areas always have the incentive to maximize subsidy. Therefore, except on very long lines of statewide importance, subsidy can most logically be provided at the local government level — the level at which the benefits of retention of service are most direct. This rule would not preclude some standard nonmarginal state assistance, given the greater taxing powers of the states.

State or Local Operation.   As noted, only one rail line (in addition to the Alaska Railroad) is state operated, but there are several municipal lines, some that have been in operation for fifty years or more. The typical policy for government-owned lines of contracting out operation to a private firm reflects several considerations, including tradition, problems of finding management, dislike of undertaking the risk, fear of inefficiency or political interference, and other considerations. Actually municipal operation offers some significant advantages. If deficits are incurred, they can be met from tax revenue without the inevitable conflict between the interests of the operators and the municipality; instead a mutual sense of responsibility develops. Most taxes are avoided. This alternative should not be rejected out of hand.

What the actual policies of the states and municipalities will be is difficult to predict. The financial position of some states is good today, but others are experiencing severe problems. But at the moment the urgency of action—compared to the time when Penn Central, the Milwaukee, and the Rock Island failed—is much less, and there is little federal stimulus, relative to a decade ago. The general shift to conservatism nationally carries over to the local governments and the states, discouraging any new activity of government. But some of the most significant action in the last decade was taken in this field by the relatively conservative states of South Dakota and New Hampshire. General political philosophy has played little part in relative state action.

Federal Policies

The current trends are for the federal government to withdraw from the rail assistance field entirely and to minimize regulation. Both reflect the desire to reduce federal spending and to minimize governmental interference with the economy. Externalities are disregarded in this philosophy, and the view is held that provision of rail service is a private and a state-local, not a federal, activity. This view, of course—as any issue of philosophy regarding the role of government and the relative roles of various levels of government—can be debated. While particular rail lines are primarily of state-local concern, the problem of continued rail service to rural areas is in a sense nationwide. But it is unlikely that a general change in federal policy will occur under the new administration, particularly in view of the federal deficit.

Were the federal government ultimately to undertake more responsibility, there would be merit in restoring the program established in the Rail Services Assistance Act of 1978 with a support program intended to be permanent. This would involve continued federal support of state planning, the provision of federal funds for assistance in acquiring and rehabilitating lines, and short-term subsidies—all to be established on a matching basis. But such a change is not likely.

Other Changing Policies

Recent legislation—particularly NERSA and the Staggers Act—while offering many benefits, adversely affected rural areas in some instances by facilitating cancellation of joint rates, elimination of reciprocal switching, changes in rail rate structures, and the use of surcharges on light traffic lines or joint rates. These became widespread in the early 1980s; by 1987, however, there was little such action. It is difficult to quantify and fully assess these changes, but several aspects are clearly detrimental to rural communities.

Joint Rates

Until recent years the major carriers had extensive systems of joint rates with connecting carriers, thus providing shippers with maximum choice in the selection of routes. The rates were typically the same but the service aspects were not. The joint rates provided overall rates based on total distance, rather than those of the separate segments of the haul, and rates on long hauls from branch line or small connecting railroad points were often the same as from points on the main line. Reciprocal switching arrangements were common, whereby railroad A would switch cars for railroad B, and vice versa, on shipments for firms with sidings on A, even though the line haul was on B, without additional charge to the shippers.

With the 3-R Act, NERSA, the Staggers Act, and the formation of CONRAIL, there was substantial movement away from this situation. The shift began with CONRAIL, which, in an effort to make itself profitable in the short run to avoid liquidation, canceled many joint rates, in part to ensure the maximum possible haul for itself. It also began to apply surcharges on remaining joint rates, as permitted by the Staggers Act. These actions hurt Norfolk Southern and CSX, which in turn retaliated. The trend also extended into the West. Reciprocal switching agreements were canceled. The results were to close gateways, lessening the choice of the shipper, and substantial additional switching charges for shippers. The basic effect was to balkanize the industry still more, with line hauls having significant rate advantages over multicarrier routes. One consequence was that some lines lost considerable traffic, to the detriment of shippers dependent on those lines. Some smaller railroads lost their "bridge" traffic, and at least one — Roscoe Snyder and Pacific — was forced to liquidate. Shippers on a few small railroads were placed at a relative disadvantage compared to those on major lines, as joint rates were canceled or revised upward. However, most of the cancellations did not adversely affect small lines but primarily various regional carriers. In a few instances the major roads used the surcharge, as authorized by the Staggers Act, as a means of discouraging the remaining traffic on lines they sought to abandon.[40]

Much of this behavior was clearly not the intent of Congress in enacting the legislation. Under Staggers, the ICC has the power to prevent cancellation of joint rates and reciprocal switching. But to date the ICC has been very reluctant to use this power. The joint rate issue was one of the major ones prompting efforts to amend the Staggers Act. The railroads have now moved away from joint rate cancellations; there were only three in 1987 compared to thirty-three in 1984 (information supplied by the Interstate Commerce Commission). Likewise the number of surcharges on light traffic lines has fallen sharply; there were 114 authorized in 1981, but only 6 in 1987. With deregulation of boxcar traffic, much of this has been placed on combination rates, in effect eliminating joint rates.

Changes in Rate Structure

Changes in railroad freight rate structures following the Staggers Act have likewise affected rural areas but in varying ways.[41] The great increase in flexibility of rates has resulted in some overall reductions in rates on agricultural products.[42] There has been an increase in availability of unit train rates, and also in many markets an increase in the availability of multicar rates, even for as few as three cars. The railroads have moved toward greater rate competitiveness with trucks on some relatively short hauls. While lower rates are beneficial, the flexibility and ability to make speedy changes in rates increases uncertainty in planning.

Of great concern to many rural shippers has been the rapid increase in use of contract rates. These are highly advantageous to larger shippers able to negotiate with the railroads for concessions. But smaller shippers are placed at some disadvantage for lack of knowledge about potential rates and bargaining power. There is also great concern about the confidentiality of the contract rates; one firm does not know what another firm is receiving. Firms not enjoying contract rates face a difficult future, often, in the case of grain, being forced to truck to the nearest elevator having contract rates.

It is also far more difficult for shippers to prove "market dominance" as a basis for complaining about unreasonably high rates, and such complaints have virtually disappeared.

Truck Deregulation

The Motor Carrier Act of 1980 had the effect of materially reducing the barriers to entry of new trucklines and allowing the existing lines to eliminate the various restrictions on commodities carried, routes, and communities served. The truckers also were given more rate flexibility; private carriers could haul for others on back hauls, and owner operators could obtain certificates to operate as common carriers more easily.

These changes, as will be detailed in later chapters, were beneficial to rural communities. But their effect upon railroad service to rural areas is less clear and must be considered in conjunction with the greater flexibility allowed the railroads in adjusting rates under the Staggers Act. Without question the change enabled truckers to get some rural area traffic away from the railroads, particularly on back hauls. In specific instances the shift to trucking has been sufficiently great to endanger continued rail service. But on the other side of the picture the railroads have much greater flexibility in reducing rates quickly to meet truck competition, and on unregulated commodities such as fresh fruit and vegetables they can adjust without notice. One consequence is that the rails have recovered a small portion of the fruit and vegetable traffic they had lost. On the other hand, in the last five years there has been a major shifting of processed foods traffic from rail to truck—to the disadvantage of rural areas served by the lines. It will be some time before the net effects can be assessed.

The deregulation of piggyback traffic has facilitated growth in this traffic, which in part benefits rural areas.

Passenger Service to Rural Communities

By 1975, as noted earlier, most rail passenger service to rural communities had been discontinued. The formation of AMTRAK resulted in the elimination of much of the remaining; AMTRAK took over only about half of the trains still operating. In general, AMTRAK service is not geared at all to the provision of service to smaller communities. Only a small portion of the rail network of the country has service, and even on the lines served, the passenger trains typically do not stop at the smaller towns, and the schedules are geared to the preferences of the major terminal cities. The future of the entire AMTRAK system is not assured, given the federal budget deficit.

Conclusion

The railroad was once the dominant and almost exclusive form of transport connecting rural communities with the outside world. The development of motor transport and the ending of passenger train and less-than-carload freight service have greatly reduced the dependence of rural communities on the railroad, and the typical small community today receives little or no inbound freight by rail. But the railroad remains the low-cost carrier for bulk shipments, primarily outbound agricultural, mineral, and lumber products, plus some inbound movements of fertilizer and materials for local factories.

For decades the railroads made little effort to abandon lines serving rural communities, in part because of relatively restrictive policies of the Interstate Commerce Commission. The last twenty years have witnessed continued declines of rail traffic on many lines (even though railroad ton mileage nationwide has been relatively stable), and increasing efforts to abandon lines. Substantial mileage was abandoned with the formation of CONRAIL and subsequent bankruptcies of the Milwaukee and the Rock Island, and the railroads have become more active in seeking to eliminate unprofitable or low-profit lines. Changes in legislation and ICC policies have made approval of abandonment much easier.

As a consequence, increasing numbers of rural communities are faced with the loss of all rail services. The evidence to date has not shown drastic adverse effects on communities losing rail service, but there has been some negative effect. The greatest fear of communities is that the loss of rail service will prevent the attraction of new economic activity requiring rail service. Shippers and communities faced with the loss of rail service must first decide whether retention of the rail service is justified, and if they conclude that it is, map strategy to retain it. This may warrant an all-out effort to prevent abandonment, approval for which, while general, is not universal. But a more positive approach in seeking to preserve service involves support for formation of local or regional low-cost railroads.

Notes

1. For example, in Indiana there were only two communities (Rising Sun and Leopold) with 1920 population in excess of 1,000 (both under 1,500) that never were served by a railroad line. There were ten nonrailroad towns with population between 500 and 1,000. In Iowa, there were only three between 500 and 1,000 that never had rail service, and none over 1,000.

2. Utah had the greatest relative number of nonrailroad towns—five over 1,000, four between 500 and 1,000. St. George, with a 1920 population of 2,000 and by 1940 of over 4,000, was one of the largest rural towns in the country never to have rail service. The large number in Utah was a product of the very long distances between communities with little in between and the Mormon colonization system, which sent out settlers to remote areas well in advance of railroads. Colorado had two nonrailroad towns over 1,000—Cortez and Meeker; California had a greater number; eleven with population between 500 and 1,000, but only three—Lakeport, San Andreas, and Mendocino—over 1,000 (all under 1,500).

3. The sample included all branch lines of the Union Pacific, Rock Island, Santa Fe, Louisville and Nashville, Missouri Pacific, Great Northern, and Milwaukee. The data were obtained from timetables of the early 1930s. This period was selected because of data availability. There had been little contraction of service by that date.

4. All of these no-service lines that were in operation in 1916 had received regular service in that year.

5. This includes those with a mixed or motor train in addition to the passenger train on 8 percent.

6. There have been several general studies of railroad abandonment, including C. R. Cherington, *The Regulation of Railroad Abandonments* (Cambridge: Harvard University Press, 1948); Michael Conant, *Railroad Mergers and Abandonments* (Berkeley: University of California Press, 1964); Interstate Commerce Commission, *Railroad Abandonment 1920–1943* (Washington, DC: Interstate Commerce Commission, 1946); U.S. Department of Transportation, *Railroad Abandonments and Alternatives* (Washington, DC: U.S. Department of Transportation, 1976).

7. The states still have power over industrial spurs, but this rule is of little consequence.

8. *Brooks-Scanlon Co. v. RR Commission of Louisiana,* 251 U.S. 396 (1920).

9. The lines were described in detail in the Preliminary and Final Plans of the U.S. Railroad Association.

10. A carrier seeking to abandon a line must file a Notice of Intent 30 days before the application is filed, and the filing must take place at least 60 days before the proposed abandonment date. If the ICC conducts an investigation of the abandonment, it must order the investigation no less than 55 days after the filing of the application, complete its hearing within 180 days, and issue its order within 120 days after the investigation is completed. This rule was designed to lessen delays.

11. U.S. Department of Transportation, *Railroad Abandonments and Alternatives* p. 30.

12. Data supplied by Interstate Commerce Commission, and *Annual Reports,* 1983, 1984.

13. Interstate Commerce Commission, Ex Parte No. 274 (Sub-No. 8), *Exemption of Out of Service Rail Lines,* November 21, 1986.

14. Good examples of approval are provided by Burlington Northern Railroad Company—Abandonment—in Fergus, Judith Basin, and Chouteau Counties, Montana, AB-6 (Sub-No. 175), decided July 26, 1984; Southern Pacific Transportation Co.—Abandonment—in Fresno County, California, AB-12 (Sub-No. 75), decided November 29, 1984; and Seaboard System Railroad, Inc.—Abandonment—in Boone, Carroll, Clinton, Hamilton, and Marion Counties, Indiana, AB-55 (Sub-No. 94), decided March 19, 1985.

15. 49 USG 1090(a)(2).

16. In Southern Pacific Transportation Company Abandonment, in Houston, Harris County, Texas, AB-12 (Sub-No. 106, Sept. 8, 1986), an application to

abandon a two-mile line, initially granted, was rejected on appeal on the grounds that the loss was incorrectly calculated.

A major element in the ICC's denial of the petition of the Southern Pacific to abandon its 134-mile Bowie-Miami line in Arizona (Southern Pacific Transportation Company — Abandonment — in Gila, Graham, and Cochise Counties, Arizona, AB-12 [Sub-No. 104], Sept. 9, 1986), was the company's failure to demonstrate losses, coupled with the loss to shippers, that would result from abandonment because of high trucking costs. The demonstration of losses element also played a part in the denial of the ICG's application to abandon its Seymour line in Illinois (Illinois Central Gulf Railroad Co. — Abandonment — in Champaign County, Illinois, AB-43 [Sub-No. 143], January 6, 1986).

17. This can be illustrated by a number of cases, for example, Los Angeles and Salt Lake Railroad Co. Abandonment and Discontinuance of Service by Union Pacific Railroad Company, in Millard County, Utah, AB-25 (Sub-No. 7), decided March 28, 1984 (the principal shipper was making primary use of trucks); Burlington Northern Railroad Company — Abandonment — in Yakima County, Washington, AB-6 (Sub-No. 197), decided July 23, 1984, in which most of the traffic was moving by truck or piggyback.

18. Burlington Northern Railroad Co. — Abandonment — in Modoc and Siskiyou Counties, California, AB-6 (Sub-No. 174), decided April 24, 1984.

19. Seaboard System Railroad, Inc. — Abandonment — in Bacon County, Georgia, AB-55 (Sub-No. 72), decided December 16, 1983.

20. Chicago and Northwestern Transportation Co. — Abandonment — in Stanley, Jones, Haakon, Jackson and Fennington Counties, South Dakota, AB-1 (Sub-No. 154), decided November 19, 1983. Note also the decision in the Southern Pacific case noted above, and CSX Transportation, Inc. — Abandonment — in Thomas and Colquitt Counties, Georgia, AB-55 (Sub-No. 181), decided June 3, 1987.

21. Interstate Commerce Commission, *Class Exemption — Acq. and Oper. of Railroad Lines under 49USG10901,* 1 ICC2d 810 C (1986).

22. Interstate Commerce Commission, *Railroad Abandonments, 1920– 1943,* Washington, DC, January 1945 (mimeo).

23. *Growth and Change,* Vol. 8, No. 2 (April 1977), pp. 8-14.

24. Washington, DC: U.S. Department of Transportation, 1976.

25. John F. Due, State Rail Plans and Programs, *Quarterly Review of Economics and Business,* Vol. 19 (Summer 1979), pp. 109–30. For a recent example, three of the projects reviewed in the *1987 Illinois Rail Plan* (Springfield: Illinois Department of Transportation, 1987) show B/C ratios of 142, 69, and 40, respectively. Three projects reported in the 1987/88 *New Jersey State Rail Plan* (Trenton: New Jersey Department of Transportation, 1987) show B/C ratios from retention of rail service of 79, 21, and 19, respectively. One line in Oregon shows a figure of 42 (*Oregon Rail Plan, 1986 Update,* [Salem: Oregon Department of Transportation, 1986]). These figures are illustrative of the high B/C ratios; many, of course, are lower.

26. The communitywide effort of Centerville, Iowa, to acquire and place back in service the rail line serving the community to avoid the danger of losing

the town's major industry is a classic example of this, but there are many others as well.

27. Two of the best sources of information, though not entirely current, are Harvey A. Levine et al., *Small Railroads* (Washington, DC: Association of American Railroads, 1982), Chap. 11; and R. Lawrence McCaffrey, Jr., and Peter A. Gilbertson, *Starting A Short Line* (Fairfax, VA: Virginia Book Distributors, 1983), Chap. 6.

28. The primary DOT sources include the Section 5050 preference share approach; Section 511, Loan Guarantee; and the Rail Services Assistance Act, for which only $15 million was appropriated in FY 1985, and $10 million is proposed for 1990.

29. John F. Due, "The Surprising Role of the States and Local Governments in Preserving Rail Freight Service," *State Government,* Vol. 58 (Spring 1985): pp. 7–12.

30. Nancy D. Sidhu, Alberta Charney, and John F. Due, "Cost Functions of Class II Railroads and the Viability of Light Traffic Density Railway Lines," *Quarterly Review of Economics and Business,* Vol. 17 (Autumn 1977), pp. 7–24.

31. Alberta Charney, Nancy Sidhu, and John F. Due, "Short Run Cost Functions for Class II Railroads," *Logistics and Transportation Review,* Vol. 13 No. 48 (1977), pp. 345–59.

32. Washington, DC: Interstate Commerce Commission, December 1986.

33. Under present legislation and policy, the ICC approves by the exemption procedure any transfer of a line from a major company to a new local company so long as the latter appears to be responsible. In past decades, while the ICC approved a number of such transfers, it was not always sympathetic, fearing that the new company would not survive, and thus required the major company to continue to operate the line. A good illustration is provided by the refusal of the ICC to allow the Colorado and Southern to abandon its Leadville line and permit a local company to take it over. Note *Colorado and Southern Railway Abandonment,* 166 ICC 470 (1930); *Denver Intermountain and Summit Acquisition,* 193 ICC 707 (1933).

34. Fairfax, VA: Virginia Book Distributors, 1983. Note also the volumes by Peter S. Fisher and Michael F. Sheehan, *Possibilities for Local, Public, and Cooperative Ownership of Short Line Railroads* (Iowa City: Institute of Urban and Regional Research, University of Iowa, 1980).

35. Interstate Commerce Commission, (Washington, DC: 1988).

36. McCaffrey and Gilbertson, *Starting a Short Line*; E. P. Patton and C. L. Langley, Jr., *Handbook for Preservation of Local Railroad Service* (National Technical Information Service, Springfield, VA, 1980), excerpted in *Resource Information for Potential Short Line Operations* (Madison: Wisconsin Department of Transportation, June 1980). Interstate Commerce Commission, *Before Your Start a Small Railroad, A Brief Overview of Things to Consider* (Washington, DC, 1988).

37. In addition to the references noted in the previous footnote, additional ones include: R. L. Banks & Associates, Inc., *Economic Study of Light Density Rail Line Operations* (Washington, DC: U.S. Department of Transportation, 1973); "Methodology for Calculating Revenues and Costs of Assuming a Short

Line Operation," *Wisconsin State Rail Plan* (Madison: Wisconsin Department of Transportation, 1981); *Short Line Costs in New York State* (Albany: New York Department of Transportation, 1974).

38. Ralph J. Moore, Jr., and D. Eugenia Langan, "Short Line and Regional Railroad Sales: Railway Labor Act Concerns," paper presented at American Railroad Conference on Small and Regional Railroads (Washington, DC, October 1987).

39. John F. Due, *The Nationwide Experience with New Small Railroads Formed to Take Over Abandoned Lines, 1971–84,* Paper No. 7, Caterpillar Tractor Co. working paper series, Bureau of Economic and Business Research (University of Illinois, Champaign-Urbana, May 1984); "New Railroad Companies Formed to Take Over Abandoned or Spun Off Lines," *Transportation Journal,* Vol. 24 (Fall 1984), pp. 30–50; *Update as of October 1986 on New Railroads Formed to Take Over Lines Abandoned or Spun Off by Major Railroads,* Paper No. 18, and *The Causes of Failure of Small and Regional Railroads,* Paper No. 21, both Caterpillar Tractor Co. working paper series, (Bureau of Economic and Business Research, University of Illinois, Champaign-Urbana, November 1986 and October 1987); Association of American Railroads, *Statistics of Regional and Small Railroads.* Washington, DC: Association of American Railroads, 1988.

40. The extreme example was Southern Pacific's actions in placing a $1,200 per car surcharge on the traffic on the Northwestern Pacific's line north of Willits, California. The effect was to end the traffic on the line, later acquired by a local company.

41. U.S. Department of Agriculture, *An Assessment of Impacts on Agriculture of the Staggers Rail Act and Motor Carrier Act of 1980* (Washington, DC: August 1982); and *Effects of the Staggers Rail Act on Grain Marketing* (Washington, DC: July 1984).

42. For illustrations, note the article by L. Orlo Sorensen, "Some Impacts of Rail Regulatory Changes on Grain Industries," *American Journal of Agricultural Economics,* Vol. 66 (December 1984): pp. 645–50.

Small Community Trucking Service

Introduction

More than 64 percent of all U.S. communities do not have rail service and thus depend primarily upon trucking for their freight transportation needs.[1] The trucking industry utilizes the 714,000-mile highway system, which is substantially more extensive than the 147,000-mile rail system.[2] If a community depends substantially upon trucking service for both inbound and outbound freight movements, a loss or reduction of dependable truck service at reasonable rates could be viewed as reducing the economic viability of the community.

At the heart of the debate in Congress over regulatory reform in the trucking industry was the issue of the importance of motor common carrier service to the viability of small, rural communities. At one extreme it was argued that deregulation would terminate service obligations and thereby lead to the cessation of for-hire motor carrier service at "reasonable" rates to small communities and other places of light traffic density. At the other extreme were those who challenged the assertion that a common carrier system requires cross subsidization of service to rural communities on light density routes with profits generated on higher-volume routes. It was argued that such a practice was irrational for the profit-oriented business firm and that it was unrealistic to think the Interstate Commerce Commission (ICC) could oversee and enforce the service obligations of the multitude of motor common carriers.

The political importance of the perceived potential adverse impact of deregulation on rural communities was clearly revealed by various provisions of the Motor Carrier Act of 1980 (MCA of 1980). For example, the provision and maintenance of trucking service to small communities and small shippers were made part of the national transportation policy goals. In addition, it required the ICC to study the impact of the act on trucking service to small communities and to submit its report to the president and Congress by September 1982. The Motor Carrier Ratemaking Study Commission, created by the MCA of 1980, was specifically instructed to examine the possible impact of the elimination of the antitrust immunity for collective ratemaking on service to rural areas and small communities.[3] Despite of, or possibly because of, the political importance of the small community issue, the MCA of 1980 sidestepped the common carrier service issue. While Congress made adequate trucking service to small communities a national transportation policy goal, it left unclear whether more competition or more vigorous enforcement of the common carrier obligation would be adopted as the means to achieving it.

Not only has the trucking industry been regulated by both the federal and state governments for more than fifty years, it has also been promoted by all levels of government for a longer period of time through government outlays for highway construction and maintenance. In 1987 more than $62 billion of government outlays went for highways with about $14 billion coming from the federal government and $46 billion from state and local governments. In 1965 the outlays from all levels of government totaled only $13 billion.[4] Given the recent increases in highway fuel taxes at the federal level and similar increases at the state level, highway outlays should continue to increase.

Several changes since 1912, the beginning of the modern era of federal government financial assistance to highway development, should be noted. First, financing has shifted from lower to higher levels of government. Local governments in 1915 provided 90 percent of highway funds while in 1965 local governments provided only 20 percent of the financing.[5] Since 1985 the percentage that the federal and state governments were responsible for remained at nearly 77 percent.[6] Second, the sources of revenue have changed. In earlier years, property and other general fund taxes were primary sources of revenue, making up about 90 percent of all funds, while in 1965 highway user charges provided 80 percent of all highway funds. Third, a greater portion of total federal and state highway revenue is being contributed by users.[7]

Although the government outlays for highways are important in meeting the transportation needs of rural communities, the recent concern about trucking transportation and the viability of rural communities has been focused on the potential impacts of the deregulation of trucking. This chapter reviews the economic regulatory policy changes made by Congress and the ICC and how the trucking firms and shippers have reacted to these changing conditions with respect to small community trucking service. The impact of these changes on rural community trucking service is analyzed. Future trends and strategies are also indicated.

Changing Federal Policies

The Motor Carrier Act of 1935, which first established federal regulation of the trucking industry, was enacted in response to a demand by the trucking and rail industries. Some states had established economic regulations of trucking before 1935, and almost all of the states eventually established economic regulation of intrastate trucking. Although legislation relevant to the federal economic regulation of trucking had been passed before 1980, no basic changes were made to the economic regulation of trucking until 1980. In the early 1970s, however, regulatory reform legislative proposals began to surface for trucking, rail, and air. Beginning in 1977, with the strong backing of President Jimmy Carter, the ICC began to reinterpret the Interstate Commerce Act in favor of more emphasis on competition and less emphasis on regulation. In fact, some consider the MCA of 1980 as simply a fait accompli of earlier ICC decisions.

Small Community Trucking Service and Economic Regulation

As noted above, the opponents of trucking regulatory reform argued that the quality of trucking service provided and the rates charged for trucking service to shippers in rural communities would be adversely affected by the easier entry and increased pricing freedoms in the trucking industry. This viewpoint was based on three premises: (1) much of the trucking service to rural communities is inherently unprofitable to serve and thus rural towns would receive little or no service under deregulation; (2) carriers cross subsidize their unprofitable service to rural towns with the excess profits allowed by economic regulations; and (3) many small towns receive service only because the ICC-regulated carriers are fulfilling their common carrier obligation to serve.[8]

The ICC has two mechanisms to induce carriers to provide service to markets that they would normally not be willing to serve. First, the

ICC can enforce the common carrier obligation to serve, which all common carriers have as a quid pro quo for receiving operating authority. The common carrier obligation to serve, one of four common carrier obligations, requires a certificated carrier to hold itself out to serve all shippers/receivers of all sizes and in all communities within the limits of its operating authorities.[9] Assuming the ICC has sufficient resources to enforce the service obligation, rural communities would be guaranteed some type of trucking service by regulated carriers.

The second mechanism for inducing carriers to serve rural communities is through the development of a cross subsidy scheme as implemented through ICC rate regulation. For example, the ICC might allow a motor carrier to raise its prices on its profitable routes to a level that would yield even greater profits if the carrier agreed to provide rural community services. Rate regulations can be used by the ICC to minimize or eliminate urban-rural rate disparities. In effect, the ICC, through its regulation of rates, can hold down rates on rural community traffic, even though more costly to serve, and can maintain higher rates on the more profitable traffic to allow the cross subsidy.

Policy Changes Relevant to Small Community Service

The cornerstones of economic regulation of the trucking industry — entry and rate regulations — began to be chiseled away by the ICC under the leadership of Dan O'Neal without the benefit of any legislative changes. The changing membership of the ICC, the strong support of the president, and the intractability of inflation through normal macroeconomic policies combined to make regulatory reform in the trucking area a reality. Dan O'Neal's replacement as chairman of the ICC, Darius Gaskins, continued and increased the administrative push for regulatory reform. Before the MCA of 1980, the ICC, through its own case-by-case decisions and rulemakings, made it easier for trucking firms to enter the industry and new markets, allowed private carriers to more effectively encroach upon the common carrier market through a liberal intercorporate hauling ruling, made contract carriers more competitive with the common carrier by eliminating the rule of eight and the restriction on having dual authority, and made common carriers more competitive with other common carriers by eliminating some of the restrictions on operating certificates. Although less active on the ratemaking side, the ICC increased the amount of ratemaking flexibility and provided more effective constraints on the actions of rate bureaus.

Through the MCA of 1980, Congress essentially endorsed what the ICC had already administratively undertaken. Although some of the provisions indicated less deregulation than what the ICC had undertaken, only the ICC's previously instituted master certificate program was specifically prohibited by the act. In certain areas such as the appropriate status of rate bureaus the MCA of 1980 pushed regulatory reform even further. The ICC, given the liberal entry policy and the rate flexibility provisions of the MCA of 1980, began granting nationwide authorities and approving rate discounting on a large scale.

Changes to Common Carrier Concept.   Congress expressed substantial concern about small community trucking service in the MCA of 1980 but refused to endorse either competition or the common carrier service obligation as the mechanism for ensuring small community service. The MCA of 1980 did not eliminate or modify the common carrier service obligation. As noted earlier, this service standard requires the carrier to hold itself out to serve indiscriminately all shippers/receivers with reasonable requests in all communities listed in its operating certificate. In 1979, Allen and Breen attempted to delineate and clarify more precisely what this phrase meant in terms of required carrier behavior.[10] Alternatively phrased, what type of protection could a rural community shipper/receiver expect from this service obligation? The ICC interpretation required the regular-route common carrier to make its services known to prospective customers and actually perform the service if demanded and reasonable. Thus, a carrier could not pick and choose customers, which implies that more is required of these carriers — regular-route common carriers — than what unregulated, profit-maximizers would tend to offer. At the same time, however, it was found that substantial managerial discretion was allowed with respect to the quantity and quality of service that a common carrier could offer and still meet its common carrier service obligation. Because the service obligation as implemented by the ICC allowed such a wide variation in the level of service — for example, frequency of service, provision of specialized equipment, and maintenance of excess capacity — common carrier behavior implied by the service obligation was found to be indistinguishable from unregulated, profit-maximizing behavior with respect to these dimensions of service.

Although the MCA of 1980 did not directly alter the common carrier service obligation, two of its provisions had an indirect impact on the concept. First, Section 20 made it easier for motor carriers to pool or divide traffic. Thus, a carrier having authority to serve a rural community could provide through a pooling arrangement its required service through another carrier also having authority to serve the same community. Since 1971 the ICC had permitted a carrier under certain circumstances to meet its service obligation through interlining with another carrier instead of providing direct service.[11] In the late 1970s the ICC took this pooling alternative arrangement one step further by sanctioning of "convenience interlining" upon proper tariff publication.[12]

Second, the ICC interpreted the new liberal entry policy of the MCA of 1980 as allowing it to grant very broad authorities to carriers, in many cases, nationwide authorities. Many firms receiving such broad authorities actually requested much narrower authorities and had neither the personnel nor the equipment to hold themselves out to serve all shippers. The ICC soon realized that its policy to grant broad authorities created a possible need to redefine the common carrier service concept. On January 27, 1981, some seven months after the passage of the MCA of 1980, the ICC opened proceedings to examine the common carrier service concept and offered alternative definitions, including having the carrier define the scope of its responsibility through its tariff or by more informal means such as advertising.[13] In March of 1983, the ICC issued the following concluding statement:

> A common carrier is not in violation of its obligations if it declines to provide service within the scope of its operating authority because such service is economically or operationally impracticable in the circumstances at the time of the service request. To the extent that prior Commission decisions may have spoken of an absolute duty to provide service to the breadth of the operating certificate, those cases are overruled as inconsistent with law and policy.[14]

An ICC staff member interpreted this changed policy as still using the certificate as a measure of the carrier's holding out but that the carrier need only provide nondiscriminatory service to the extent of its actual operating capabilities.[15] This new definition at a minimum reduces the scope of the responsibility of a carrier and possibly eliminates any meaningful constraint on the previously prohibited practice of traffic selectivity. The impact of this change on small community service depends upon the degree to which the common carrier service obligation was enforced in past years and to what degree rural community trucking service is profitable and thus will be provided by carriers without regulatory intervention. Both of these issues are discussed below.

Changes in Level of Competition. Although proponents and opponents of deregulation disagreed about the degree of competition Congress intended to inject into the trucking industry via the MCA of 1980, the administration of the act by the ICC has been procompetitive. In addition, there was disagreement about what the impact of this added competition would be in terms of the quantity and quality of trucking service to rural communities.

On the positive side, it was argued that rural communities would have a much larger number of potential trucking firms to serve them. The number of ICC-regulated carriers has increased from about seventeen thousand to more than thirty thousand.[16] In addition, the removal of restrictions on operating certificates of common carriers and on the operations of private carriers has added to the number of potential carriers serving rural communities. Easy entry into the industry and into new markets forces the existing carriers to provide better service at reasonable rates. Furthermore, the new competition with flexible rates should produce more price-service options from which the shipper/receiver in the rural towns can select.

On the negative side, it was argued that the lack of entry control would dilute the profits being earned on the more lucrative routes which would prevent the carriers from cross subsidizing the rural community traffic. In addition, the reduced rate regulations might allow the carriers to more easily raise rates in small communities to reflect either the higher costs of providing the service or the lack of competition in these markets despite more competition in the industry in general. The net effect of these countervailing forces on the provision of service to rural communities has been the object of a number of studies that are reviewed below.

Nature of Demand and Supply of Rural Community Trucking Service

Before reviewing the available data on the impact of the regulatory changes on the costs and the quality and quantity of trucking service to rural communities, the nature of transportation demand and supply in these communities will be examined.

Nature of Transport Demand in Small Communities

The studies conducted on the issue of the effects of trucking deregulation revealed a great diversity in the types and sizes of businesses located in rural communities. Despite the diversity, it appears that rural community businesses are characteristically small. Most do not have a professional transportation staff or the wherewithal to expend much effort making transportation decisions. They appear to cope relatively well with their environment, however, because they tend not to have complex distribution needs, which are usually local or regional in nature. In addition, the incoming freight to rural community businesses comes from a small number or origins. One study revealed that 40 percent of small community businesses receives freight from a single source origin and 60 percent receives freight from less than ten origins. Also, many small community businesses are part of much larger distribution chains with sophisticated traffic departments, for example, Western Auto. The routing and other problems associated with distribution are handled by the chain's traffic department.[17]

In a 1978 nationwide study of 205 small and rural communities (defined as communities between 1,000 and 25,000 in population), 46 percent of the shippers were found to be engaged in retailing, 33 percent in manufacturing and processing, and 11 percent in wholesaling. In the smallest communities (1,000 and 2,500 in population), the percentage of businesses involved in retailing was much larger (73 percent). For the communities between 10,000 and 25,000, the percentage engaged in retailing dropped to 40 percent. The larger the community, the more important manufacturing was to the community. The other types of businesses — wholesaling, agriculture, mining, and construction — also were found to vary in terms of importance but never collectively matched either retailing or manufacturing in terms of importance.[18]

Although there are substantial variations in shipment characteristics of shippers in rural communities, certain common features have been found. Rural communities, particularly communities of less than 5,000 residents, have much more inbound traffic than outbound, reflecting the importance of retailing in smaller communities noted above.[19] In one of the more comprehensive rural community trucking studies, Kidder indirectly confirmed this imbalance of traffic found in earlier, regional-oriented studies, and also was able to determine the predominant type of freight service required by each of the 474 firms on which interviews were conducted. All 474 firms had inbound freight but only 226 had outbound freight. Of the receivers of inbound traffic, 130 were classified as needing small package service, 258 needing less-than-truckload (LTL) services, and 66 needing truckload (TL) services. Of the shippers of outbound freight, 99 were classified as needing small package service, 78 needed LTL services, and 49 required TL services.[20] In a nationwide ICC study required by Section 28 of the MCA of 1980, a profile of shippers in rural communities ranging in population from 100 to 15,000 was created. The study found a substantial range of traffic among the shippers extending from less than 1 shipment per month to over 1,200 shipments per week. About 80 percent of the respondents received between 1 and 10 shipments per week and the same percentage sent between 1 and

10 shipments per week. The range in shipment size among the shippers was also large with the most frequent shipment size being less than 500 pounds.[21]

Although data on the types of carriers that rural community shippers tend to use undoubtedly reflect both the types of services demanded and the types of services supplied, they do suggest the potential impact of deregulation on small community shippers. The ICC study found that a very small percentage of rural community shippers/receivers relied solely on private carriage (about 1 percent). More than 23 percent relied solely upon for-hire motor carriage. The data also indicated the shippers use many different types of transportation services.[22] Table 3.1 contains the results of the survey conducted by the ICC in 1982, which revealed that a large number of different types of transportation services are used and that there are substantial differences between types of transportation

Table 3.1. Transportation used by rural community shippers, Interstate Commerce Commission—Section 28 study

Type of Transportation (by size of community)	Percentage of Shippers Using Service in Last Six Months	
	Inbound	Outbound
UPS		
5,000–15,000	92.0	41.9
Under 5,000	93.9	38.6
General freight		
5,000–15,000	69.4	27.5
Under 5,000	67.6	20.1
Private truck		
5,000–15,000	68.8	36.9
Under 5,000	73.1	34.9
Parcel post		
5,000–15,000	51.9	37.5
Under 5,000	65.5	40.7
Bus package		
5,000–15,000	30.3	16.0
Under 5,000	26.8	10.3
Air freight		
5,000–15,000	14.6	6.0
Under 5,000	13.6	5.2
Other parcel		
5,000–15,000	11.2	5.5
Under 5,000	12.6	5.2
Railroad		
5,000–15,000	6.5	2.7
Under 5,000	5.4	1.6
Other		
5,000–15,000	0.8	0.1
Under 5,000	2.4	1.6

Source: Interstate Commerce Commission, *Small Community Service Study* (Washington, DC: Interstate Commerce Commission, 1982), Table A-2.

Note: Data based upon questionnaires returned by 786 small, rural community shippers surveyed in July 1981.

used for inbound and outbound freight. In addition, a significant difference between shippers in communities with five thousand residents or less and shippers in the larger small communities, five thousand to fifteen thousand persons, was found with respect to transportation use.

In her detailed study of shippers in small communities in three southern and three northern states, Kidder found a substantially greater relative use of private carriage for outbound traffic than for inbound traffic. Table 3.2 provides a summary of her findings. Supplementing these findings are the results from the nationwide survey conducted by the Senate Commerce study cited above, which are summarized in Tables 3.33, 3.4, and 3.5. This study found that shippers tended to ship all or nothing by a particular form of carriage—more than 60 percent of the shippers indicated that all of their outbound traffic moved by only one type of carrier. Second, manufacturers were found to be more reliant on common carriage than were the all-industry respondents. Third, there was less reliance on common carriage by firms in small communities for inbound shipments.

Table 3.2. Transportation demand by rural community shippers, Kidder study, 1981–1982

	Number	%	Cumulative %
Scope of business (distance of shipments)			
Town only	192	40.7	40.7
Within 100 miles	160	33.9	74.6
Intrastate only	12	2.5	77.1
Regional	56	11.9	89.3
National	35	7.4	96.7
International	17	3.3	100.0
Type of inbound traffic			
Primarily small package	139	28.6	28.6
Primarily less-than-truckload	258	56.8	85.4
Primarily truckload	66	14.5	100.0
Type of outbound traffic			
Primarily small package	99	20.8	20.8
Primarily less-than-truckload	78	16.5	37.3
Primarily truckload	49	10.3	47.6
No outbound	248	52.3	100.0
Percentage of inbound freight tonnage by private carriage			
None	173	36.5	—
Less than 10	52	11.0	—
10–50	64	13.5	—
50–90	65	13.7	—
Over 90	120	25.3	—
Percentage of outbound freight tonnage moved by private carriage (only the 226 shippers with outbound traffic)			
Less than 10	31	13.7	—
10–50	49	21.8	—
50–90	26	11.5	—
Over 90	120	53.0	—

Source: Alice Kidder, *Impact of Regulatory Reform on Shipper/Receiver Freight Service in Selected Rural Communities, 1982: A Second Follow-Up Study* (Washington, DC: Department of Transportation, 1983), Table 1.

Table 3.3. Shipments moved by type of motor carrier (percentage of respondents)

	Percentage of Shipments				
	0	1 to 19	20 to 79	80 to 99	100
All industry					
Inbound					
Common	22.3	14.5	21.4	9.4	32.4
Exempt	98.2	0.2	0.0	0.8	0.4
Private	39.1	9.0	19.0	15.7	17.2
Contract	91.8	2.8	1.2	1.4	0.8
Special	96.2	1.4	0.4	0.4	0.8
Outbound					
Common	37.6	15.0	14.0	7.1	27.0
Exempt	96.6	0.4	0.8	0.4	1.8
Private	36.4	9.5	11.1	11.9	30.5
Contract	87.6	2.2	3.5	5.8	0.9
Special	98.7	0.0	0.4	0.0	0.9
Manufacturers					
Inbound					
Common	10.1	21.0	31.9	15.9	21.1
Exempt	96.7	0.0	1.7	1.6	0.0
Private	27.7	21.0	30.3	17.6	3.4
Contract	82.4	9.3	5.8	0.8	1.7
Special	76.5	11.8	10.0	1.7	0.0
Outbound					
Common	14.0	20.7	19.9	20.7	24.7
Exempt	91.9	4.9	2.4	0.0	0.8
Private	37.9	19.0	16.6	20.7	5.8
Contract	80.2	7.4	6.6	3.3	2.5
Special	90.1	4.2	4.9	0.8	0.0

Source: U.S. Congress, Senate, Committee on Commerce, Science, and Transportation, *The Impact on Small Communities of Motor Carriage Regulatory Revision* (Washington, DC: U.S. Government Printing Office, June 1978), Exhibit IV-6.

Note: Data based on personal interviews conducted in 1978 of more than 500 shippers in 205 small, rural communities.

Table 3.4. Reliance on common carriage, by community size (percent of respondents)

	Inbound		Outbound	
Population	Not reliant	Heavily reliant	Not reliant	Heavily reliant
All industry				
1,000 to 2,500	50.0	32.5	50.1	41.6
2,500 to 5,000	35.5	43.8	56.9	33.3
5,000 to 10,000	40.8	34.0	49.9	29.3
10,000 to 25,000	30.2	50.3	52.2	38.8
Manufacturing				
1,000 to 2,500	41.7	33.2	44.5	33.2
2,500 to 5,000	32.3	32.3	40.4	37.6
5,000 to 10,000	18.1	45.7	30.4	52.3
10,000 to 25,000	26.7	40.0	20.0	63.3

Source: U.S. Congress, Senate, Committee on Commerce, Science, and Transportation, *The Impact on Small Communities of Motor Carriage Regulatory Revision* (Washington, DC: U.S. Government Printing Office, June 1978), Exhibit IV-7.

Note: "Heavily reliant" is defined as use for 80 percent or more of shipments; "not reliant" is defined as under 20 percent use. Data are based on personal interviews conducted in 1978 of more than 500 shippers in small, rural communities.

Table 3.5. Reliance on private carriage, by community size (percent of respondents)

Population	Inbound		Outbound	
	Not reliant	Heavily reliant	Not reliant	Heavily reliant
All industry				
1,000 to 2,500	40.0	42.5	66.7	25.0
2,500 to 5,000	49.0	33.6	43.1	48.5
5,000 to 10,000	38.1	37.4	44.0	40.0
10,000 to 25,000	60.3	24.1	49.1	41.9
Manufacturing				
1,000 to 2,500	41.5	25.1	47.2	33.3
2,500 to 5,000	38.7	29.1	40.7	37.4
5,000 to 10,000	50.2	18.1	74.0	17.3
10,000 to 25,000	66.7	10.0	73.4	13.3

Source: U.S. Congress, Senate, Committee on Commerce, Science, and Transportation, *The Impact on Small Communities of Motor Carriage Regulatory Revision* (Washington, DC: U.S. Government Printing Office, June 1978), Exhibit IV-8.

Note: "Heavily reliant" is defined as use for 80 percent or more of shipments; "not reliant" is defined as under 20 percent use. Data are based on personal interviews conducted in 1978 of more than 500 shippers in small, rural communities.

Nature of Transportation Supply in Rural Communities

As the data in the tables mentioned above clearly indicate, shippers in rural communities have a number of transportation alternatives from which to choose. It is clear that many of the shippers in these rural communities, especially communities with greater emphasis on the retailing industry, rely primarily on private carriers and small package specialists such as UPS and bus package service. Communities vary somewhat in terms of their reliance upon common carriage depending upon the region in which the community is located and the amount of manufacturing activity in the community. The Motor Carrier Ratemaking Study Commission concluded that common carriage is important to small communities but not necessarily critical.[23]

Characteristics of General Freight Service to Small Communities.   In a study of general freight carriers in eight small communities in the Northwest, Breen and Allen found that most of the direct service to rural communities was provided by the smaller interstate carriers.[24] On the other hand, the data in the Continuous Traffic Study (CTS) indicated that the large interstate carriers provide their share of rural community service. The CTS data support the position that the types of carriers that serve rural communities do not appear to be significantly different from those that serve large communities.[25] Available 1980 data indicate that traffic carried by regulated carriers has a slightly higher probability of moving under class rates and a slightly higher probability of being in a higher rating if it originates in a sparsely populated county.[26]

As one might expect, a lower density of freight activity is found in rural areas, making it more difficult to serve. Most (80 percent) of the traffic originating in rural communities is destined for counties in metropolitan areas and the same percentage of traffic destined for the communities originated in counties in metropolitan areas. Interestingly, the freight imbalance found in small, rural communities apparently is no different than what is found in many smaller metropolitan areas.[27]

The most distinguishing characteristic of rural community trucking service is the prevalence of interlining. Table 3.7 contains data on the degree to which interlining was used in 1976 and 1980, several years after ICC regulatory reform took place but before the MCA of 1980 was implemented. The Beale's Code, which is used in Table 3.7, is presented in Table 3.6. Less than 30 percent of all shipments between urban areas

Table 3.6. Calvin Beale's metro adjacency codes

Code	Definition
1	County of SMSA. SMSA population at least 1,000,000 in 1970
2	County of SMSA. SMSA population 250,000–999,999 in 1970
3	County of SMSA. SMSA population 50,000–249,999 in 1970
4	County with at least 20,000 urban residents, contiguous to an SMSA
5	County with at least 20,000 urban residents, not contiguous to an SMSA
6	County with 2,500–19,999 urban residents, contiguous to an SMSA
7	County with 2,500–19,999 urban residents, not contiguous to an SMSA
8	County with no urban residents, contiguous to an SMSA
9	County with no urban residents, not contiguous to an SMSA

Source: Motor Carrier Ratemaking Study Commission, *Collective Ratemaking in the Trucking Industry* (Washington, DC: Motor Carrier Ratemaking Commission, June 1, 1983), Chap. 8, exhibit 2.

Note: An urban resident is a resident of a place or township with 2,500 or more inhabitants in 1970. A county is contiguous to an adjacent SMSA if at least 1 percent of workers in the county commute to the SMSA.

Table 3.7. Percentage of shipments interlined by year, by Beale's Code for shipment origins and destinations

Beale's Code	For Shipment Origins		For Shipment Destinations	
	1976	1980	1976	1980
1	25	17	21	14
2	28	19	26	17
3	41	30	39	29
4	42	31	43	35
5	54	40	48	39
6	52	43	56	45
7	59	49	55	48
8	63	57	60	53
9	66	59	64	61

Source: Motor Carrier Ratemaking Study Commission, *Collective Ratemaking in the Trucking Industry* (Washington, DC: Motor Carrier Ratemaking Commission, June 1, 1983), Chap 8, exhibits 22 and 23.

were interlined for these years, while over 50 percent of all shipments destined to or originating in totally rural counties were interlined. The degree of interlining decreased slightly during the five-year period.[28]

Rates for Small Community Trucking Service.   In addition to the nature of the types of general freight trucking services offered to shippers in rural communities, it is important to note the cost factor. Data on rates offered to rural community shippers are not as good as the data on service. The ICC, as part of its Section 28 study, conducted an analysis that allows some comparison of rates offered to rural community shippers with rates offered to urban shippers. The effects of deregulation on the rates offered to rural community shippers will be discussed later. Using Beale's 1970 code and CTS data for the years 1976 and 1980, a time by which some of the ICC regulatory reform administrative actions had taken effect, the ICC ran regressions that allowed a comparison of the rates for moving a typical shipment to or from a rural community with rates for a similar movement to or from a larger, more urban community. The results, reported in Tables 3.8 and 3.9, indicate that in 1976, the more heavily regulated period, rates varied little by size of community. The key question, which will be addressed later, is whether this resulted from ICC regulation or market forces at the time. By 1980, the evidence appears to indicate that the rate structure had shifted slightly in favor of smaller or more remote communities.[29]

Table 3.8. Comparison of estimated revenue for typical shipments by size of origin and destination in 1976 and 1980

Year	Larger Beale's 1, 2, 3, 4, & 5		Smaller Beale's 6, 7		Smallest Beale's 8, 9	
	Origin	Destination	Origin	Destination	Origin	Destination
1980	$54.92	$54.98	$53.20	$54.11	$49.19	$50.96
1976	37.12	37.24	37.95	35.82	36.24	38.58

Source: Interstate Commerce Commission, *Small Community Service Study* (Washington, DC: Interstate Commerce Commission, 1982), Table 8.

Table 3.9. Comparison of estimated revenue for typical shipments, by remoteness from urban areas of origin and destination in 1976 and 1980

Year	Large Beale's 1, 2, 3, 4, & 5		Small Contiguous Beale's 6 & 8		Small Noncontiguous Beale's 7 & 9	
	Origin	Destination	Origin	Destination	Origin	Destination
1980	$54.92	$54.98	$53.72	$55.53	$52.50	$52.64
1976	37.12	37.24	38.69	36.33	37.15	36.13

Source: Interstate Commerce Commission, *Small Community Service Study* (Washington, DC: Interstate Commerce Commission, 1982), Table 9.

Profitability of Small Community Trucking Service. The question of profitability of small community service is related to the issue of the nature of transportation supply and was a very important issue in the debate preceding the MCA of 1980. Rural community markets have certain characteristics that make them more costly to serve than urban areas. For example, the low density of traffic and imbalance between inbound and outbound tend to increase the costs of providing service. Past studies have found, however, that rural community service can be and is profitable for certain carriers. Carriers serving rural towns reduce the frequency of service, operate "peddle runs," impose extra charges ("arbitraries"), and take advantage of the less congested nature of rural areas and the more flexible employee practices.[30]

Effects of Deregulation
on Rural Community Trucking Service

A number of studies conducted before the MCA of 1980 was enacted and before the ICC regulatory reform administrative actions had been undertaken strongly suggested that deregulation would have minimal adverse effects on the amount, quality, and cost of rural community trucking service. For example, a number of studies found that traffic selectivity—behavior that is not consistent with the common carrier service obligation—was found to take place in a large number of situations. In their study in the Pacific Northwest, Breen and Allen found that the regulated common carriers, particularly the larger ones, behaved more like unregulated profit-maximizers than common carriers.[31] This finding is supported by several other studies conducted in the late 1970s.[32] Although less numerous, other studies indicated that the rural community trucking service was profitable for the carriers.[33] In addition, the studies revealed as indicated above that shippers in small communities had available and used several different types of trucking services, including private carriage, UPS, and bus package service. The basic conclusion from these studies was that regulation was neither effective, based upon the finding that traffic selectivity was pervasive, nor necessary, based upon the finding that small community trucking service was profitable. In fact, many economists argued that with easier entry into the industry and into specific markets, rural communities would likely have better service after deregulation.

Sufficient time has now passed to examine the actual impact of deregulation on rural community trucking service. A number of studies have been undertaken, one by congressional mandate, that have attempted to measure the impact of federal trucking deregulation on the service provided and the rates offered to rural community shippers. Several other studies have examined the impact of trucking deregulation at the state level. The results of these studies are summarized below.

Effects of Federal Trucking Deregulation

A number of studies have been conducted ranging from a nationwide study by the ICC to a number of studies examining the impact in one state. The studies range from one by Kidder (1985), who developed a longitudinal study of the effects in six states, to studies looking at only one postderegulation point in time and comparing the service and rate levels to a preregulation period of time. Sponsors of the studies include the ICC, the federal DOT, and state government agencies. Despite the diversity of approaches taken, sponsorship, duration of time covered, size of sample used, and the actual states covered, the results have been remarkably consistent. Beilock and Freeman, in a study of small community studies, concluded, "The overwhelming weight of the evidence gathered to date clearly shows that deregulation of regulatory reform has had either a neutral or moderately positive impact on the quality and level of service offered, and the rates charged to nonurban shippers/receivers."[34] Several of the more important studies are reviewed below.

The Kidder Study.   In the most thorough longitudinal study of the effects of relaxation of trucking regulations and more competition on the level and cost of trucking service in small communities, Alice Kidder has conducted four follow-up studies to the one she initially conducted in the 1978–1979 time period. The initial study concentrated on six hundred shippers and receivers in six target areas within North Carolina, South Carolina, and Georgia. In 1981 a follow-up survey was undertaken of service levels of some of the six hundred respondents in the initial survey. In addition, 243 rural firms in the states of Maine, New York, and Pennsylvania were interviewed in the fall of 1980.

In 1982 a second follow-up study was undertaken that involved the reinterviewing of the shippers and receivers in the southern sample (North Carolina, South Carolina, and Georgia) and the northern sample (Maine, New York, and Pennsylvania). In June 1983 Kidder conducted a third round of follow-up interviews on some 495 firms. The shippers selected for this third round represented manufacturing, wholesaling, retailing, construction, and other types of firms. Firms chosen were located in counties where the rural population constituted 70 percent or more of the total. In May and June of 1985 Kidder conducted a fourth and final round of follow-up interviews with more than 200 firms randomly selected from the firms originally sampled. Thus, the Kidder studies encompass many observations for each of five different time periods and from two different regions in the country.

The basic results indicate that only 4 percent of the respondents in the third follow-up survey reported a decline in quality of service, which Kidder defined as timeliness and security of the service. Frequency of service, which was considered separately, has declined in each of the last two follow-up observation years indicating that motor carriers are adjusting their pickups and deliveries to account for the level of demand. Freight rates in the third year follow-up survey increased although many respondents did not know if the increase was greater than the increase in cost of living. Kidder noted that these findings suggest that the carriers are adjusting the charges for freight service to less accessible areas although she did not collect data on urban-rural comparisons.[35]

Kidder's overall conclusion in the fourth follow-up study was that service quality and quantity have not diminished with regulatory reform for the vast majority of shippers in rural areas. The number of competing carriers has actually increased in rural areas. Very little has changed for most shippers since the first study was conducted in 1978–1979. These shippers rely heavily upon UPS for small package service and make considerable use of private carriage. Generally acceptable levels of service are available from an array of certified carriers. Carriers are making adjustments with respect to rates and frequency of service. Rates have adjusted upward in rural areas with the steepest rate increases found in the most remote areas.[36]

Section 28 ICC Study.   Congress mandated a thorough investigation of trucking service to small communities to determine if regulatory reform had any adverse effects on rural community shippers.[37] The ICC used a shipper survey that was mailed to about 1,200 randomly selected businesses in randomly selected small communities. The businesses were broken into two groups with each group asked to comment on the prior six-month period. The three mailings were January 1981 (Group 1), July 1981 (repeated for Group 1 and added Group 2), and January 1982 (repeated for Group 2). Each mailing was considered a phase. In comparison with the Kidder study, this study had the advantage of using a nationwide sample but the disadvantage of a shorter time period over which to observe changes in carrier and shipper behavior.

The report considered the impact of deregulation upon service and rates. In terms of service availability, the study found that over the three phases of the shipper survey, service availability changed very little.

Shippers reporting service availability improvement ranged from four to eight times higher than those reporting poorer service availability. With respect to on-time performance and loss and damage, the two main dimensions of the ICC's quality of service variable, the study concluded that the record was fairly consistent in all three phases or time periods. The only exception was that in Phase 1 of the study, shippers indicated that they were having more difficulty in resolving loss and damage claims than they had prior to 1980.[38]

The ICC also examined the issue of the effect of regulatory reform upon the freight rates charged to small community shippers and receivers. Because of the inability to audit freight bills and the unreliability of survey data on rate levels, the ICC decided to use the CTS data. Having access only to the 1976 and 1980 CTS data at the time of the study, the ICC was forced to perform the analysis upon the assumption that 1976 represented the preregulatory reform era whereas 1980 was viewed as a more competitive time period due to the administrative regulatory reform measures undertaken by the ICC. The results indicated that rates to and from small communities increased less rapidly in the period of regulatory reform than rates to or from large cities (see Tables 3.8 and 3.9).[39]

The Iowa Study.   During April 1986 the Iowa Department of Transportation conducted a survey to determine the effects of the federal regulatory reform of motor carriers on regulated trucking service to Iowa's smaller communities. With few exceptions, the large urban areas (over fifty thousand population) were excluded from the survey and thus it addressed the issue of the impact of deregulation and increased competition on rural areas of Iowa.[40]

More than 500 mail-back survey questionnaires to motor carrier users were distributed: 160 to businesses contacted for the 1980 Iowa DOT study titled "Motor Carrier Service to Small Communities in Iowa,"[41] and 360 to additional shippers and receivers selected from a list of businesses provided by the Iowa Development Commission. An attempt was made to survey shippers in each of the state's ninety-nine counties.

The survey indicated that certified common carrier was the most highly used type of motor carrier with 71 percent of the shippers using the regulated motor common carrier and that LTL was the most typical shipment size. The results strongly indicated the lack of any adverse effects of regulatory reform at the federal level on small rural shippers in Iowa. Forty percent of the respondents stated that their service had improved, 10 percent noted a decrease in the level of service, 22 percent said there was no change, and 28 percent did not respond (assumed by the Iowa DOT staff to reflect no change in service). In terms of rate changes, 11 percent of the respondents noted increases in rates, 18 percent noted a decrease in rates, and 71 percent did not respond to the rate change question. There was no correlation between a decrease in service/ higher rates and the size of the community. There was a correlation, however, between the size of the firm and service/rates.

Other Studies.   Several other studies analyzing the impacts of federal trucking regulatory reform on rural community trucking service in particular states or regions had similar results. Borlaug conducted a field study of motor carrier service to six small communities in Nevada and Oregon one year after the passage of the MCA of 1980. She found that the shippers and receivers were satisfied with their overall level of service and that service had not deteriorated since the 1980 act was passed.[42] The state of Washington found no significant change in loss and damage settlements, transit times, or the number of carriers used between the preact and postact period.[43] A study of the impacts of the MCA of 1980 on the trucking service to small towns in Minnesota by Harper, though detecting some additional rate discrimination in favor of large community shippers since regulatory reform, found that shippers in small communities generally thought regulatory reform was a positive development.[44]

Effects of State Trucking Deregulation

All but two states (New Jersey and Delaware) established fairly extensive economic regulations of at least the common carrier trucking industry. Many of the states patterned their regulatory systems after the federal trucking economic regulatory system established by the Motor Carrier Act of 1935. Although most state regulatory agencies continue to base trucking regulation, in whole or in part, on the traditional system, changes at the state level are beginning to occur, most in keeping with the new federal policy. Alaska, Arizona, Florida, Maine, Vermont, and Wisconsin have recently deregulated intrastate trucking. Other states, South Dakota and California, for instance, have substantially lessened their controls over intrastate trucking. Florida was the first state to totally deregulate its intrastate motor carrier industry—on the same day, July 1, 1980, that the MCA of 1980 became law. Maine next deregulated intrastate trucking. In the latter half of 1982, the intrastate trucking industries in Arizona and Wisconsin were deregulated. In a survey of state transportation regulating agencies in mid-1982, it was determined that out of the forty-seven states responding, six states had deregulated or were moving toward deregulation, ten states were regulating in line with federal regulation, twenty-nine states were not changing regulations, and two states were moving toward stricter regulation.[45]

The findings with respect to the impact of state deregulation on rural community service have definite implications for the total impact of trucking deregulation at the federal level. Although the states can only regulate intrastate traffic, it has been argued that intrastate regulation of small community service has important impacts on interstate service. For example, in rural communities that generate insufficient traffic to support the operations of more than one trucker, a variety of contractual carrier arrangements are made that consolidate and delegate the performance of the service to the community to a single carrier. A variety of arrangements, such as pooling, leasing interline agreements, and contract drayage, exist that allow the intrastate carrier to provide both intrastate and interstate service without holding the operating authority for the interstate service. Therefore, examining whether intrastate service is offered to a community provides insights into whether a community will be able to receive interstate service. In addition, it has been argued that carriers willing to provide intrastate service in a community should have little difficulty obtaining similar interstate authority.[46] Finally, intrastate operations of an interstate motor carrier are subject to state regulations in the same manner as are exclusively intrastate operations.[47]

Several studies of the impact of state reforms have been performed with the focus on the states of Florida, Arizona, and Wisconsin.

Studies by Beilock and Freeman.   Beilock and Freeman conducted studies in both Florida and Arizona.[48] In Florida they surveyed shippers/receivers in urban and nonurban areas in June 1981 and June 1982, one and two years respectively after total economic deregulation of intrastate trucking. The sample in both years consisted of 144 shippers/receivers. Their research indicated that deregulation had improved or at least not harmed the quality and quantity of service-rate options. They also found that service had improved more for the urban shipper/receiver than for the nonurban shipper/receiver.

In Arizona they conducted surveys at three different times — June 1982, November 1982, and July 1983 — which represented a pre- and two postderegulation time period observations. The sample sizes ranged from 90 to 127 in the three surveys. Both rural (areas outside of Phoenix and Tucson areas) and urban shippers/receivers appeared to have experienced some rate relief and improvements in the quality and quantity of

service. As with the case of Florida, the urban shippers/receivers benefited more than the rural shippers.[49]

Studies by Pustay.   Pustay's studies differed from most of the others by
looking at states other than Florida and by not using the survey technique.[50] Pustay studied the nature of state regulation in four states
(Florida, Texas, Ohio, and South Dakota) — which ranged from no regulation (Florida) to very restrictive regulation (Texas) — and the quality
and quantity of trucking service provided to rural communities in each
state. By comparing the unregulated state's results (Florida) with the
highly regulated state's results (Texas), Pustay was able to make some
general statements about the impact of state regulatory reform
measures. South Dakota had undergone substantial reforms in 1981,
particularly in the area of entry decontrol, while Ohio, though not deregulated to the degree of South Dakota, was not as restrictive as Texas in
its intrastate trucking regulations.

Pustay compared the intrastate and interstate service offered to
sampled communities in each of the four states in the fall of 1976 and
1982. The 1976 observation obviously represents a prereform time period, while the 1982 observation — two years after Florida deregulated
and one year after South Dakota partially deregulated intrastate trucking — represents the postreform time period. For each state a sample of
fifty communities with populations of less than two thousand was developed. The *National Highway and Airway Carriers and Routes,* a guide
which lists the common carriers providing inbound service to a particular community, was used to determine the level of service offered to each
community for both time periods. Pustay acknowledged that this is a
simple and limited measure of service but the methodology avoided the
problems associated with using the survey technique.

Pustay's basic findings indicate that interstate service has improved
since the Motor Carrier Act of 1980 was passed. In addition, deregulation in Florida appears to have led to major improvements in intrastate
trucking service to small communities, which is a finding somewhat
stronger than the findings in studies using the survey technique. In contrast, little change in intrastate small community service resulted from
reforms passed in South Dakota.

The Wisconsin Study.   Effective October 1, 1982, Wisconsin deregulated
intrastate for-hire motor carriers. The Wisconsin transportation commission was required to study the impact of intrastate trucking deregulation upon the shippers and trucking firms in the state.[51] The transporta-

tion commission was required to submit the report to the legislature by July 1, 1983, which did not allow an adequate amount of time for the impacts of deregulation to be fully realized. Despite this shortcoming, the study merits a brief review.

Overall it was found that the large majority of shippers (about 96 percent) reported that trucking service performance since deregulation was as good or better than before deregulation. Only about 2 percent reported that availability of carriers had deteriorated since deregulation. Less than 1 percent of the respondents stated that the freight had not arrived in good condition at least as often as before. Ninety-six percent indicated that claims were settled to their satisfaction at least as often since October 1, 1982, as before. The data on rates revealed no homogeneous pattern on rate changes. Sixty-seven percent of the shippers said they were satisfied with deregulation while 27 percent had no opinion. Only 6 percent were dissatisfied.

Because of concerns about the impact of deregulation on service to rural areas and small communities, respondents were grouped into urban, partially urban, and rural categories based upon their location in the state. It was found that the sales and shipment volumes of the three groups were quite similar. Except for a few questions, the responses from shippers from all three location categories were not significantly different. The authors of the report concluded that the shippers in both urban and rural areas have roughly similar opinions about the effects of deregulation.[52]

The California Study. In 1980 the state of California revamped its regulation of intrastate trucking by replacing minimum rates with transition rates and by allowing thousands of "permitted" carriers to enter into the common carrier component of the trucking industry. In short, this action, which has been called reregulation, injected substantially more competition into the intrastate trucking industry — including the LTL sector. The basic regulatory framework for intrastate trucking remained the same as it was in 1980. In a study based on a December 1983 survey of shippers using intrastate trucking in California, the hypothesis suggesting that higher rates and poorer service to small towns and rural areas would result from this reregulation was examined.[53] The survey results indicated that there was a difference between urban and rural shippers in terms of LTL rate changes. While 59 percent of the shippers in urban areas experienced decreased rates, only 38 percent of the rural firms indicated decreases. Forty-two percent of the rural shippers experienced LTL rate increases in contrast to the 28 percent of the urban shippers that faced rate increases. However, in the assessment of quality of service, rural and urban shippers did not differ in any significant way. Interestingly, 87 percent of the shippers in both urban and rural areas favored continuation of reregulation over the more restrictive regulation or favored complete elimination of state controls of rates and routes.

Strategies for Preserving Trucking Service to Rural Communities

The majority of the studies of the impacts of trucking deregulation on the quantity, quality, and cost of regulated trucking service to rural communities have found the impacts to be neutral or positive. Given these findings, it is reasonable to find few governmental strategies to maintain service. The trucking firms have already employed strategies consistent with profit maximization that have enabled rural communities to maintain adequate trucking service at reasonable rates.

Governmental Strategies

Unlike the legislation that enabled airlines and railroads to abandon communities more easily, the MCA of 1980 did not establish any federally funded subsidy programs that would alleviate any potential, transitional trucking problems in rural communities created by regulatory reform. As noted above, Congress was very concerned about the impact of trucking regulatory reform on service to small communities but did not indicate how that service would be maintained—through more vigorous enforcement of the common carrier obligation or through more competition in the trucking industry. The ICC's actions and the congressional inaction clearly indicate that the move toward more competition was the federal strategy adopted. The ICC weakened the common carrier obligation and increased the level of competition—both actual and potential—by an easy entry policy. The majority of the studies on the impacts of this strategy suggest it was the correct one.

Of eleven midwest and mideast states, by 1985 only one state had developed any strategies to help maintain trucking service to small communities.[54] The majority of state officials contacted indicated that state regulation of intrastate carriers and competition was adequate to maintain trucking service to rural communities. Many of the eleven states were moving or had moved to make their economic regulation of intrastate trucking more in line with the nature of federal regulation. Illinois was in the preliminary stage of developing a brokerage concept with the aid of a computerized network of multimodal services available. Overall, however, the state officials appeared to view deregulation at the federal level as neither reducing the level of service nor increasing the cost of trucking service.

Private Sector Strategies

Both carriers and shippers can take action to help maintain a certain quality and quantity of trucking service to rural communities. Because the initial results of deregulation indicate that rural community trucking service has neither declined in either quality or quantity nor increased unreasonably in terms of costs, it is not surprising to find little written on strategies taken by the private sector to maintain rural community trucking service.

Earlier studies revealed that shippers responded to inadequate and/ or high-cost general freight service by switching to UPS and private carriage when feasible. The private carriage option for shippers usually involved either switching to their own trucks, which might be nothing more than using a van or pickup to transport freight to and from the nearest large city, or switching to suppliers that deliver in their own trucks. These studies tended to suggest that shippers relied upon these market adjustments and not on available ICC complaint alternatives. The use of shipper associations in rural communities was not considered to be feasible by many shippers as a solution if a community were to lose its regulated certificated trucking service completely.

Carriers have continued the practice of interlining as a mechanism of serving rural communities. Some carriers in Florida, where deregulation of intrastate trucking has occurred, have added intrastate service to complement their interstate service in order to increase their utilization of terminals and the probabilities for obtaining a back haul. Certain carriers have added significantly to their terminal systems and have increased their service levels to rural communities by placing many smaller terminals in rural areas. Possibly most important is the individual decision made by numerous trucking firms to serve rural communities. This decision is now a feasible strategy, given the easy ICC entry regulations for certificated trucking firms.

Notes

1. American Trucking Associations, Inc., *Small Town Blues* (Washington, DC: American Trucking Associations, 1976), p. 8.

2. Transportation Policy Associates, *Transportation in America,* 6th edition (Washington, DC: Transportation Policy Associates, 1988), p. 21. It should be noted that the 714,000-mile highway figure includes only federal-aid primary, secondary, and urban-extension highways with exclusions.

3. See Public Law No. 96-296, Sections 4 [National Transportation Policy], 28 [Small Community Service Study], and 14 [Rate Bureaus].

4. Transportation Policy Associates, p. 26.

5. Charles A. Taff, *Commercial Motor Transportation* (Centerville, MD: Cornell Maritime Press, Inc., 1980), p. 60.

6. U.S. Department of Transportation, Highway Statistics—1985, (Washington, DC: Department of Transportation, 1985), p. 16.

7. Taff, p. 60.

8. See Karen L. Borlaug, "The Impact of Deregulation on Small Community Trucking Service," paper presented at the Eastern Economic Association, Philadelphia, April 1981, for additional discussion of these premises.

9. The four common carrier duties are the duty to serve, the duty to deliver, the duty to charge reasonable rates, and the duty not to discriminate.

10. Benjamin J. Allen and Denis A. Breen, "The Nature of Common Carrier Service Obligations," *ICC Practitioners' Journal,* Vol. 46, No. 4 (May-June 1979): pp. 526–49.

11. See *Consolidated Freightways Corporation of Delaware, et al., Pooling,* 109 M.C.C. 596, 607 (1971). The primary reason supporting the change in ICC policy was the appearance of the energy crisis. A more critical interpretation would note that many firms before the 1971 decision were not providing direct service but only indirect service through informal pooling arrangements. The policy change in 1971 could be viewed simply as a fait accompli for those carriers.

12. "Convenience interlining" allows a carrier by means of a simple tariff publication to provide through service to its authorized points by interlining at the gateways as interchange points where joint through routes are applicable.

13. *Elimination of Certificates as the Measure of "Holding Out,"* Ex Parte No. MC-77 (Sub-3), January 27, 1981.

14. Notice, *Elimination of Certificates as the Measure of "Holding Out,"* Ex Parte No. MC-77 (Sub-3), March 15, 1983, p. 2.

15. Statement of Beryl Gordon, Office of Legislative Counsel, Interstate Commerce Commission, accompanied by William Southard, director, Office of Transportation Analysis, hearing before the Senate Committee on Commerce, Science, and Transportation, on Oversight of the Motor Carrier Act of 1980. 98th Cong. 1st sess., December 15, 1983.

16. American Trucking Associations, Inc., *American Trucking Trends—1986* (Washington, DC: American Trucking Association, Inc. 1986), p. 13.

17. Motor Carrier Ratemaking Study Commission, *Collective Ratemaking in the Trucking Industry* (Washington, DC: Motor Carrier Ratemaking Commission, June 1, 1983), pp. 316–17.

18. U.S. Congress. Senate. Committee on Commerce, Science, and Transportation, *The Impact on Small Communities of Motor Carriage Regulatory Revision,* Committee Print (Washington, DC: U.S. Government Printing Office, June 1978), pp. 43–44.

19. See Denis A. Breen and Benjamin J. Allen, *Common Carrier Obligations and the Provisions of Motor Carrier Service to Small Rural Communities* (Washington, DC: Department of Transportation, 1979), pp. 102–03; and Con-

gressional Budget Office, *The Impact of Trucking Deregulation on Small Communities: A Review of Recent Studies,* Staff Working Paper, February 1980, p. 3.

20. Alice E. Kidder, *Impact of Regulatory Reform on Shipper/Receiver Freight Service in Selected Rural Communities, 1982: A Second Follow-Up Study* (Washington, DC: Department of Transportation, 1983), pp. 8–9.

21. Interstate Commerce Commission, *Small Community Service Study* (Washington, DC: Interstate Commerce Commission, 1982), p. 9.

22. *Ibid.,* p. 8.

23. Motor Carrier Ratemaking Study Commission, pp. 317–19.

24. Breen and Allen, p. 108.

25. Motor Carrier Ratemaking Study Commission, p. 320.

26. *Ibid.,* pp. 321–22.

27. *Ibid.,* pp. 322–23.

28. *Ibid.,* pp. 323–42.

29. Interstate Commerce Commission, *Small Community Service Study,* pp. 16–24.

30. Motor Carrier Ratemaking Study Commission, pp. 323–24. A "peddle run" route is one which originates and terminates at a carrier's terminal and covers a predetermined geographical area. The area served is usually rural but tied into one or more larger communities.

31. Breen and Allen, p. v.

32. For example, see Karen Borlaug, et al., *A Study of Trucking Service in Six Rural Communities* (Washington, DC: U.S. Department of Transportation, November 1979); and Paul McElhiney, *Motor Common Carrier Freight Rate Study,* prepared for Federation of Rocky Mountain States, Inc., Denver, CO. May 1975.

33. See U.S. Department of Transportation, *Economic Analysis and Regulatory Implications of Motor Common Carrier Service to Predominantly Rural Communities,* prepared by R. L. Banks and Associates, Inc., June 1976; and Michael W. Pustay, John W. Drake, and James R. Frew, *The Impact of Federal Trucking Regulation on Service to Small Communities,* DOT-OS-70069 (Washington, DC, 1979).

34. Richard Beilock and James Freeman, "Deregulated Motor Carrier Service," *Transportation Journal,* Vol. 23, No. 4 (1984), p. 30.

35. See Alice E. Kidder, *Third Follow-up Study of Shipper/Receiver Mode Choice in Selected Rural Communities, 1982–1983* (Washington, DC: Department of Transportation, 1984), pp. 58–62 for additional discussion of Kidder's findings for the initial and first three follow-up studies.

36. Alice E. Kidder, *Fourth Follow-up Study of Shipper/Receiver Mode Choice in Selected Rural Communities, 1984–1985* (Washington, DC: Department of Transportation, 1985), pp. 28–30.

37. See Interstate Commerce Commission, *Small Community Service Study* for additional discussion of the ICC's findings.

38. *Ibid.,* pp. 10–14.

39. *Ibid.,* pp. 16–24.

40. Iowa Department of Transportation, Office of Economic Analysis, "Results of a Shipper Survey to Determine the Effects of: 1) Federal Deregula-

tion of Motor Carriers Providing Trucking Service to Iowa's Smaller Communities; and 2) The Availability of Designated Highway Routes for Larger Vehicles Used by Motor Carriers Serving Iowa's Smaller Communities" (Ames: Iowa Department of Transportation, May 1986).

41. See W. H. Thompson, R. D. Voorhees, and K. B. Boberg, "Iowa: A Baseline Laboratory of Motor Carrier Service to Small Communities," *ICC Practitioners' Journal,* Vol. 48, No. 4 (1984): pp. 431–41.

42. Karen L. Borlaug, *A One-Year Assessment of the Motor Carrier Act of 1980: Small Community Trucking Service in Nevada and Oregon* (Washington, DC: U.S. Department of Transportation, 1981), p. vi.

43. Washington State Department of Transportation, *Impacts of Trucks and Railroad Deregulation on Transportation Operations and Economic Activity in the State of Washington* (Olympia: Washington State Department of Transportation, 1982).

44. Donald Harper, "Consequences of Reform of Federal Economic Regulation of the Motor Trucking Industry," *Transportation Journal,* Vol. 21, No. 4 (Summer 1982): pp. 35–58.

45. Richard Beilock and James Freeman, "Motor Carrier Perceptions of Intrastate Motor Carrier Regulations and Regulators," *ICC Practitioners' Journal,* Vol. 51, No. 3 (March-April 1984): p. 277.

46. Michael W. Pustay, "Regulation of the Intrastate Motor Freight Industry in Ohio," *ICC Practitioners' Journal,* Vol. 50, No. 4 (May-June 1983): p. 431.

47. Donald V. Harper, *Economic Regulation of the Motor Trucking Industry by the States* (Urbana: The University of Illinois Press, 1959), p. 82.

48. See Beilock and Freeman, "Deregulation Motor Carrier Service," for additional discussion.

49. *Ibid.,* p. 79.

50. Michael W. Pustay, "A Comparison of Pre- and Post-Reform Motor Carrier Service to Small Communities," *Growth and Change,* January 1985, pp. 51–52.

51. The Wisconsin Office of the Commissioner of Transportation, *Deregulation of Wisconsin Motor Carriers,* 1983, pp. 50–56.

52. *Ibid.,* pp. 69–71.

53. N. Gail Frey et al., "Effects of Reregulation of the California Intrastate Trucking Industry," *Transportation Journal,* Vol. 24, No. 3 (1985): pp. 4–17.

54. In November 1985, officials in state departments of transportation in Iowa, Illinois, Indiana, South Dakota, North Dakota, Missouri, Kansas, Nebraska, Wisconsin, Minnesota, and Michigan were interviewed via telephone.

Small Community Bus Service

Introduction

The intercity bus has long been associated with the need for affordable transportation among residents of small communities. The flexibility and relatively low start-up costs associated with bus operation were largely responsible for its introduction in the early 1900s. No single date is associated with the beginning of intercity bus service, but the use of buses spread rapidly in the early 1900s stretching beyond urban areas into the surrounding communities and then on to intercity service. With increasing interest in motor transportation and automobile ownership came improved road surfaces and the opportunity for expanding service. In the years before World War I, hundreds of small companies began providing local and regional bus service. Then when the growth of the automobile began to impact the demand for passenger rail service in the 1920s, the railroads themselves began substituting bus service in low-density areas. This trend accelerated through the 1920s and early 1930s with railroads infusing significant capital into the bus industry.[1] By 1928 there were about forty thousand common carrier buses with an estimated 10 percent of them in interstate commerce. They carried about 3 million passengers.[2]

The Impacts of Changing Regulatory Policies

State Regulation

State regulation of buses began early with Pennsylvania leading the way in 1914, but by 1930 all states except Delaware had regulations. The regulations imposed by the states varied considerably, however. Some emphasized safety of passengers while others focused on the impact of buses on road and bridge deterioration. Still others noted concerns for the social consequences of unregulated fares and route selection. In general, early regulation was directed toward highway protection and passenger safety. During the mid-1920s, however, state regulation increasingly focused on such economic considerations as competition and fares. In this regard, states generally tried to apply to buses the principles and procedures previously employed in regulating railroads and large-scale, capital-intensive public utilities.[3] This led to considerable focus on the financial stability of existing carriers and a concern about the impact that duplication of service by more than one carrier would have on costs of service. In effect this led to the development of route monopolies. State regulatory commissions gave existing carriers first priority on route expansion as long as the service adequately provided for the public interest. Only if an existing carrier failed to provide adequate service would the state commissioner authorize a competing service. Stability in operating conditions was viewed as a necessity.

In retrospect this application of public utility regulation to buses may have been inappropriate given the relatively small investment needed to initiate bus service. Competing services would have potentially benefited travelers through lower fares and higher quality of service, while lower equipment utilization and higher unit costs would not have placed an undue burden on individual bus companies.[4]

Given the propensity toward stability and route monopoly, however, mergers and consolidations were prevalent in the 1920s. As the demand for longer haul trips increased, the trend toward mergers increased. "The present and basic structure of the emerging intercity bus industry, therefore, was to a significant extent determined by regulatory forces and patterns prevalent within the industry in the late 1920s."[5]

The most outstanding example of the impact of mergers is the development of Greyhound Lines, Inc. Greyhound, the dominant Class I carrier, began in the Midwest in 1926 when it was organized as a holding company for the securities of other bus companies. An aggressive management and favorable economic factors enabled Greyhound, which took its present name in 1930, to absorb other smaller companies. This spared the new company the start-up expenses incurred by competitors.

By 1929 the company had acquired sufficient operating authority to operate from New York to the West Coast, allowing it to make more efficient use of equipment and maintenance facilities and to assure more effective management of operations. The result was more convenient through-service and presumably lower fares for passengers. In the early 1930s, Greyhound acquired many railroad bus subsidiaries and offered long distance competition for passenger trains.[6]

By the mid-1920s the bus industry had achieved considerable economic stability since "state grants of public convenience and necessity" had insulated the industry from new carrier entry. But the power of state regulation over such economic issues as fares and service quality was dissipated in 1925 when the Supreme Court invalidated state regulations that were not primarily concerned with matters of safety. Economic regulation was deemed to be the responsibility of the federal government as defined in the interstate commerce clause of the Constitution. In a study published in 1928, the Interstate Commerce Commission recommended that dual economic regulation replace state regulation in this area.[7]

Federal Regulation

This movement toward federal regulation was reinforced by bus operators who were concerned about the inequities attributed to state regulation. Some states, for example, required bus companies to post bonds even if they did not stop within state borders. One small bus operator commented in 1928 that he would not object to regulation by the ICC because that would assure that all companies would be treated equally. State power, he feared, might be used in an "unfriendly way."[8]

S. A. Markel of the National Bus Association testified at the Congressional Hearings in 1928, "We find in a number of states, duplication of service, service that is not dependable, and a number of operators whose solvency might be questioned and have nothing to answer for damages, and a chaotic condition with respect to the interstate operation of motor carriers."[9]

In light of these concerns about state regulatory commissions, it is rather surprising that the federal regulatory legislation introduced in 1928 provided for enforcement by state boards. The legislation was not passed in 1928 and a similar bill was introduced in 1930. At that time testimony by opponents of federal regulation underscored concerns about potential impacts on bus service to small communities. Day Baker of the Smaller New England Bus Lines testified that regulation would limit competition, which is healthy to the development of the bus business, and "restrict to a very great extent the development and expansion of those out-of-the-way routes, which might not appear profitable to the larger established companies, but would under competition be promoted by the individual pioneer. . . . Competition on various bus routes should be allowed for some time to come, so that . . . bus service may be established in every district, rural as well as urban, throughout the country for the benefit of the public at large."[10]

Again, the bill failed passage. When introduced again in 1935, enforcement was left ultimately to the ICC. Joseph Eastman, federal coordinator of transportation, took care to point out, "the bill does not undertake to eliminate competition in transportation in any way but it does undertake to place that competition on a better and sounder plane."[11]

As passed, the federal Motor Carrier Act of 1935 provided that carriers apply to the ICC, rather than to state boards, for certificates of "public convenience and necessity." These would be issued to any qualified applicant that filed a written application and was found "fit, willing, and able properly to perform proposed services as will be required by the present or future public convenience and necessity."[12]

The act was not intended to preempt state authority over interstate travel but did provide for a considerable federal regulation of regular route service between fixed terminals across state lines. The carriers were required to file security bonds and insurance policies with the ICC. The commission was also to rule on the reasonableness of fare changes. Carriers were to post thirty-day notices of intended fare changes with the commission, which was charged with preventing excess charges as well as promoting safety and uniform accounting and statistics. Certified carriers could carry newspapers, baggage, and express packages, as well as passengers, and could also run charter service. The ICC was also to provide for joint rates between points. Mergers were allowed even with railroads but only if the carriers involved made application to the commission and notified all appropriate state governors and all other interested carriers and if public hearings found "that public interest would be promoted."[13] Requests for permission to cancel service were carefully reviewed by the ICC in the light of the requirements for "present or future public convenience and necessity," and route duplication was avoided through entry procedures stringently enforced by the ICC. The ICC had to declare a route vacant and a qualified carrier had to prove "public convenience and necessity" required service before it could apply to provide service there.

The Motor Carrier Act of 1935 did, however, have the effect of limiting competition, since existing carriers were issued certificates without requiring further proof that "public convenience and necessity" would be served by such an operation[14] as long as they operated over the same routes as they did in 1934. This grandfathered in the powerful Greyhound system. In 1936 a voluntary association of small bus companies, many of which had ties to railroads, formed the National Trailways Bus System to counter Greyhound's dominance in the interstate bus industry. Restricted by the Motor Carrier Act from merging, the companies in the Trailways system emphasized joint policies, including interline transfer tickets, consolidated terminals, coordinated schedules, joint supervision, and a common logo.

Impacts of Regulation on Service in Communities

Although clearly affecting the pattern of competition among intercity bus carriers, the act did not affect service to small communities detrimentally. On the contrary, small towns were knit into a national network. In fact, bus service and ridership expanded considerably in the 1940s reaching a peak of 1,320 million passengers and 27 billion passenger miles in 1945.[15]

Declines in service to small communities came in response to declines in ridership precipitated by the increased availability of automobile transportation from the 1950s through the 1970s. By 1977, 84 percent of all households owned at least one auto, and 37 percent of the households had more than one auto.[16] Bus ridership declined to only 1.8 percent of all passenger traffic. Nevertheless, the bus industry continued to provide inexpensive service to passengers without access to automobiles—the old, the young, and the low-income population. Buses served fifteen thousand communities in 1981, fourteen thousand of which had no other form of public transportation. They carried 375 million passengers in 1981, a considerable decline from the peak in 1945 but still more than any other type of carrier. In addition, they provided package express service, without stringent size and weight restrictions, for businesses in smaller metropolitan and rural areas.[17]

Nevertheless, the ubiquity of bus service, which had contributed to its rise in the 1930s and 1940s, was by the 1970s contributing to the economic woes of the bus industry. Providing regularly scheduled service to small communities that could generate two or three passengers a week was clearly not cost efficient. Consequently, service to a large number of these small communities was cut during the 1970s. Service to others was retained in large part because of requirements of state regulated bodies and the ICC requirements stemming from the Motor Carrier Act of 1935.

Between 1969 and 1979 over 185 locations lost service and new stops were only added in the suburbs.[18] Service frequency to small communities and balance also declined significantly in the decade 1969–1979. One study noted an 11 percent decline in one-way intercity schedules serving small cities. Unbalanced, inconvenient schedules made it almost impossible for residents of an increasing number of small towns to complete short distance shopping trips in one day. Once-a-day bus scheduling proliferated, covering 43 percent of the routes examined in one national study.[19] The same study pointed out that the existence of bus routes on highways did not necessarily mean that on-line rural residents had easy access to bus transportation, since scheduled stops were frequently miles from residences, and the practice of unscheduled stops was applied inconsistently. By 1978 one case study noted that only 42 percent of the small towns sampled had access to intercity bus service.[20]

Movement toward Deregulation

Even with these cuts the bus industry profits continued to decline and the industry urged the repeal of federal regulations so as to permit route reorganization and to open up competition. Again, discussion revolved around potential impacts on service to small communities. Said a representative of the National Association of Regulatory Utility Commission, "Loss of this service could prove to be devastating not only to individual bus riders who depend on the service, but to communities at large who are finding themselves increasingly isolated particularly in light of diminishing airlines and Amtrak availability."[21]

Of particular concern was the fear that deregulation would reduce the incentive for cross subsidy of routes—the practice whereby a carrier making sufficient profit on a well-traveled route was required to continue service on an unprofitable connecting route to small towns. A small bus operator from South Dakota noted that total deregulation would allow Greyhound to continue to serve the city of Sioux Falls while dropping service to Mobridge, a town generating only twelve riders.[22] Others countered these arguments with such comments as, "in the near term service to small towns seems no more threatened than to larger cities." Based on available financial data "the bus industry is healthier in rural areas than in highly urbanized areas."[23]

The state of Florida had deregulated truck and bus transportation in 1980 in response to pressures to open up the market to competition, and Florida's two-year positive experience in a deregulated environment was a major factor in reassuring concerned congressmen about potential effects of deregulation. In Florida, fears that deregulation would lead to chaos with fly-by-night operators ripping off consumers in small towns had not materialized. Greyhound had dropped service to fifteen small towns in central Florida but had increased its service mileage 8 percent. Similarly, Trailways had dropped service to eight small towns in northern

Florida but had increased its service mileage by 7.5 percent. Half of the small towns dropped were picked up by replacement service and all had continuing service available between nine and twenty-one miles away. No complaints had been received from small Florida towns regarding loss of service. In fact, the only protest was by four individuals in Apalachicola where once-a-week Greyhound service was discontinued.[24]

These positive reports helped to reinforce the arguments of Class I carriers that the straitjacket imposed by federal regulation was preventing the opportunity to make a profit especially since other modes had already been deregulated.[25] According to the 1948 Reed-Bulwinkle Amendment to the Motor Carrier Act, industrywide requests for fare increases were proposed by the National Bus Traffic Association and reviewed by the ICC to assure that they were nondiscriminatory, just, and reasonable and set at the lowest level consistent with providing service.[26] Industry complaints were not so much with federal fare regulation as with the inequities caused by distinctions between interstate rates set up by states and the interstate rates. The major concern with federal regulation was with restrictions on exiting from unprofitable routes and on abandoning unprofitable stops.

Cost Function

The question as to whether there is an economy of scale in the intercity bus industry has been the subject of inquiry for a number of economic studies over the last decade.[27] Such studies have been hampered by the limited availability of comparable data, the skewed nature of existing data reflecting an industry dominated by a duopoly. They have also been challenged by the need to break out scheduled from unscheduled service and to differentiate among aspects of the service mix — charter, local, express, and package. Distinguishing between the effects of "density" of service (uniform expansion over a fixed route) and network economies (feeder and interlining service) remains an important challenge.[28]

As early as 1984 it was clear that deregulation would not provide a quick solution to the declining profits of intercity bus companies. In that year Greyhound barely broke even — in part because of high drivers' salaries — while Trailways made a small profit and the independents made a bit larger profit.[29] These figures offered little encouragement to small operators considering routes running through low-density rural areas. Table 4.1 uses 1981 figures to demonstrate the differential in average costs and revenue for entire intercity bus systems and for the portion of each system running through Iowa, a state with a relatively low population density.[30] As is apparent, the operating costs were some-

Table 4.1. 1981 expense/revenue comparisons

	Iowa expenses/ bus mile	Systemwide expenses/ bus mile	Iowa revenue/ bus mile	Systemwide revenue/ bus mile
Class I				
Greyhound	1.95	1.95	1.79	2.03
Trailways	1.62	1.65	1.33	1.48
Jefferson	.51	2.07	.49	2.19
Jack Rabbit	1.34	1.34	1.19	1.41
Midwest Coaches	.96	1.07	1.10	1.28
Scenic Hawkeye	1.03	1.01	1.07	1.25
Class II				
River Trails	1.01	1.31	.99	1.52

Source: Derived from Iowa Department of Transportation, *1983 Iowa Intercity Bus Plan.*

what lower for the Iowa portion of the routes than for each system as a whole, but revenues were also generally less. For only two independent Class I carriers did revenues slightly exceed expenses. For the one Class II bus for which data was available, expenses far exceeded revenues for the Iowa portion. The lower operations cost for intercity bus service is not surprising, given the limited schedules available and the limited revenue that is attributable to the small number of riders. What is clear, however, is that there is no clear evidence that a smaller bus company can run more profitably in low density areas.

One study underscored the importance of a company's maintaining a mix of services in order to balance out costs and revenues generated by charters and regular route service, for example. There is evidence that charter and regular route services can be produced jointly at lower costs than separately.[31] This should encourage small companies to continue to perform local regular route service as well as charter service, but unfortunately the marginal costs for both are high, especially in an area with a scattered population. At least one study noted the basis for some government intervention in the bus industry in order to encourage economic efficiency. However, it noted that government help in encouraging service cooperation among firms might achieve the same goals as regulation of entry and pricing.[32]

The Bus Regulatory Reform Act of 1982

As passed in 1982 the Bus Regulatory Reform Act (BRRA) responded to the expressed demands of bus operators for deregulation but it also attempted to provide for the needs of small communities. The impact on small communities and those over sixty years of age was to be carefully monitored by the Motor Carrier Ratemaking Study Commission until at least 1985.[33]

The stated purpose of the act was to remove regulatory controls since "Federal and State regulatory structure has tended to . . . inhibit market entry, carrier growth, maximum utilization of equipment and energy resources . . . and overly protective regulation has resulted in operating inefficiencies and diminished price and service competition." In order to counter these negatives, the ICC was to "do everything in its power to promote competition in the motor bus industry."[34]

Specific responsibilities of the ICC were listed as follows: (1) to promote competitive and efficient transportation services, (2) to allow a variety of quality and price options to meet changing market demands, (3) to allow the most productive use of equipment and energy resources, (4) to enable efficient and well-managed carriers to earn adequate profits, attract capital and maintain fair wages, (5) to maintain service to small communities and small shippers and interstate bus services, (6) to provide and maintain commuter bus operations, and (7) to promote intermodal transportation.[35]

These provisions represented a radical departure from the traditional legislation that had encouraged route monopoly as a means of furthering efficiency and effectiveness. Now competition was to be the means of achieving the same goals. Yet that competition was not to trade benefits to small communities or to lose sight of the potential for intermodal cooperation.

Specifically, entrance of new bus companies was encouraged especially as replacement service in areas where rail, air, or other bus service had been terminated. The old requirement that applicants for a certificate must prove that the proposed service was consistent with "present or future public convenience and necessity" was replaced by the requirement that applicants prove only that they are "fit, willing and able," to meet safety and minimum financial requirements and to provide service. The minimum level of financial responsibility was fixed at $5 million for any vehicle over sixteen passengers and $1.5 million for vehicles up to fifteen passengers. This responsibility would be demonstrated by insurance or a surety bond. As before, a certificate of a motor carrier was to include authority to carry newspapers, baggage, packages, or mail as well as passengers. If in agreement with state law, carriers could also carry charter and regular route passengers in the same vehicle. Protests were limited to competing carriers that were "willing and able to provide service that meets the reasonable needs of the traveling public" and had indeed "performed the service described in the application within the last 12 months."[36]

Exit policy was similarly made more permissive. A carrier wishing to discontinue service or reduce service to once a day would file a petition with the state affected and then notify the governor, appropriate state agencies, and interested local governments. If no one objected within 20 days, the petition would be granted. The state would have 120 days to decide a contested request. If, however, the state denied the petition, the carrier could appeal to the ICC, which would require those opposing the petition to demonstrate that discontinuance "is not consistent with the public interest" and that continuing service "will not constitute an unreasonable burden on interstate commerce." The nature of this unreasonable burden was defined to include public financial burden in the form of subsidies. The petitioner would be required to present an estimate of the annual subsidy, which would be required to continue service, as well as evidence of the amount of traffic, revenue, and financial assistance that would be required to continue service.[37]

The matter of discriminatory rates, which was a result of different state and federal rate review processes, was also addressed. States would continue to enjoy authority over fares and schedules on interstate service, but the act included the provision (section 6B2d) that "it is the sense of Congress that each state should revise its standards and procedures for rates, rules, and practices . . . to conform to . . . practices applicable to interstate transportation . . . within 2 years." The ICC would assume jurisdiction over a rate, rule, and practice in interstate transportation that would place "an unreasonable burden on interstate or foreign commerce."[38]

The impacts of such far reaching legislation were expected to be considerable. With the potential for streamlining their routes, bus companies expected to again become profitable. Meanwhile, small communities awaited the generation of replacement service, which the proponents of the legislation had argued would come from new small operators encouraged by the relaxed entry requirements. During the 1982 hearings, for example, Cornish Hitchcock, director of the Transportation Consumer Action Project, pointed out that since there is no economy of scale in the bus industry, small companies can compete adequately with large.[39] Economists agreed that the dominance of two large firms in the bus industry was not a factor of the market economy but rather of an artificial economy propped up by regulation.[40]

The subsequent impacts of the legislation especially upon small towns has been the subject of considerable investigation not only by the Motor Ratemaking Study Commission and the mandated oversight hearings, but by independent researchers as well. Most studies have focused primarily upon aggregate numbers of abandonments but it is important also to reflect on the impacts on residents of small communities as well as the level of replacement service generated.

The Nature of Demand for Bus Service in Small Cities

Impacts on Small Town Residents

The expectation was that impacts of the BRRA would vary among communities relative to the availability of alternative forms of transportation and the characteristics and persistence of riders, noted both in the number of riders boarding at a stop and in the level of protest accompanying discontinuance of service. A broad-based analysis of such impacts would be most difficult to achieve since accurate data on ridership by stop is not available. Neither the bus companies nor state regulatory agencies kept such data even before deregulation, and since deregulation, record keeping is solely at the discretion of the private companies. Consequently, information on ridership and alternative travel modes must be obtained on a stop-by-stop basis from former ticket agents.

One study considering the experience of small town residents focused on Iowa, a state well known for its rural, small town orientation. During the oversight hearings after the Bus Deregulation Act, Iowa was repeatedly discussed as an exemplar of impacts in rural areas. Forty-one percent of the 3 million residents of Iowa live in towns under 2,500 population.[41] Also, the intercity bus has traditionally been the primary form of transportation for rural Iowa. Over three hundred communities are still served by at least one intercity bus a day while air service is only provided to twenty Iowa cities and is directed outside the state.

The target population of ticket agents was identified from among the thirty-seven regularly scheduled stops listed for discontinuance in the May 15, 1984, report submitted by the Motor Carrier Ratemaking Study Commission.[42] For thirty-four of these stops, addresses and telephone numbers of former ticket agents were found in the back issues of the (Iowa) *Transit Atlas*. A review of these stops in conjunction with Russell's guide indicated that not all had actually been eliminated.[43] Nevertheless, they were retained in the sample for comparative purposes. It was also felt that responses of riders to a temporary reprieve from discontinuance would provide further insight into the potential ridership from small communities, which had been initially deemed marginal by the bus industry.

A review of the findings from the survey indicated that one-third of the responding locations still had bus service and two-thirds had lost service as a result of deregulation. None of the stops had or continues to serve large numbers of passengers. The numbers ranged from about eight a month to about sixty per month. As might be expected, larger numbers of passengers had used those stops with continuing service. While 68.8 percent of the stops where service had been discontinued handled less than ten passengers a month, all those with continuing service handled more than ten passengers a month. Thirty-seven percent of these handled over fifty passengers a month. All these figures are well below the median of fifty departures per week for an average small town as identified in the Senate Committee on Commerce, Science and Transportation study of bus service in small towns.

Package handling differed similarly between stops with continuing service and those stops with canceled service. Of these stops where service was discontinued, 43.8 percent had handled ten or less packages a month and 81.3 percent had handled fifty or fewer packages a month. Among those stops with continuing service, 62.5 percent had handled over fifty packages a month. Nevertheless, there were some surprises. One canceled stop had handled over a hundred packages a month. There were also two canceled stops that had sold over fifty tickets a month. Hence, if impacts are measured only in terms of numbers of people inconvenienced, reports from these Iowa towns would clearly indicate minimum impact. However, assessment must also consider the type of riders inconvenienced.

The literature generally indicates that bus passengers differ from passengers on other modes of transportation in that a larger proportion are senior citizens and have lower incomes than either train or air passengers. Across the country, college-age students also form a large percentage of bus riders. The implication is that bus passengers include more who are disadvantaged and far more who are captive riders than do other modes of public transportation. Among various states that have conducted analyses of the characteristics of bus riders, the proportion of seniors and youth riders differ as do reports of income level. For example, a Tennessee study presented a series of passenger profiles for different cities and indicated that the age of typical passengers was twenty years in Chattanooga, Memphis, and Nashville, whereas the average passenger was between fifty-six and sixty-five years old in Cookville. The average income of Tennessee bus riders was between $7,501 and $15,000 in 1981.[44] In the state of Washington, 30 percent of bus riders were under the age of twenty-five and 30 percent were over sixty years old, while 40 percent of the riders had family incomes of less than $10,000.[45]

Among the former ticket agents responding to the survey in Iowa, half reported that over 75 percent of the former riders were senior citizens. This proportion differed considerably for those Iowa towns that still had bus service. Sixty-two percent of these reported that less than half of their riders were seniors. Few ticket agents indicated any sizable number of young riders. An income-related question was not possible on a survey directed toward ticket agents.

Another general observation regarding bus travelers is that they travel shorter distances than do train or air travelers. For example, one report noted that the average distance of a bus trip was only about 125 miles.[46] The reports from the Iowa ticket agents seemed to confirm this finding. Among the former ticket agents, 62 percent noted that more than three-quarters of the passengers traveled less than 100 miles and within Iowa. That proportion was somewhat less for stops with continuing service. In three-quarters of those communities, 50–74 percent of the passengers bought tickets for trips of less than 100 miles. Except for towns near the state borders only a small proportion of stops had riders traveling out of state. Among those locations with discontinued service, only 25 percent reported that a substantial number of passengers had purchased out-of-state tickets. Sixty-two percent of the stops with continuing service indicated substantial interstate travel; most trips were to neighboring Omaha, Nebraska, or to Sioux Falls, South Dakota. Only one location, which is near a large lake with boating and camping facilities, indicated substantial long-distance interstate travel.

The primary trip purposes for those riding the bus was generally noted as "visiting friends and relatives" or "for social or recreational use." This was also true for by far the largest proportion of riders in surveys conducted in Oregon, Georgia, Texas, Michigan, Wisconsin, Idaho, Indiana, and Tennessee and recorded in a study by the Motor Carrier Ratemaking Study Commission. A 1978 report of the American Bus Association noted that 88 percent of bus trips were for personal visits or recreation. Although no quantifiable data on trip purpose could be acquired from former ticket agents, anecdotal reports obtained at the conclusion of the follow-up telephone interviews would confirm that Iowa's bus riders also travel for family visits or recreation. Trips to school by college-age youth appear to be highly seasonal and not a substantial factor in the towns surveyed.

Since 1976 senior citizens and other transportation-disadvantaged people in Iowa have been provided an increasing amount of short-distance public transit service for trips to the doctor, social service agencies, personal business locations, congregate meal sites, shopping, and handicapped training programs.[47] However, only two ticket agents were aware of a rural public transit service. Outside of the automobile, only intercity bus service can provide for independent recreational travel and visits to family and relatives outside of town. Reports supplied by ticket agents underscored the former riders' reliance on the intercity bus for this service and the lack of adequate replacement service to fill this need. For example, one agent commented on a former passenger who had to cancel her annual vacation trip because there was now no way to get to a city about sixty miles away where the tour group assembled. Other agents commented that the former passengers just do not have the opportunity to travel outside town any longer. They underscored the traditional independence of older Iowans. This would prevent them from asking friends or relatives to drive them to other towns or cities. Quantifiable information on whether or not former riders had driver's licenses and/or access to automobiles could not be obtained from ticket agents. Nevertheless, anecdotal information gained in the telephone interviews would seem to confirm the findings of the Motor Carrier Ratemaking Commission in assessing impacts of deregulation on older Americans. That report noted that based on riders' surveys in Georgia, Washington, Texas, Wisconsin, and North Carolina, approximately one-third of the intercity bus passengers had either no driver's license or no vehicle available for the trip.[48] The overwhelming majority of the ticket agents who noted a high proportion of senior-citizen riders also noted that these people had no other means of travel.

The distance to the nearest continuing bus stop is, of course, another measure of relative impact given the availability of means to get there. The motor carrier commission study reported that surveys of riders and households in North Carolina found that 68 percent of the respondents lived within nine miles of the nearest bus stop. In Tennessee, 63.4 percent of the bus passengers lived within ten miles of a bus stop.[49] Among the small towns losing service in Florida, all were within nine to twenty-one miles of continuing service.[50] The findings in Iowa suggested an average distance that was considerably farther than in either of the other states. The range reported was from one to thirty-six miles with 69 percent of the former agents noting that the next stop was over eleven miles away. Thirty-seven percent stated that the next stop was over twenty miles away. For only two locations had discontinuance had minor impact. In these cases, streamlining service had moved the stop from a downtown location to the highway one mile away. For those towns with the nearest bus stop over twenty miles away, the impact of discontinuance was effectively to eliminate intercity bus travel for the residents unless they had personal access to an automobile.

As indicated above, persistence of the ridership can be determined in part by the number of passengers who board the bus at a specific stop. Another important measure in determining salience of demand for service, however, is the level and regularity of protest generated by the discontinuance. In Iowa, as in Florida, little formal protest has been noted. There have, however, been two exceptions. In one town slated for discontinuance, a local church leader mobilized citizens to protest the fact that residents in the town's senior-citizen home would be denied transportation. The effort was most successful. One of the hearings relating to the Bus Deregulation Act was held in that small town and Greyhound dropped plans to bypass the town. Unfortunately, since then ridership from that town has fallen off considerably. Only about twenty people a month bought tickets in 1984 compared to about eighty a month in 1982. Package shipments used to gross about four hundred dollars a month, but by 1984 the figure had fallen to about two hundred dollars. The agent felt that the publicity surrounding the initial plan to drop the stop continued to affect usage. People regularly called in and were surprised that the stop was still functioning.[51]

In one other town the ticket agent urged disappointed riders to write to the company complaining about discontinuance. They did but received no response. Then they made no effort to follow up with the Iowa DOT or the Transportation Regulatory Authority. For at least one community, service was withdrawn so abruptly that even the ticket agent was not informed; consequently, no formal protest was initiated. With deregulation, bus companies have not always felt it necessary to announce discontinuance although that is specified in the act. Consequently, an unprofitable route in west-central Iowa was informally abandoned.[52] The ticket agent of another town seemed to sum up the feelings of many, "It's too late." (Nothing can be done.) "We were talked out of railroads on a national level (now we are losing our buses too)."

A number of ticket agents, however, reported informal protests. Former riders came in and complained about service cancellation. Two years after service discontinuance, a number were still receiving calls requesting information about bus service and expressing concern that there is no longer a bus stop near by. Sixty-two percent of the discontinued stops had recorded informal protests. All stops that had handled over ten passengers a month noted informal protests as did half of those that had had less than ten per month. The amount of protest was not significantly related to either the proportion of riders traveling out of state nor to the distance they generally traveled within the state. The percentage of former riders over age sixty also was insignificantly related to the amount of informal protest received. Concern over elimination of specific stops, therefore, appeared not to be linked to any segment of the transit-oriented public. Despite the small number of actual riders involved, the effects on the quality of life of individuals living in these small towns have been substantial.

Dissatisfaction regarding discontinuance of bus service generated comments regarding the increased cost in shipment as well as greater reductions in the type of packages that could be shipped. All former ticket agent respondents indicated that without bus service, shipments generally go by United Parcel Service (UPS). Yet, Iowans, much like others affected by discontinued bus service, quickly discovered that UPS does not offer weekend delivery and does not handle irregularly shaped packages or packages weighing over fifty pounds. One former agent indicated that a major firm in his town had to make arrangements to transport materials to the nearest bus stop seventeen miles away since UPS could not handle the size and shape of his products.

The impacts of deregulation have not, however, been all negative. Among several of the stops still operating, the number of passengers has increased since dedicated bus riders have made the effort to travel from discontinued stops to the closest available stop. After a number of stops on U.S. Highway 6 were closed, Greyhound initiated a new stop at an exit on Interstate 80 ten miles farther south. This stop was also designated as the rest stop for Greyhound buses traveling along the interstate. Consequently, six to eight buses have stopped there each day and riders have gotten off to make purchases at the restaurant while the buses refueled. The income generated by this change has been considerable and additional employees have been hired to handle the rush periods. The relative benefits of this change would need to be weighed against the inconvenience to residents of the small towns in traveling to this highway stop.

In general, the impacts of the discontinuance of Iowa stops upon the economy of the towns involved has been minimal. Few of the basic businesses of the ticket agents were adversely affected. Three agents indicated a loss in revenue from package service, but the others indicated that there was so little financial return associated with package shipping that it wasn't worth the paperwork involved. The majority indicated that so few residents were passengers or shippers that the economy of the towns was relatively unaffected.

The costs involved in continuing regular bus service to towns generating as few as ten passengers a month are no doubt prohibitive, and if bus service is to continue at all, companies must have the right to streamline service as has been advocated by Greyhound and other bus companies. Nevertheless, the BRRA held out the promise of replacement service to those affected communities.

Assessing the Level of Demand

One important consideration that is only beginning to be recognized in this context is the importance of distinguishing between need and demand for intercity bus service. This distinction is important for assessing the potential for successful replacement services. Numerous studies have attempted to define need for bus service in terms of the proportion of residents in an area corresponding to a set of characteristics associated with bus riders. Bus riders tend to be older and have lower incomes than those using air or train service. For example, 16 percent of bus riders are sixty-five or older as compared to 9 percent of train riders and 6.8 percent of air travelers. At the other end of the spectrum, 33.6 percent of bus travelers are under eighteen as compared to 15.2 percent of train passengers and 8.6 percent of air passengers. In 1977, 19.3 percent of bus travelers had an income under five thousand dollars, a factor true of only 9.9 percent of train passengers and 4.8 percent of air passengers. Bus riders also travel shorter distances: 69 percent traveled less than six hundred miles as compared with 59 percent of those on trains and 11 percent of those on airplanes.[53]

Although no separate surveys were conducted of intercity travelers in rural areas, the expectation is that the characteristics of rural residents riding buses mirror the national averages. Rural areas are, however, home to a sizable senior population creating a relatively large pool of potential bus riders. Consequently, two major studies have focused on the proportion of seniors in towns where service was abandoned as a major factor in examining the impacts of abandonment on specific communities.[54] One study focused on income levels in towns where service was abandoned or replaced.[55] These proportions may well indicate the relative level of a potential pool of bus riders, but they do not in themselves indicate the level of demand for replacement intercity bus services. Even elderly and low-income residents in those areas may well have become accustomed to automobiles or shared ride travel and may no longer be interested in bus service. Other indicators of demand must be considered including past ridership levels, protests over abandonment, community support for bus service, the length of time without service, and the relative proximity to continuing service.

Past ridership must be viewed in association with information about the adequacy of the past service. Communities with infrequent service limited to odd hours are unlikely to generate sufficient ridership to justify replacement service.

The level of public protests must also be viewed in context. Effective protest requires leadership and coordination, factors frequently missing in smaller communities. A study of fifteen states with a sizable number of discontinued stops reported no concerted effort to halt abandonment in rural areas. Protests were instead presented initially to the ICC by carriers when states had denied the right to eliminate or cut service. Almost all petitions were granted in favor of the carrier. Among the few isolated examples of citizen protest, all resulted in either a delay of abandonment or continuation of the route with state subsidy. What seems to be needed is an effort to organize groups of potential riders (seniors, low-income citizens, blue-collar workers, etc.) in an effort to get a reading of resident interest and demand for service. Community support is essential to the development of successful replacement service.

The length of time a community is without service is also a crucial factor. When residents must be reintroduced to the concept of bus travel, the process, at best, takes time. At worst, it has all the hazards of introducing a new service for which there is no preestablished interest to build upon.

The relative proximity to other services is a factor generally mentioned at the time of abandonment. However, this factor also is relative. The adequacy of the other service and the means of accessing it must also be considered.

Once the level of demand for replacement service is assessed, it is possible to consider the adequacy of the service designed to meet that demand.

Replacement Service

Regular Route

As indicated above, the expectation with the passage of the Bus Deregulation Act in 1982 was that small bus companies that had been prevented from moving in on routes already technically serviced by larger carriers would begin operations between smaller cities in rural areas. The experience of the two years since deregulation has not confirmed that expectation but rather has indicated a continuation of trends established long before 1982. There were approximately 21 percent fewer communities receiving service in 1982 than in 1975 and 20 percent fewer communities receiving services in 1984 than in 1982.[56] The record on replacement service has not shown a dramatic increase. In the first year after deregulation an American Association of State Highway and Transportation Officials (AASHTO) survey noted that only sixty cities in nine states had received regular intercity bus replacement service. Forty-five of those cities were in the under–five thousand population class. When these figures were compared with the 480 cities losing all service in that year, 405 of which were in the under–five thousand population class, the record is not impressive. Only 7.8 percent overall and 7.3 percent in the under–five thousand population group received replacement service. In addition, 280 cities (207 under five thousand population) had their service cut by 50 percent or more. The record was only partially mitigated by the fact that 128 cities (69 in the under–five thousand population class) that had not had bus service before gained regular route service in 1982. In the second year, as Figure 4.1 indicates, the record improved somewhat to 13 percent replacement overall (117 out of 899) and 11 percent replacement (81 out of 713) for places under five

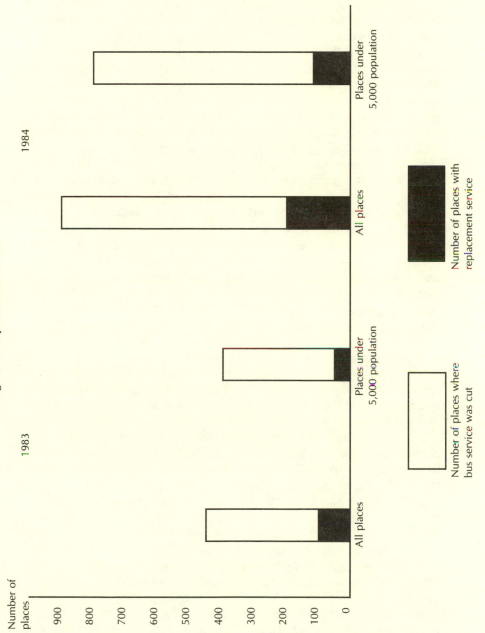

Fig. 4.1. Replacement record.

thousand. In addition, 159 new cities (102 in the under–five thousand group) gained service in the second year.[57] This record certainly does not represent any improvement over the replacement record for the period 1975–1982 prior to deregulation when service initiations equaled 26 percent of the terminations.[58]

Russell's guide listed fifty-four new bus companies in June 1985 as compared with November 1982, but that must be balanced against the seventy-two bus companies that were listed in 1982 but no longer listed in 1985. This represented not the expected gain but rather a net loss of 25 percent. Granted, a quick review of Russell's guide cannot account for mergers or small companies that do not choose to be listed, but it does indicate the lack of any abrupt change in the established pattern regarding bus company entrance into regular route service.

Most of the places listed in the AASHTO survey as having acquired replacement service were served by expanded routes of existing carriers.[59] Although 225 applications for regular route authority to operate a total of 46,686 route miles were filed in the first year after the passage of bus deregulation, it is difficult to determine the extent to which those applications represented the potential for replacement service to points abandoned by another carrier. Such information is not included on the application forms.[60]

Charter Service

What is clear is that the big gains since deregulation have been in the area of charters. Even in the period before deregulation, small non-Class I carriers carried 89.4 percent of the charter and special services.[61] In some states charters had served to compensate for operating nonrevenue-producing routes in rural areas. Now that it is no longer required to run a regular route in order to be approved for charter service, new charter companies have been entering the field at a rapid rate. According to one study, 1,706 applications (88.4 percent of all applications) were for charter authority in the first year of deregulation, 764 by existing firms and 942 by first-time applicants. This represented a 511 percent increase over the average of the previous five years.[62] In Ohio, for example, 80 percent of the requests for contract permits were for charter rather than for regular route service. In fact, out of the seventy bus companies operating in Ohio in 1985, sixty-four were charter companies.[63] New low-cost charter operations with about three buses can easily undercut traditional companies trying to balance out losses on a regular route with revenues from a charter service. As a result, small traditional bus companies are apparently being forced to exit. This observation was made in interviews with representatives of transportation departments in several eastern states but cannot yet be verified by independent data.[64] The effect of such developments would certainly impact negatively on regular route service to small communities. At the least, increased charter service does not compensate for the loss of intercity bus service in rural areas.

Express Service

The other major trend since the BRRA has been increased service between metropolitan areas over interstate highways. Telephone interviews with fifteen state department of transportation representatives underscored this trend, which is understandable in the light of the BRRA since it urges the reduction of cross subsidies between routes or types of service.[65] Nevertheless, the trend directs regular route service away from small self-contained communities. Even if intercity bus service were retained in a neighboring community or out on the highway, there would typically be no local transit system linking the points.[66] Fortunately, the Motor Carrier Ratemaking Study Commission found that this trend was more noticeable among larger than smaller bus companies. Smaller companies were not as likely to eliminate even marginally profitable rural service in response to reduced profits because of the level of competition experienced on their better routes.[67] Moving into unprofitable routes abandoned by another carrier, however, would certainly provide more of a challenge for a small operator, a challenge that few have accepted.

In April 1985 Greyhound, the giant of the American intercity bus industry, launched a franchise program that it hoped would stimulate greater interest among small operators in assuming marginal rural routes. From 1974–1984 Greyhound's ridership plummeted 40 percent, and profits were half the 1974 levels. Faced with these declining profits, Greyhound developed a plan in 1985 to spin off 10 percent of its routes, primarily segments of less than five hundred miles each. The hope was that operators with lower operating costs might be able to make money from them. The concept was that short haul routes (under five hundred miles) could provide service at more convenient travel times, albeit with increased transfers, than would the cross-country bus and therefore better serve the needs of residents of smaller communities.[68] Franchisees had the benefits of the Greyhound name, insurance, advertising, sales outlets, driver training programs, management assistance, and maintenance and service. In exchange they agreed to pay a franchise fee of five thousand to ten thousand dollars over a period of five years for a two- or three-bus fleet respectively, royalties of two hundred dollars or 10 percent of profits each month, and contribute to the cost of advertising.[69]

The franchise program, however, never served as a significant stimulant to replacement service or retension of service in nonmetropolitan areas. Seven franchises were initiated in 1985, and five were still operating in 1988. Litigation initiated by the drivers' union halted expansion of the program from 1986 to 1988. Among the franchises developed, most represented expansions of existing companies but several of these have been so successful as to expand their routes farther.

While the franchise concept was new to Greyhound, Trailways, its chief competitor, had been encouraging independent non-Class I carriers even before the passage of the BRRA. Over the two-year period from 1982 to 1984 Trailways transferred operating authorities to twenty non-affiliated carriers. In fact, over fifty independent, non-Trailways affiliated carriers were members of the National Trailways Bus System by 1984. This coordinated network provided the potential for feeder runs to larger carriers and helped supply replacement service to a number of smaller communities. Although thirteen marginal route independent affiliates with the Trailways bus system abandoned service from 1982 to 1985, eight new companies replaced them, according to Russell's guide.[70]

Nevertheless, spinning off marginal routes was not successful in solving the financial problems of the parent lines. By December 1986 the problems of decreasing ridership and increasing costs forced the owners of Greyhound to divest themselves of the company. The new owners included the former head of Trailways who then six months later filed to take over Continental Trailways. It is too soon to determine the full impacts of these changes on service to small communities, but there are some reasons for optimism. For example, in an effort to cut costs Continental Trailways had applied to the Colorado Public Utilities Commission for permission to halt service on the unprofitable routes in southwestern Colorado in 1987. Although the state denied the request to stop service in areas unserved by another bus company, the Interstate Commerce Commission overrode the state and granted Trailways permission to abandon the routes in question. Before the ruling could take effect, however, Greyhound took over Trailways and announced a one-year moratorium on canceling any former Trailways stops. Greyhound reserved the right to reassess the situation after July 1988.[71]

Greyhound also announced a Rural Connector Service that would link their through route with rural public transit and local taxi service. All connecting service would be included on Greyhound schedules and passengers would be able to purchase through tickets. Launched with considerable enthusiasm in Tennessee in November 1987, the program is showing some signs of success.[72] For example, passengers from two rural routes outside Johnson City, Tennessee, are now connecting with Greyhound routes at a common terminal.[73] In North Carolina four pilot projects are connecting rural public transit vans and taxis with Greyhound routes. Similar programs were introduced in twelve states by December 1988. The passengers pay Greyhound a supplement of two dollars for the connecting service and Greyhound pays 10 percent of the outbound fare back to the connecting service. Difficulties in transferring packages among various types and sizes of vehicles and the insurance problems involved have discouraged all but one connector route from handling shipping services.[74] A parallel program, the Greyhound shuttle, goes one step farther by allowing Greyhound commission agents to lease vehicle from Greyhound lines and to operate them in rural areas or small towns as connectors to Greyhound's intercity system. A pilot of the shuttle in Sandusky, Ohio, provided positive indications of the program's potential.[75] As with any new service it will take time to test these programs. In fact, success will rest largely on the ability to reintroduce rural riders to bus service. If the current efforts are successful, Greyhound plans to test them in other parts of the country as well.

These private industry efforts at generating replacement service are well intentioned but their success must be measured in their ability to generate sufficient profit for all involved, and in the bus industry profits are dependent upon ridership. The ability of small communities to generate sufficient sustained ridership to support bus service remains to be seen.

One regional carrier, Jefferson Lines, has placed major emphasis on working with communities to stimulate ridership. The management of Jefferson Lines distributes publicity kits to the leaders of communities that they serve. Using the kits, towns can generate public meetings focused on bus service and citizens can share their concerns directly with representatives of Jefferson Lines. Response has been outstanding in Oklahoma and the model is now being tested in other states as well. These efforts along with tourist packages have helped increase ridership substantially.[76]

Alternative Service

Publicly funded alternatives to intercity bus service have the advantage of surviving with deficits and consequently have been an approach used extensively in low-density areas. Unfortunately, there is no common or consistent source of information regarding publicly funded or assisted approaches to intercity bus service. In fact, in some cases only local service providers are familiar with the type and extent of replacement service provided by rural public transportation. In an effort to generate such information a telephone survey was conducted of rural public transportation coordinators and intercity bus coordinators in a sample of fifteen states in July 1985 with a follow-up on May 1988. States selected for inclusion in the study had lost a disproportionately large number of bus stops after deregulation. The sample was also intended to reflect a broad geographic distribution and a range of state-sponsored responses to the need for intercity buses in rural areas. Unfortunately, specific quantitative service data was not available to test the relative success of the operations discussed.

States varied widely in their response to the need for replacement intercity transportation. Emphasis ranged from state subsidies for replacement service to specialized safety or marketing programs. Other states considered replacement service a matter of local prerogative, which was left up to the rural public transportation providers. Among the fifteen states surveyed, for example, three emphasized a continuing extensive state subsidy system available for intercity service and three stressed specialized state programs focused on marketing or safety. Two other states indicated use of limited federal funding to assist with operating replacement service and specific routes. The remaining eight states determined that local communities or counties were closest to the needs of their residents and consequently the public rural transportation service that they monitor is best able to determine the extent of need for replacement service. They can choose to operate feeder lines, stimulate the construction of cooperative terminals, or foster public-private cooperation.

Section 18

The one federal program that all states have relied upon for basic funding of operating assistance for rural intercity transportation providers is Section 18 funding authorized by the Urban Mass Transportation Act of 1964 as amended. This program, which was initially funded at $70 to 75 million, was funded at only $64.6 million in 1987. It is administered very differently in each state since each is required only to submit an annual project plan to the Urban Mass Transit Administration (UMTA), which in turn reviews the plans only to insure that they are in keeping with the general purpose of Section 18: to provide transportation to the general public living in the rural areas. The directive is so broad as to include the possibilities for subsidies for intercity carriers as well as county van service. To date, both capital and operating expenses are allowable. The proportional amounts allocated to operating and capital expenses vary among the regions of the country. For example, from 1984 to 1986 the states of the Northeast allocated 63.5 percent to operating expenses and 27.3 percent to capital expenses while the western states allocated an average of 45.5 percent of their funding to operating assistance and 42.6 percent to capital assistance. A number of states have opted to transfer funds from the more restrictive Section 9 to this program.[77] All state public transit coordinators surveyed applauded the Section 18 program and urged increased funding levels for it. They felt that any failings of the program were due to inadequate funding.

Because of the limited amount of funding available few states have changed their substantive approach to funding allocation since 1982. Distribution between small urban and rural projects differed among the states although most of the states surveyed allocated about one-third of the funding available to projects in small urban areas and the rest to projects in rural areas. Since awards were based on the merit of specific proposals, however, the ratio varied both among states and overtime within individual states. Only one state, Wisconsin, considered establishing a prioritizing system for distribution of operating subsidies that would rank projects as (1) urban services, (2) rural and Indian services, and (3) intercity services. This would have favored more densely populated areas much as do private operators. As with any prioritizing system this concept generated considerable concern among those assigned a lower rank, and UMTA intervened by restricting states from setting priorities for distribution of Section 18 funds. Consequently Wisconsin backed away from this concept and continued to use the more typical approach of awarding subsidies based on proposals submitted by all eligible providers.[78]

Only two of the fifteen states surveyed have directly subsidized private intercity service providers with Section 18 funds, and one of these (Wisconsin) is now insisting that private companies present their requests through a public agency. In three of the other states, funds were distributed to counties that then had the discretionary power to subcontract with private carriers if they felt that to be the best way of meeting service objectives. The remaining states distributed Section 18 funds to public agencies on the basis of project proposals. The number of projects funded ranged from five in Wyoming to forty-two in Kansas with the average being about twenty-five, a range fairly typical of that reported for the United States as a whole in 1986. In seven of the fifteen states one or more of the projects served a multicounty area, thereby providing the potential for an alternative to intercity bus service.[79]

Most states distributed funds primarily to public transit services that operated primarily within a county. A number of these services did run dedicated trips across county lines but only for such purposes as visiting health facilities, for example, in the Cincinnati and Dayton areas of Ohio. Such specialized services of rural public transportation are, however, more akin to charter services than a substitute for intercity bus service. In fact, this type of activity on the part of federally funded public transit providers prompted UMTA to issue a regulation in April 1987 that would bar publicly funded services from providing charter service if at least one private operator was willing to provide services. The FY 1988 appropriation bill in November 1987, however, directed UMTA to exempt from that regulation any nonprofit operator that could demonstrate "clear need" for the service or that the service was needed by the handicapped. A compromise measure exempted providers of services for the handicapped with 501C funding from the UMTA regulation and required only that public providers inform potential client groups of available private charter services.[80] This competing interest in charter service is understandable given the efficiency of operating this type of service and the potential for private company profit.

Unfortunately, however, regular route rural service has neither appeal. Intracounty systems funded through Section 18 include both dial-a-ride and fixed-route systems and provide primarily for nearby shopping, personal business, and medical trips. Although open to the general public, as required in the legislation, most serve senior citizens primarily. In only three of the states surveyed were the rural transit coordinators aware of Section 18 funded services being used extensively for work trips.

North Carolina initially subsidized two intercity routes that were threatened with abandonment in 1983. One route transported workers from the eastern part of the state to the Outer Banks while the other provided continuation of service in a rural mountain area. Even the subsidy and more regularized service was insufficient to generate adequate ridership on the western route, which was again abandoned in 1987. Service to the Outer Banks, however, has met with greater success. This service carries maids and cooks from lower-income sections of the eastern shore cities to their places of employment in hotels and restaurants on the Outer Banks. Ridership, which had declined, was increasing substantially, and several private providers began vying for the Section 18 subsidy to provide service in the area. The state DOT responded by turning over the Section 18 money to the appropriate counties to contract for the service and to monitor the operation. In April 1988 when Carolina Trailways threatened to reduce service to the southeastern part of the state, the North Carolina DOT entered into a contract with that carrier to provide six daily trips. The contract provided for Section 18 funds to offset revenue losses of up to four cents a mile for the first six months of operation and up to two cents a mile for an additional year.[81]

Similarly, in Louisiana two intercity projects provided for work trips in otherwise unserved areas, but in this case both routes were directed toward New Orleans. One route, which served low-income workers in the southern part of the state, had an increasing ridership. The other route served workers from the more affluent suburbs. Section 18 funds paid 50 percent of the deficit of both routes, but even with this help, the suburban route was to raise fares in order to help cover costs.

In Georgia, one county service operated a Section 18 funded subscription service for workers across the Clay County line into Alabama. Other counties also operate intracounty work trip routes in Georgia. In Wyoming, Section 18-funded projects served two other target groups— college students and skiers.

Where Section 18 subsidized projects served a multicounty area, there was the potential that they could serve as feeders bringing riders from rural areas to remaining bus stops along the interstates. However, only four rural public transit coordinators actually noted formal efforts to generate such transfer points. In Pennsylvania, one five-county system was coordinating with Trailways to arrange for a feeder service. Considerable effort was expended on feeder services in Iowa, albeit as a special demonstration using an UMTA grant rather than Section 18 funds. A special state effort was being made to encourage Section 18 project recipients to include feeders and transfer points in their upcoming transit development plans. In Louisiana, also, parishes that were having financial difficulty in running services were being advised to cut out service to urban areas and instead link up with Greyhound or other private carriers. In Illinois, some rural public transit van programs acted as short-distance feeders. In the other states, there were no formal efforts to encourage transfer points, although all surveyed felt that informal connections were possible, particularly for outgoing passengers traveling through a county seat which still had intercity bus transportation.

In several locations in the sample states, public transit providers with strong community support took stronger steps toward cooperation with intercity bus lines. In Cadillac, Michigan, and in Clarksville, West Virginia, local dial-a-ride systems encouraged transfers by building garages to serve both local and intercity public providers. In Clarksville, Greyhound used the Central West Virginia Transit garage. Cadillac, Michigan, secured a two hundred thousand dollar grant to build a terminal for dial-a-ride and intercity bus and taxi.

The small urban system in Johnson City, Tennessee, made the same type of offer to Trailways. When Trailways threatened to abandon the stops in Johnson City, the city offered to build a terminal that would serve Trailways and the small ten-bus city transit company. This terminal has now been passed along to Greyhound, and the city has also added human services offices to the building to assist senior citizen riders.

To date, little else has been done to encourage more general feeder programs with Section 18 providers. However, as indicated above, there was some renewed interest in feeder services by fall 1987 with the initiative coming from regional private carriers as well as Greyhound. Many of the rural public transit coordinators interviewed felt that the transfers connected with feeders would discourage rather than encourage additional riders. They felt that all but the transit dependent would find transfers most inconvenient. In one location in northern Michigan, however, a substantial group of transit-dependent people continue to transfer buses at 2 A.M. even in the winter.[82]

State Subsidy Programs

According to the joint survey on changes in state intercity bus programs and policies conducted by AASHTO and the National Association of Regulatory Utility Commissioners in October of 1983,[83] ten of the forty-eight states responding indicated that they had an existing state subsidy program for intercity bus transportation. These subsidy and/or state operating assistance programs helped to insure alternative intercity bus service when private intercity bus companies accelerated their retreat from rural areas. Among the states sampled in the current study, three states—California, Michigan, and Pennsylvania—had the most comprehensive state programs and all were sufficiently unique to warrant further discussion.

In California, the state operating assistance program was well established before the Bus Deregulation Act of 1982. One-quarter of 1 percent of the state sales tax is returned to the counties according to a population-based formula for use for public transit. In fact, only twenty-five of the eighty intercity bus companies in California were private. When Greyhound announced cancellation of ninety-nine stops, 91 percent of the people affected already had access to public transit. Even after Greyhound withdrew, the average distance to an intercity bus stop was still only ten miles, which is the national average. Rather than undercutting Greyhound, however, the counties also provided a user-side subsidy system so that individual riders paid the same price to ride on Greyhound as on the county-sponsored public vehicle. Greyhound then billed the county for the rest of its usual fare.

Similarly, in Pennsylvania a state subsidy was available for intercity buses. Eleven routes were subsidized—four Greyhound, three Trailways, and four independent. To be eligible for a subsidy, a carrier had to serve routes over thirty-five miles, go through at least two counties, and serve a rural population base. For example, Greyhound at first filed to abandon the Philadelphia to Scranton route in 1982. It then withdrew its request in favor of a subsidy to help defray operating costs of $2.48 a mile. The subsidy to help cover operating costs, was to continue as long as the route's revenues did not drop below 40 percent of costs.

A complementary Pennsylvania state program, "Section 203," funded through state lottery funds, provided user subsidies for senior citizen trips up to thirty-five miles in length. Beginning with planning money in 1980, the program has expanded to include more than eighty transit companies from across the state. By 1985 it provided up to 90 percent of the costs for a senior citizen trip. The additional 10 percent of the fare is usually picked up by an area agency on aging. The program has been most successful in raising ridership although 95 percent of the riders on the participating services are seniors. Other passengers pay up to ten dollars for unsubsidized trips on the same services. Although the thirty-five-mile limitation does not allow this program to substitute for most intercity travel, it is possible for a senior to use a local cooperating service to travel to an intercity bus stop. In at least one small city, schedules are coordinated to encourage such transfers.

In Michigan, the state moves beyond subsidies to actually purchase intercity routes abandoned by private carriers, provided that the abandoned bus was the only form of intercity service for rural residents. The routes are bid out to operators who are expected to meet specific safety requirements and to build up patronage within a two-year period. Since the primary objective is to provide service, the state will pull out of a route if a private operator wishes to serve the same area. To date, the program has worked well in sparsely populated areas like the thumb area of the state.

Other State Programs

Operating subsidies, however, whether federal or state, may not necessarily be the long-term answer to the problems of providing intercity bus transportation in rural areas. Continued subsidies may, in fact, only temporarily prop up services that need more serious attention.

As indicated above, the critical requirement for effective rural intercity bus service is sufficient ridership. As long as ridership continues to decline, continued service cannot be assured. Three of the states surveyed, Michigan, Minnesota, and Iowa, are attempting to address factors that may be contributing to declining ridership. Again, their approaches are sufficiently unique to warrant more extensive discussion.

In Michigan, state efforts have concentrated on bus safety and the upgrading of equipment. The concept is that people are reluctant to ride on old vehicles that may be of questionable quality and potentially unsafe. Consequently, the state department of transportation has launched a program that provides new vehicles to rural systems, with the hope of improving not only safety records but also the image of the system, thereby building confidence in it and encouraging greater ridership.

Participating companies were provided with new buses and a safety certificate that required them to have safety inspections at a state-operated maintenance facility twice a year. In exchange for the new equipment, the operator would agree to serve areas with a regular schedule at least five days a week and would agree to pay back the state in six years with 5 percent interest. At the end of the six years, the title of the vehicle would be turned over to the operator. The target group for the program was clearly the small intercity bus operator in a rural area. New operators who wanted to operate along major highways have not been able to participate because of limited funds. As such, the program has been credited with retaining continued safe service for workers in northern Michigan where three small companies operated new buses over scheduled intercity routes. Ridership has increased in northern Michigan and stabilized elsewhere.[84]

A more direct approach to declining ridership has been developed in Minnesota where the Department of Transportation has launched a targeted market analysis to test for potential ridership in rural areas. The objective was to discuss potential needs for intercity bus transportation with those who are most likely to be affected—the rural residents themselves. Considerable effort was expended through newspapers, radios, and visits to senior citizens' groups to generate focus discussions that consider a number of service alternatives ranging from changes in schedules and routes to alternative types of service providers and equipment. Reactions in groups ranging in size from two to forty were taped and assessed.

The analysis along one rural route, for example, indicated insufficient potential ridership to justify continued service. Efforts were continuing to build focus groups of current and potential riders to consider expanding service on some specific routes and service alternatives on other routes. The state DOT also began working with private employers and chambers of commerce to generate focus groups of potential riders. The approach had the benefit of gaining information on level of need before an operator invested in a specific route. Naturally no system could accurately predict ridership, but having a prereading of potential and the appeal of specific alternatives seemed preferable to investing time and energy in a pilot project, which would test only one alternative.[85]

Iowa also was moving toward a market analysis approach to determining needs for intercity bus. In a six-month period ending in May of 1985 the Iowa DOT, assisted by an UMTA 4-I project grant, tested five types of feeder service ranging from taxi and van to connecting bus service. The program featured aggressive marketing of the feeder services including radio, TV spots, local newspaper features, and presentations in senior-citizen centers and service clubs. Handouts and TV spots announced an 800 toll-free number for free information on connecting services and towns. Despite all efforts however, the program generated only about 125 riders per month. Envisioned as an opportunity for rural riders to reexperience bus travel, the feeders actually only served as a replacement service for one town. For other towns the feeders actually reintroduced the intercity bus to residents who had not had that option for up to fifteen years. The disappointing responses may have been attributable in part to this introduction of a "new form" of travel after residents had become accustomed to automobiles or shared-ride travel.

Unlike the Minnesota program, these pilot feeders were expected to generate their own demand. No needs studies or focus groups preceded their introduction. The experiment showed the need for such pretests and Iowa now plans to develop focus groups and market analysis as a preliminary step in determining interest in specific feeder routes.

Efforts to stimulate ridership were not limited to the state level. A number of local efforts sparked by chambers of commerce have been noted as well. In Georgia, the DOT reported numerous promotions organized by local merchants to encourage riding on county buses. One of the most determined and thoughtful efforts was in Fort Bragg, California, where the city effected a positive schedule change. The bus had run from Fort Bragg to San Francisco in the morning and returned in the evening, a schedule that was most agreeable with workers and shoppers, but layover costs for the driver led the company to reverse the schedule, and ridership from Fort Bragg plummeted. Community interest was sufficiently high that the Chamber of Commerce agreed to pay the driver's layover cost in order that the original schedule could be restored.[86]

Unfortunately, no pre- and postridership reports were available to compare the relative success of these various programs or to compare the level of ridership on these services with that on similar systems in areas without a major effort to improve ridership.

Assessment

The lack of comparable quantitative data on ridership by route clearly limits the depth and accuracy of assessment of the adequacy of responses to meeting the needs for continuing intercity bus service in rural areas. With deregulation any requirement for regular consistent record keeping was eliminated, making the task of analysis even more complex. Nevertheless, some observations may be derived from the above descriptive account of private and public efforts at replacement service to small communities. These observations include (1) a prognosis for replacement service, (2) a review of the potential for rural public transit as an alternative, (3) an overview of the potential for public-private partnership, (4) a request for more information on saliency of demand for rural service, (5) a review of the role of federal subsidies, and (6) an overall conclusion.

Replacement Service

Clearly it is unrealistic to expect that bus companies can be forced to retain unprofitable stops. The belief that easing requirements for entry into service will generate large numbers of replacement carriers to pick up marginal stops also seems unrealistic given the experience of the past two years. Replacement levels will probably remain about as they are. Spinning off unprofitable or marginal routes in the hopes that others will be challenged to and be able to make them profitable also seems to be a rather unrealistic solution to replacement service. Local companies might be able to operate at more convenient times thereby generating a somewhat higher ridership, but most intercity routes in rural areas are destined to operate with relatively low ridership and marginal profits. The BRRA removes much of the incentive for cross subsidizing such rural routes through charters, since small companies can enter the more profitable charter service without any obligation for also running a rural intercity route. It is not surprising that a major development since the BRRA has been the rise in new charter companies. With BRRA there is also little incentive for companies to enter the rural intercity market when a combination of charters and express or subscription service holds out a far greater possibility of profit with the same capital investment as for a rural intercity route. In fact, in some areas small companies that had used charters to cross subsidize rural routes have found that with BRRA new charter-exclusive companies are undercutting their traditional charter business and jeopardizing their efforts to continue unprofitable rural routes.

Publicly Funded Alternative Systems

The experience of the last two years has indicated that continuing to provide intercity service in many rural areas is more of a public service than a target for private enterprise. That would indicate the need for publicly funded forms of alternative service. However, rural public transit as provided in most areas cannot substitute for intercity bus service. In most areas it is operated by a social service agency within a specific county and serves the needs of a specific clientele. As required by federal funding, most such services also carry the general public on a space-available basis, but operating times and routes make that provision of limited utility to the general traveling public. Rural public transit can only meet the needs for intercity bus service if it travels in sufficiently large multicounty regions and has schedules and routes that appeal to a broad base of the general public.

Public-Private Cooperation

Linking rural public and continuing private service would seem to be a natural solution. Until the advent of the Greyhound experiment, however, there were few efforts to provide feeder programs that would link rural public transit with private intercity buses at continuing stops. In most states there has been no encouragement for feeder programs and transfers are arranged only on an informal basis for specific passengers. Such systems work to some degree for outgoing passengers but make a return trip almost impossible. Only in Iowa was there a major state-initiated effort to encourage feeder programs linking local services with private intercity carriers in locations along an interstate. The Iowa experience pointed out that feeder systems won't self-generate passengers. A considerable effort in publicizing the program is essential to reassure passengers especially about the return trip. Any reports of unsuccessful transfers such as long waits between vehicles can undo months of effort in generating riders. Only with the full cooperation of all parties, including the operators of the transfer stop (restaurant owners, gas station owners, etc.), can such a system work effectively, and then only by building a tradition of success can it generate riders. The complexity of operating such a system is enough to discourage some. To expect successful feeder programs to develop on an ad hoc basis by local initiative is unrealistic. The Greyhound initiative seems to offer far more promises.

Public-private cooperation in building joint terminals has eliminated a major problem in facilitating transfers through cooperative scheduling and providing a safe, convenient location for the wait between buses. This venture worked successfully in such locations as Clarksville and Cadillac when private companies and the public saw mutual benefit in the cooperative venture. Opportunities for such cooperation are, however, usually limited to larger communities.

The Level of Demand for Service

Other examples of local initiative working to continue or modify intercity bus service speak to a major factor in providing either replacement or alternative service—saliency of demand. Where communities have mobilized efforts to retain service, bus companies have responded positively. It is much more difficult for bus companies or even publicly sponsored services to monitor informal protests or to respond to the needs of individuals.

The Minnesota effort and the parallel program in Iowa, as well as the Jefferson Lines–sponsored public meetings, are viable approaches to gaining insight into the level of demand for intercity buses in rural areas—a factor critical to the interest of any replacement service. The Michigan bus safety program is an indication that rural workers will ride a safe, convenient service when offered. The experiment in the outer banks of North Carolina reconfirms the popularity of convenient, well-scheduled service among low-income rural workers. Efforts in rural areas with less well-defined work destinations have not fared as well.

Out-of-pocket cost of service is another important consideration in determining demand. Both Pennsylvania and California have minimized this factor for senior citizens through state subsidies. Ridership among the rural elderly in those states is relatively high. The Minnesota study, however, indicated that some members of the general public would be willing to pay one dollar more than the existing fare if service were reliable and schedules convenient. Obviously, fare levels as well as other considerations in demand must be assessed for each area.

Federal Subsidies

The level of federal subsidy is limited. All states surveyed emphasized the need to continue the Section 18 program. Nevertheless, this program cannot begin to meet the needs of all rural residents. A scattershot effort all over a state is unlikely to create much of an impact. If viable alternative service is to be generated or existing service is to be effectively subsidized, it is important to use the federal money where there is a demonstrated need or demand for service. Only one state, Wisconsin, has considered setting up a formal priority system for allocating Section 18 funds. Such a system may well be needed as long as the priorities are regularly reviewed and are sufficiently flexible to respond to demonstrated needs. Since federal money is limited, it is also critical that it be reinforced by state and local funding if adequate service is to be provided.

Conclusion

Six years after the BRRA went into effect it is safe to say that the act has not benefited small rural communities. The hope that ease in entry requirements would generate replacement service was generally ill-founded. What has happened after BRRA in terms of replacement service is very similar to what happened before. The potential for using publicly funded rural transit as an alternative form of service or as a feeder service has not been consistently explored among the various states, nor has there been sufficient determination to use state programs to bolster the federal Section 18 program. If effective intercity service is to continue in rural areas, it will take a clear indication of public demand for that service and a public willingness to help meet that demand. Avenues for public-private partnerships are available but in a deregulated environment they will not be explored unless communities can demonstrate demand and private companies can perceive the potential for profit.

Notes

1. Interstate Commerce Commission, *Intercity Bus Industry,* (Washington, DC: Interstate Commerce Commission).

2. *Ibid.*

3. *Ibid.,* p. 38.

4. Interstate Commerce Commission, *The Intercity Bus Industry, A Preliminary Study,* (Washington, DC: Interstate Commerce Commission, Office of Transportation, 1978), pp. 1, 2.

5. *Ibid.,* p. 3.

6. *Ibid.,* p. 4.

7. *Ibid.,* p. 5.

8. Statement of Burton Thomas, operator of the Gray Line of Boston, in U.S. Congress, hearings before the Committee on Interstate and Foreign Commerce of the House of Representatives, 70th Cong., 1st sess., April 1928, on Regulation of Interstate Motor Buses on Public Highways, H.R. 12380.

9. Statement of S. A. Markel, in U.S. Congress, hearings before the Committee on Interstate and Foreign Commerce of the House of Representatives, 70th Cong., 1st sess., April 1928, on Regulation of Interstate Motor Buses on Public Highways, H.R. 12380.

10. Statement of Day Baker, Small New England Bus Lines, in U.S. Congress, hearings before the Committee on Interstate and Foreign Commerce, House of Representatives, 71st Cong., January 1930, on Regulation of Interstate Motor Buses on Public Highways, H.R. 7954.

11. Statement of Joseph Eastman, federal coordinator of transportation, in U.S. Congress, hearings before a subcommittee of the Committee on Interstate

and Foreign Commerce of the House of Representatives, 74th Cong., 1st sess., February 1935, on Regulation of Interstate Motor Carriers, H.R. 5262, 6016.

12. 1935 hearings, Section 307.

13. *Ibid.,* Section 306.

14. *Ibid.*

15. ICC, *Intercity Bus Industry,* p. 42.

16. *Ibid.,* p. 27.

17. Motor Carrier Ratemaking Study Commission, *A Report to the President and the Congress of the United States, Part II, Implementation of the Bus Regulatory Reform Act of 1982: The Impact on Older Americans and Effect on Interstate Bus Service,* May 15, 1984, p. 16.

18. ICC, *Intercity Bus Industry,* p. 42.

19. U.S. Department of Transportation, *Intercity Bus Service in Small Communities* (Washington, DC: Department of Transportation, 1980), pp. 20–22.

20. U.S. DOT/UMTA, *An Inventory of Transportation Services in Places of Less than 10,000 Population Outside of Urbanized Areas,* prepared by North Carolina A and T State University, Greensboro, NC, 1978, p. 4.

21. Statement of John Shapleigh, representative of the National Association of Regulatory Utility Commissioners in U.S. Congress, hearings before the Subcommittee on Surface Transportation of the Committee on Commerce, Science and Transportation of the U.S. Senate, 97th Cong., 2nd sess. on H.R. 3663, Deregulation of the Intercity Bus Industry, March 8, 1982.

22. Statement of Lowell Hansen of Jack Rabbit Lines, 1982 hearings.

23. Statement of Cornish Hitchcock, director of Transportation Consumer Action Project, 1982 hearings.

24. Statement of George Sheldon, Government Operations Committee, Florida House of Representatives, 1982 hearings.

25. Statement of William McCracken, senior vice-president of Greyhound, Inc., 1982 hearings.

26. ICC, *Intercity Bus Industry, A Preliminary Study,* (Washington, DC: Interstate Commerce Commission, 1978).

27. Fred Fravel, "Returns to Scale in the U.S. Intercity Bus Industry," *Transportation Research Forum,* Vol. 19 (1978): pp. 551–60; Fred Fravel, Helen Tauchen, and Gorman Gilbert, *Economies of Scale in the U.S. Intercity Bus Industry,* DOT-RC–92025 (Washington, DC: Department of Transportation, July 1980); Helen Tauchen, Fred Fravel, and Gorman Gilbert, "Cost Structure of the Intercity Bus Industry," *Journal of Transportation Economics and Policy,* Vol. 17, No. 1 (January 17, 1983): pp. 25–48; Martin Williams and Carol Hall, "Returns to Scale in the United States Intercity Bus Industry," *Regional Science and Urban Economics,* Vol. 11 (1981): pp. 573–84.

28. ICC, *Intercity Bus Industry,* pp. 49, 50.

29. *Ibid.,* 54.

30. Iowa Department of Transportation, *1983 Iowa Intercity Bus Plan,* Draft, February 1983.

31. Tauchen, Fravel, and Gilbert, p. 45.

32. *Ibid.,* pp. 42–45.

33. The Motor Carrier Ratemaking Study Commission was requested to monitor impacts on the aged and small towns. AASHTO has also mentioned site abandonments as has a team of researchers from Indiana funded by the U.S. Department of Transportation. Private studies have also attempted analysis of deregulation.

34. Public Law 97-261, 97th Cong., The Bus Regulatory Reform Act of 1982, September 20, 1982.

35. *Ibid.*

36. *Ibid.*

37. *Ibid.*

38. *Ibid.*

39. Statement of Cornish Hitchcock, 1982 hearings.

40. ICC, *Intercity Bus Industry,* pp. 34–35.

41. U.S. Department of Commerce, Bureau of the Census, *General Population Characteristics, Iowa, 1980* (Washington, DC: U.S. Government Printing Office, 1982).

42. Motor Carrier Ratemaking Study Commission, *A Report to the President and the Congress of the United States, Part II, Implementation of the Bus Regulatory Reform Act of 1982.*

43. *Russell's Official National Motor Coach Guide for the U.S., Canada, Mexico, and Central America* (Cedar Rapids, IA: Russell's Guides, 1985).

44. *Tennessee Intercity Bus Study,* Vol. I (J. R. Wilbern and Associates), Tennessee Department of Transportation, January 1981.

45. Intercity Bus Study, Study Report, Washington, Oregon, Idaho, (Washington, DC: Department of Transportation, January 1982).

46. ICC, *Intercity Bus Industry,* p. 3.

47. Iowa Department of Transportation, *1983, Iowa Intercity Bus Plan* (draft), February 1983, p. 7.

48. Motor Carrier Ratemaking Study Commission, *A Report to the President and Congress, Part II, The Implementation of the Bus Regulatory Reform Act of 1982,* pp. 274, 310, 311.

49. *Ibid.,* pp. 383–84.

50. Statement of George Sheldon in U.S. Congress, hearings before the Subcommittee on Surface Transportation of the Committee on Commerce, Science and Transportation, U.S. Senate, 9th Cong., 2nd sess., March 8, 1982, on H.R. 3663, Deregulation of the Intercity Bus Industry, p. 118.

51. Interviews with Iowa DOT Transit Division spokesperson and with ticket agents, July 1985.

52. Interviews with Iowa DOT Transit Division spokesperson and with a spokesperson for the Iowa Transportation Regulatory Authority, July 1985.

53. Motor Carrier Ratemaking Study Commission, *Report to the President,* May 1984, p. 383.

54. *Ibid.,* and Clinton Oster and Kurt Zorn, *The Impacts of Regulatory Reform on Intercity Bus Service* (Bloomington, IN: University Research Office of the U.S. Department of Transportation, September 1984).

55. Oster and Zorn.

56. *Ibid.,* p. 28.

57. Francis B. Francois, American Association of State Highway and Transportation Officials, statement for submittal to the Subcommittee on Surface Transportation, Senate Committee on Commerce, Science and Transportation relating to Oversight of the Bus Regulatory Reform Act of 1982, November 1983, 1984.

58. Oster and Zorn, p. 29.

59. Fred Fravel, "Intercity Bus Service Changes Following the Bus Regulatory Reform Act of 1982," paper presented at the annual meeting of the Transportation Research Board, January 1985, Table 7.

60. *Ibid.,* pp. 13, 14.

61. Intercity Bus Industry, p. 9.

62. Fravel, "Intercity Bus Service"; Intercity Bus Industry, p. 75.

63. Interview with a spokesperson for the Ohio Utility Commission, June 14, 1985.

64. Interviews with spokespeople for rural transportation services and Section 18 in Ohio, Pennsylvania, North Carolina, and West Virginia, June 12–16, 1985.

65. Fravel, "Intercity Bus Service," p. 22.

66. Intercity Bus Industry, p. 83.

67. Fravel, "Intercity Bus Service," p. 24.

68. Ripley Watson, "Greyhound Lines Steering New Path to Profit," *Des Moines Register,* April 12, 1985, p. A–3.

69. Greyhound System Franchise Agreement Packet (Phoenix: Greyhound Lines, Inc., 1985), pp. 15–18; telephone interview with Greyhound spokesperson, May 1988.

70. *Russell's Official National Motor Coach Guide for the U.S., Canada, Mexico, and Central America* (Cedar Rapids, IA: Russell's Guide, Inc., 1982, 1985).

71. U.S. Department of Agriculture, Office of Transportation, *Final Report on the North Central Regional Symposium on Rural Intercity Passenger Transportation, December 7–9, 1987* (Washington, DC: U.S. Department of Agriculture, 1988).

72. Randy Isaacs, Greyhound Lines, Inc., presentation at the annual meeting of the Transportation Research Board, Washington, DC, January 1988.

73. Telephone interview with rural transportation providers, Johnson City, Tennessee, May 17, 1988.

74. Telephone interview with spokesperson for North Carolina DOT, May 18, 1988.

75. Greyhound Lines, Inc. "Greyhound Shuttle Service Program Manual" (Dallas: Greyhound Lines, Inc., April 1988).

76. U.S. Department of Agriculture, Office of Transportation, *Final Report.*

77. George Rucker, "Section 18: The Last Three Years, Summary Data," paper presented at the annual meeting of the Transportation Research Board, Washington, DC, January 12, 1988.

78. Interviews with spokespersons for the Wisconsin DOT, August 1985 and May 1988.

79. Rucker; interviews with spokespersons from transportation departments in fifteen states.

80. Martin Sabo, "UMTA Charter Regulations—A Fair Compromise," *Passenger Transport,* Vol. 45, No. 44, November 2, 1987; Telephone interview with representative of UMTA's National Resource Center of the Rural Transit Assistance Program, May 1988.

81. Telephone interviews with spokespersons for the North Carolina DOT, June 1985 and May 1988.

82. Telephone interviews with spokespersons for the state rural public transportation program in Louisiana, Georgia, Wyoming, West Virginia, and Michigan, June 1985 and May 1988.

83. Francis B. Francois, American Association of State Highway and Transportation Officials, November 1983.

84. Telephone interviews with spokespersons for state public transportation programs in California, Michigan, and Pennsylvania in June 1985, with updates in 1988.

85. Telephone interviews with spokesperson for Minnesota DOT, June 1985 and May 1988.

86. Telephone interview with spokesperson for California DOT, June 1985, with follow-up in January 1988.

Small Community Air Service

Introduction

Air transportation service is a highly valued "commodity" for a small community. The availability of commercial air service (and the quality of this service) is one important community characteristic firms include in their facility location decisions. Thus, the industrial and economic development potential of a small community is, in part, dependent upon its ability to attract and retain quality air service. Similarly, the impact of existing air service upon the mobility of the community's citizenry is an important factor in measuring the attractiveness of the community as a place to live. The importance of air service in small, rural communities is even more pronounced as they, by definition, have greater locational disadvantages to overcome.

As a consequence, the impact of economic deregulation of the airline industry upon air service in small communities has been a major concern of these communities and of federal and state transportation policymakers. The airline deregulation legislation was passed in 1978. Virtually all small communities have experienced changes in the quality of their air service, and a large number have suffered significant reductions in service during this time.

In this chapter a review of economic regulation as it pertains to small community air service will be presented, and the changes in service levels that have occurred since deregulation will be investigated. Additionally, trends, issues, and potential problems pertaining to the commuter airline industry and government involvement in air transportation to small communities will be addressed.

Changing Federal Policies: Preregulation

Route Authority

Airline economic regulation commenced with the passage of the Civil Aeronautics Act of 1938. The thrust of this legislation was to promote the development of the U.S. air transportation system, which at the time consisted of a small number of large (for the time period) carriers who were heavily dependent upon airmail revenues. Toward this end the regulatory agency, the Civil Aeronautics Board (CAB),[1] was granted broad authority over industry and market entry, pricing, inter-airline operating agreements, mergers and consolidations, and subsidy.

As noted by one author, the CAB was very conscious of the need to promote financial stability in the airline industry and to avoid destructive or "excessive" competition among the carriers.[2] As a result, it strictly regulated entry to the industry and entry to and exit from specific air transport markets. Evidence of the CAB's effectiveness in controlling the number of firms in the industry may be found by viewing the segment known as the domestic trunk carriers. Initially, sixteen trunk lines were "grandfathered" by the CAB. By 1978, the year of legislated deregulation of passenger service, their number had dwindled to eleven as a result of mergers and consolidations. No new trunk carriers were certificated during the forty years of stringent CAB control though many applications were submitted to the CAB.[3] Similarly, the CAB exercised strict control over individual airline markets through its issuance of "certificates of public convenience and necessity." Competition was controlled by (1) limiting the number of carriers serving a given route, and (2) imposing conditions or restrictions upon the carriers' service (e.g., specifying intermediate and junction points, prohibiting or requiring stops or through service). An important aspect of the regulatory system, particularly in light of our focus on small community service, was the inability of carriers to lawfully suspend or abandon service without CAB approval.

Until the mid-1940s, scheduled air passenger service to communities with a population less than fifty thousand was limited. When such a community received scheduled service, it was usually because the aircraft technology of the day required frequent stopovers on long-haul routes. The development of faster, longer, and longer-range aircraft during World War II, however, led to the use of this type of equipment by the postwar airlines. Consequently, short haul, low-density flights became less attractive to carriers as they sought to increase aircraft productivity and available seat miles per day by flying longer-distance segments.[4]

The reduction of trunk carrier service in short haul, low-density markets and the formation of many new airlines that wanted to fly short haul markets (with DC-3s purchased at low prices from the government after the war) produced political pressure upon the CAB to expand the air transportation system to the smaller and more isolated communities of the country.[5] The CAB in 1943 announced that it would study the feasibility of such "feeder" service. The following year saw the beginning of the "local service experiment" that led to the development of the local service airlines.

Local Service Airlines. The 1943–1944 CAB investigation of local, feeder, and pick-up air service computed traffic data for eighty-eight cities with populations of less than fifty thousand that had received air service as of September 1940. The results of this study confirmed the CAB's concerns over the profitability of airline service to these communities as even the largest group, those communities with populations between twenty thousand and fifty thousand, averaged only 13.4 arriving and departing passengers per day.[6] The CAB believed that surface transportation competition would depress profit levels on air service at these cities. However, the CAB relented to the pressure from proponents of feeder service and decided to approve such service on an experimental basis.

The CAB's primary concern for the financial well-being of the trunk lines was evident in its approach to certifying new service in these small communities. First, the CAB opted to establish a new class of carrier to provide this service rather than to allow or require the trunk lines to do so. The CAB recognized the advantages of utilizing the existing carriers vis-à-vis creating a new class of airlines: less initial capital outlay, ability to offset losses on local service with profits from long-distance operations, history of experience in the business of air transportation, and better quality of service as measured by size and comfort of aircraft.[7] However, the fear of a drain on trunk line profits led to the decision to create a new class of feeder airlines, which became known as the "local service airlines," even though "the proposals from the new carriers emphasized 'economy and less luxurious standards of service' with smaller aircraft . . . and the elimination of stewardesses and some ground personnel."[8] Second, the CAB initially imposed the requirement that a local service carrier's flights had to originate and terminate at points on its certificate and to stop at every intermediate point. Though the latter condition assured more frequent service to intermediate points than would otherwise have occurred, the primary intent was to prevent the local carriers from providing direct competition to the trunk lines.[9] The CAB later modified this policy to allow some nonstop service, but the insulation of trunk line markets from local service carrier competition remained an objective of CAB regulation until 1966.[10]

The CAB was also concerned with the potential cost to the government of air service to small communities, and incorporated two safeguards into its process of awarding routes for feeder service: (1) authorizations were limited in time (usually three years), and (2) operations were to be confined to those that did not require excessive levels of subsidy.[11] (Small community subsidy programs will be discussed in a later section.) Additionally, in selecting feeder routes the CAB cited, as "guiding principles," the probability of financial success and local need. However, as Morgan notes, population density and length of the feeder link seem to have exerted greater influence on these decisions.[12]

In spite of the CAB's "safe" approach to small community service regulation, the local service carriers required and received a substantial amount of subsidy during the late 1940s and early 1950s. The CAB, in response to recommendations of the 1953 Air Coordinating Committee report, initiated a program of route strengthening for the local service airlines in an effort to reduce the level of subsidy to both them and the trunk carriers. The CAB's approach consisted of three actions: (1) liberalization of the route restrictions imposed upon the local service carriers, (2) transfer of the lowest volume trunk line points to the local service airlines and the addition of new routes for the locals, and (3) the establishment of a "use it or lose it" policy that stated that small communities that could not meet the minimum requirement of five passengers per day would lose their air service.[13] The actions proved to be ineffective in reversing the trend of ever-increasing subsidies.

Beginning in 1966 the CAB once again embarked upon a program of route strengthening. The approach taken at this time represented a significant departure from the existing regulatory philosophy, which had kept the local service carriers from competing head-to-head with the trunk lines. The CAB began selecting locals over trunks for new nonstop authority on many new routes, including certain high-density routes, and permitting the locals to overfly hubs in order to carry more traffic point to point. (These new routes were not eligible for subsidy.) Additionally, three mergers among several locals were approved by 1972. These mergers and the awarding of long-haul routes in high-density markets changed the size and route structure of many locals to more closely resemble those of the smaller trunk lines.[14] As Molloy observes, "the natural result of these changes was a predictable decrease in emphasis on small communities. . . . The dramatic shift came in the late 1960s when the local service airlines moved into the jet era. The lower unit costs of the jets were simply too tempting. The only problem, of course, was that the higher seating capacity and faster speeds meant a shift to a different route structure than that previously operated."[15]

As the locals wished to abandon much of their small community service and the CAB wished to reduce subsidy levels for this service, the CAB in 1973 adopted a new policy whereby the smaller commuter airlines could be substituted for locals in small community markets. With CAB approval, the locals could contract service to the smaller commuters that had smaller equipment more suitable economically for these markets. The commuter airlines received all or part of the federal subsidy for serving these routes, but the locals remained responsible for the provision of these services should the commuters fail.[16]

Commuter Airlines. The CAB's willingness to allow commuters to substitute for local service airlines in small communities on a subsidized basis led to significant growth in commuter operations and an increasingly more important role for them in small community service during the 1970s. A brief history of the economic regulation and development of the commuter airlines follows.

As mentioned earlier, the availability of surplus military transport planes and a large number of military pilots returning to civilian life resulted in a tremendous influx of new airlines providing nonscheduled, or air taxi, service in short haul, low-density markets immediately after World War II. An estimated 2,730 nonscheduled operators existed in 1946. However, the local service experiment and a general lack of managerial skills for most air taxi operators created an attrition rate so large that fewer than 50 were still in operation in 1951.[17]

The rapid growth of nonscheduled operators caused the CAB to reassess their exemption from economic regulation.[18] The CAB's investigation into nonscheduled air transportation culminated in the decision, announced in May of 1946, to continue with the exemption but to require these carriers to provide the CAB with information about the extent of their transportation services. Also, the CAB assumed the power to issue cease and desist orders if it found a nonscheduled carrier "engaging in unfair methods of competition."[19] In 1947 the CAB established two categories of nonscheduled carriers, "large" and "small" irregular carriers, and imposed operating restrictions upon them. Originally, small irregular carriers, the forerunners of today's commuter airlines, were limited to using aircraft with a gross takeoff weight not to exceed 10,000 pounds, or three or more planes whose aggregate takeoff weight did not exceed 25,000 pounds. In 1949 the CAB experimentally granted exemptions to the commercial operations of aircraft having a gross takeoff weight of 12,500 pounds or less. These exemptions were made permanent in 1952 with the adoption of Economic Regulation, Part 298.[20] Part 298 did, however, require the small irregular carrier, or air taxi, to register with the CAB; carry CAB-prescribed levels of passenger and property insurance; provide the CAB with copies of scheduled fares, rates, and charges; and file quarterly reports providing information on passenger, cargo, and mail operations. Also, Part 298 permitted the air taxis to enter into cooperative arrangements with the scheduled air carriers.[21]

The growth of air taxi operations was negligible until the mid-1960s. The major impediment to their growth, the nonavailability of appropriate air craft, and the removal of this barrier are discussed by Molloy.

> The principal reason that scheduled air-taxi service was nonexistent in this period (1952–1965) was that the available aircraft were either too large, for example, the DC-3, or too small, for example, the utility aircraft, to meet the demands of the low-density markets that the Part 298 carriers were supposed to serve. . . . The key to the development of the commuter industry as we know it today was the technological breakthrough in power plants for small aircraft. The development of the lightweight turboprop engine in 1964 resulted in the introduction of such aircraft as the DeHavilland Twin Otter and the Beech 99. This permitted, for the first time, the operation of fifteen- to eighteen-seat aircraft under the 12,500-pound limitation of Part 298.[22]

Coinciding with the new technology that provided air taxis with suitable aircraft for their markets was the CAB's new route strengthening program for local service airlines that began in 1966. The locals' subsequent de-emphasis of small community service created many new markets for the air taxis. As a result, in 1969 the CAB established a subclass of small irregular carriers known as commuter air carriers, officially defined as those operators who perform at least five round trips per week between two or more points and publish a flight schedule.[23] Part 298 was amended to strengthen the reporting requirements, but the commuter airlines were exempt from the normal economic regulations that applied to the scheduled airlines. In 1972 the CAB removed the 12,500-pound weight limit and allowed commuters to operate aircraft seating thirty or fewer passengers and having payload capacity of up to 7,500 pounds.[24]

The role of commuter airlines in the U.S. air transportation system increased dramatically during the 1970s. Between 1972 (the year before the CAB allowed locals to contract small community service to commuters) and 1980 commuter enplanements in the forty-eight contiguous states grew at an average annual rate of 13.6 percent. In 1972 commuter service to outlying regions where commuter service developed earlier and more rapidly (e.g., Alaska, Hawaii, and the Caribbean) accounted for 40 percent of total commuter enplanements. By 1980 this service accounted for only about 20 percent as a result of the rapid growth of commuter operations on the mainland.[25] As will be discussed later, the role of commuters in small community service has become even more important since airline deregulation.

Subsidy Programs

The CAB was empowered by Section 406(a) of the Civil Aeronautics Act of 1938 to establish rates of compensation for the hauling of mail. The CAB viewed the mail revenues as important to the development of the nation's air transportation system, and set rates with this objective in mind. Thus, the initial subsidies for the promotion and development of the airline industry (and, hence, the air transport system) were provided by the U.S. postmaster general. Airline subsidies did not become a CAB budget item until October 7, 1953.[26]

From 1954 to 1960 the CAB, under Section 406, implemented a program whereby subsidy rates were determined on a carrier-by-carrier basis. The subsidies were, in essence, allocated on a cost-plus basis as they were designed to make up the difference between costs and revenues and produce a reasonable return on the carrier's investment. As Table 5.1 indicates, virtually all operating subsidy monies from 1959 until 1978, the year deregulation legislation was enacted, went to the local service carriers. In addition, most of the subsidy paid to the trunk lines was for small community service in the New England states.[27]

The cost-plus nature of the 406 individual carrier-based subsidy created a number of administrative problems and, in general, did not provide an incentive to the airlines to operate in a cost efficient manner.[28] Consequently, the CAB in 1961 established a "subsidy class rate" system for the local service airlines. This approach with frequent modifications in the subsidy formula remained in effect until the termination of the 406 subsidy program in 1983.

The class rate subsidy program was intended to reduce the administrative burden on the CAB and to promote cost efficient operations by the local service carriers. Rates were based on standard industry costs per available seat mile that varied inversely with the carrier's systemwide average traffic density. As some carriers had more favorable operating conditions that produced excess benefits for them, the CAB introduced a profit-sharing plan that required a carrier earning a return on investment

Table 5.1. Section 406 subsidy payments to U.S. domestic airlines serving 48 contiguous states, fiscal years 1954–1981

Fiscal year	Amount of Subsidy (thousands of $)				Number of Points Served
	Trunklines	Local service	Regionals	Total	
1954	3,822	24,299	—	28,121	—
1955	2,773	22,358	—	25,131	539
1956	1,790	24,122	—	25,912	540
1957	1,522	28,444	—	30,016	546
1958	2,283	32,703	—	34,986	547
1959	1,201	36,450	—	37,651	558
1960	—	51,498	—	51,498	567
1961	—	56,300	—	56,300	562
1962	—	64,835	—	64,835	561
1963	—	67,700	—	67,700	543
1964	2,566	65,482	—	68,048	539
1965	3,475	64,412	—	67,887	524
1966	3,089	58,671	—	61,760	518
1967	2,477	55,240	—	57,717	514
1968	1,343	47,982	—	49,325	517
1969	—	40,513	—	40,513	517
1970	—	34,830	—	34,830	474
1971	—	55,940	—	55,940	470
1972	—	62,160	—	62,160	461
1973	—	60,206	—	60,206	441
1974	—	68,619	—	68,619	417
1975	—	57,573	1,812	59,385	394
1976	—	64,658	4,017	68,675	—
1977	—	70,561	4,391	74,852	—
1978	—	69,097	4,840	73,937	380
1979	—	66,132	5,894	72,026	—
1980	—	63,387	9,404	72,791	248
1981	—	72,897	8,502	81,399	—
Total	26,391	1,487,069	38,860	1,522,320	

Source: Office of Technology Assessment, "Impact of Advanced Air Transport Technology," Part 3 (Washington: Government Printing Office, February 1982), pp. 15–16, as reported by Molloy, p. 68.

above the CAB-prescribed limit to return a portion of its excess earnings.[29]

Due to the rapid escalation of subsidy levels during the early to mid-1960s, the CAB attempted to reduce subsidy through its route strengthening policies and by substituting revenue sharing for profit sharing. The CAB expected the local service airlines' increased revenues from the new longer-haul, high-density markets to reduce their subsidy needs. Though subsidies did decline dramatically between 1967 and 1970 while the revenue-sharing approach was in effect, so did the local carriers' profits. Collectively, they lost an average of almost $40 million per year during this period.[30] Consequently, the CAB abandoned the revenue-sharing approach in 1970.

The various class rate formulas in affect during the 1970s were similar in that subsidies were paid on the basis of (1) the number of days each subsidy-eligible point was served, (2) the number of departures from each of these points, and (3) the number of plane-miles flown in this service. A revenue offset was made for the number of revenue passengers and revenue passenger-miles generated on subsidized flights.[31] As can be seen in Table 5.1, subsidy levels rebounded immediately to pre-1968 levels.

Criticisms of 406 Class Rate Subsidy Program.   The 406 class rate subsidy program has been widely criticized for being excessively costly while failing to maintain quality air service in small communities. A major criticism of the program was its "orientation towards preserving the financial health of the airlines rather than assuring adequate service for subsidized communities."[32] More specifically, it has been argued that class rate subsidies encouraged reductions in both service levels and quality of service at small communities through its policy of subsidizing local carriers' acquisition and operation of jet aircraft. A discussion of these criticisms follows.

Though intended to be more cost-effective and more closely tied to service levels than the individual rate technique, the class rate program was amended to include a "need adjustment" subsidy intended to help carriers earn a reasonable return on the investment in subsidized operations. The CAB allowed the carriers to include a portion of the capital investment in jet aircraft in their subsidy-eligible investment base. The allowable part of the investment was determined by the amount the aircraft was used in subsidy-eligible markets vis-à-vis ineligible markets.[33] Since subsidy rates were based only on the volume of service (i.e., the basis referred to in the preceding section) and not the quality of service (e.g., service at desirable times, nonstop vs. multiple-stop service) at eligible points, the subsidies, in effect, hastened the local carriers' acquisitions of aircraft that were more suitable for the long-haul, high-density markets the locals were now allowed to serve.[34] Hence, the subsidies expedited the abandonment of small communities by the locals. Additionally, the manner by which subsidies were allocated often gave incentives to the local service carriers to provide a lower quality of service in small communities. Meyer and Oster describe how the class rate subsidy produced such perverse results.

> Because of the offset for revenue passengers and revenue passenger miles, a conveniently scheduled flight was likely to earn less subsidy (although more passenger revenue) than an inconvenient one. Thus an aircraft used to fly both subsidy and nonsubsidy routes generally could earn more revenue plus subsidy by flying the nonsubsidy route during the peak period (when there were more passengers) and the subsidy route during the off-peak period (when there were fewer passengers). Furthermore, because a subsidy was paid for each aircraft departure from an eligible point (up to a limit), more subsidy could be earned by an aircraft flying a multistop route among subsidy-eligible points than by an aircraft flying nonstop or one-stop routes.[35]

The failure to base subsidy rates on quality of service sometimes led to better, albeit more costly (to the government), service in small communities. For example, local service carriers were subsidized to fly large jet aircraft at low-load factors in some markets where commuter airlines operating smaller aircraft could have made a profit without subsidy.[36] To the extent that passengers prefer jet service to commuter service, the small communities benefited from better service. (On the other hand, frequency of service might be adversely affected.) However, the level of subsidy required in such cases exacerbated the general problem of too high subsidies under the 406 program.

General Impact on Small Community Service.   The inability of the 406 subsidy program to maintain adequate service in small communities may be evidenced by the reduction of service in a significant number of small communities. Between 1968 and 1978 the CAB deleted 127 points from carrier certificates after concluding that the cost to the government exceeded the benefits of this service. At 58 other points, local service carriers were permitted to suspend service so long as commuter replacements could be found. An additional 64 points suffered local carrier service suspension without replacement service provided.[37]

Changing Federal Policies: Deregulation

Small Community Air Service Program

The passage of the Airline Deregulation Act of 1978 (ADA), Public Law 95-504, caused additional concern among many small communities that further erosion of their air transport service would occur. Because the ADA granted certificated carriers greater pricing freedom and eased the restrictions on route entry and exit, many small communities in the low-density and short haul markets feared, at worst, losing all certificated air service or, at best, suffering only a reduction in such service and an increase in fares. As a result, Congress, cognizant that its new policy of relying upon market forces rather than government regulation would adversely affect many small communities, included some protection for the communities in the ADA. Section 419, entitled Small Community Air Service, guaranteed the continuation of essential air service to all eligible points in the country. Congress defined essential air service (EAS) in Section 419(f) as

> scheduled air transportation of persons to a point provided under such criteria as the Board determines satisfies the needs of the community concerned for air transportation to one or more communities of interest and insures access to the nation's air transportation system at rates, fares and charges which are not unjust, unreasonable, unjustly discriminatory, unduly preferential, or unduly prejudicial . . . and in no case shall essential air transportation be specified as fewer than two daily round trips, 5 days per week or the level of service provided by air carriers to such point based on the schedules of such air carriers in effect for calendar year 1977, whichever is less.

The ADA identified as eligible for EAS protection all points that were certificated as of October 24, 1978 (the date the ADA was enacted), whether or not they were actually receiving certificated air service and those points that were decertificated between July 1, 1968, and October 24, 1978. The CAB was given the task of determining which points from this latter group required a guarantee of EAS. The CAB was also mandated to establish EAS levels for each eligible point within one year of passage of the ADA, and was directed to guarantee that these levels of service be provided, with federal subsidy where needed, for the subsequent ten years. Five hundred and fifty-five eligible points were identified in the forty-eight contiguous states, 480 certificated points (68 having suspended service), and 75 points that were decertificated between July 1, 1968, and October 24, 1978.[38] Table 5.2 lists the numbers of eligible points by state.

Table 5.2. Number of eligible points by state as of October 24, 1978

State	Certificated Points — Active	Certificated Points — Suspended	Decertificated Points (deleted between July 1, 1968 and October 24, 1978)	Total
Alabama	9	—	—	9
Arizona	5	4	1	10
Arkansas	6	2	1	9
California	26	3	25	54
Colorado	12	—	—	12
Connecticut	3	3	—	6
District of Columbia	1	—	—	1
Florida	20	1	3	24
Georgia	9	1	2	12
Idaho	5	1	1	7
Illinois	12	3	—	15
Indiana	6	4	2	12
Iowa	9	1	—	10
Kansas	12	—	—	12
Kentucky	5	1	1	7
Louisiana	7	—	—	7
Maine	5	2	1	8
Maryland	1	2	—	3
Massachusetts	6	—	—	6
Michigan	23	—	—	23
Minnesota	11	1	—	12
Mississippi	10	1	—	11
Missouri	7	1	3	11
Montana	14	1	—	15
Nebraska	13	—	—	13
Nevada	4	—	1	5
New Hampshire	3	—	4	7
New Jersey	3	3	—	6
New Mexico	9	1	—	10
New York	12	9	2	23
North Carolina	13	—	2	15
North Dakota	8	—	—	8
Ohio	7	2	3	12
Oklahoma	6	1	3	10
Oregon	9	1	3	13
Pennsylvania	12	7	—	19
Rhode Island	1	—	—	1
South Carolina	5	—	2	7
South Dakota	9	—	—	9
Tennessee	7	—	2	9
Texas	18	6	5	29
Utah	3	—	1	4
Vermont	2	1	1	4
Virginia	9	—	1	10
Washington	6	4	2	12
West Virginia	9	1	—	10
Wisconsin	11	—	3	14
Wyoming	9	—	—	9
	412	68	75	555

Note: Compiled from Civil Aeronautics Board, Bureau of Pricing and Domestic Aviation, *List of Eligible Points* (January 1979).

The following sections focus on the determinations of EAS levels and the Section 419 subsidy program for air transportation in the forty-eight contiguous states. Hawaii and, particularly, Alaska have quite different EAS needs and were treated separately and differently by the ADA and the CAB. They will not be included in this treatise.

Guidelines for Individual Determinations of Essential Air Service Levels

In order to facilitate the establishment of EAS levels for each eligible point the CAB developed a set of guidelines that, according to the CAB, were to be used "as a framework for individual determination, not as an ironclad formula."[39] These guidelines addressed the relevant and important factors to be considered: designated hubs, type of airline equipment, frequency of flights, maximum available capacity to be guaranteed, time of flights, and number of stops permitted. The CAB's determinations of these guidelines and the rationale behind each are delineated in the *Federal Register.* A summary of the general guidelines follows.

Hubs. The CAB required service to one or two hubs (but never more than two) to meet EAS standards. Two hubs would be selected if the eligible point had close commercial, geographical, and political ties to both hubs and sufficient traffic to support two daily round-trips to each hub (or enough traffic to support one daily round-trip to each hub if the community requested such service). A hub was defined as a point enplaning more than 0.05 percent of the total enplanements in the United States.

In designating hubs the CAB considered several factors — the extent to which candidate hubs provide access to the national air transportation system; the commercial, geographic, and political ties between candidate hubs and the eligible point; the traffic levels to candidate hubs, as indicated by traffic studies and origin and destination data; distance of hubs from the eligible point; and the size of candidate hubs. EAS did not usually require service to a particular airport at a hub. However, the CAB intended to review requests for service to a specific airport at a multiairport hub city on a case-by-case basis with the determining factor being whether such a designation was necessary to ensure adequate access to the transportation system and convenient access to the hub city for local traffic.

Equipment. The CAB's general policy was to not specify the size or type of aircraft. The following requirements were, however, stipulated: all aircraft had to be sufficient to accommodate passengers and accompanying baggage, larger aircraft may be required over long distances, all aircraft had to meet FAA safety standards, all aircraft were required to have two engines and be operated by two pilots, pressurized and air-conditioned aircraft were required when absolutely necessary to provide usable air service at the eligible point, and aircraft had to be accessible to passengers by stairs rather than over the wing.

Frequency of Flights. Consistent with the statutory EAS requirement, the CAB determined EAS to require at least two round-trip flights each weekday, plus two round-trips over the weekend from the eligible point to the designated hub, unless the point was receiving less than that in 1977 and could not support such service at 60 to 65 percent average load factors. EAS levels would be increased if historic traffic data and studies of traffic potential indicated that more frequent service was necessary, if the capacity available to the eligible point was being shared with traffic destined for an intermediate stop or a point beyond the eligible point, or if smaller aircraft were being used with the result being insufficient capacity. The CAB also intended to establish a two-tier level for EAS for eligible points with seasonal traffic levels.

Maximum Available Capacity. The CAB ruled that only under unusual circumstances would EAS levels be fixed at a number of flights that would accommodate more than eighty passengers each day at the eligible point (forty enplanements and forty deplanements). The CAB contended that a guarantee of 120 available seats each day (60 seats in each direction) would generally meet this eighty passengers per day standard. This was later changed to 160 available seats. Eligible points might receive a guarantee of more than 160 seats each day if the number of stops between or beyond an eligible point and its hub resulted in the available aircraft capacity being shared with passengers at those intermediate or beyond points, if the distance between the eligible point and its hub required the use of large aircraft, if the eligible point was extremely isolated, if the eligible point had suffered an abrupt and significant reduction in service that warranted a temporary increase in maximum guaranteed capacity, or if some other unusual circumstance existed. In the event of a service reduction at an eligible point receiving self-sufficient air service, the CAB would generally not guarantee more than 75 percent of the present level of service to a maximum of 160 available seats each day.

Time of Flights.   To qualify as EAS, flights had to depart at times considered reasonable in view of the purposes for which the local passengers were traveling. For travel that was primarily local, at least one flight in the morning and one in the late afternoon or evening would be required. If travel was primarily to connect with other flights, flights emanating from and returning to the eligible point had to be designed to link with those connecting flights.

Number of Stops Permitted.   The CAB permitted a maximum of two stops between the eligible point and its hub, unless a larger number was agreed to by the community. One-stop or nonstop service might be required if necessary to make the service usable.

Determination of Essential Air Service Levels for Specific Communities

As mentioned earlier, the CAB intended to use the general guidelines as a framework for assessing the initial EAS needs for each eligible point. Specific circumstances at an eligible point might warrant a departure from the general guidelines. In order to gauge the air transport needs of the various communities the CAB relied upon existing traffic and other data and surveyed each community via mailed questionnaires. Seven major factors influenced the CAB's determinations of EAS for certificated points: (1) traffic volume (generated by the eligible point and between the eligible point and candidate hubs); (2) the degree of isolation (measured in terms of road mileage between the eligible point and nearest hubs); (3) current air service (at the eligible point and at potential hubs — number of carriers, flight frequencies, and destinations); (4) quality of service considerations (indicated by degree of circuity of flights for travelers from the eligible point to their final destinations); (5) nonstop air mileage between the point and its designated or potential hubs; (6) economic activity at the point (in broad classifications such as agriculture, industry, and tourism); and (7) community views.[40] Addus sampled several CAB orders covering EAS determinations at sixty points and discovered traffic volume to be the dominant factor in determining EAS levels and economic activity to be the least important factor. He found hub designation to be the most important factor affecting EAS eligibility, while type of equipment (followed closely by flight frequency and scheduling) was the least.[41]

Addus also reviewed the EAS determinations of these sixty communities to compare the CAB's findings with the communities' views. In general, he found community outlooks exerted little influence on EAS determinations. Of particular note, the CAB's decisions ran counter to community views in fifteen of the sixteen cases where a community expressed a view on flight frequency, in all twenty-seven cases concerning type of equipment, and in twenty-six of the forty-seven cases concerning hub designation.[42] According to Addus,

> most of the communities expressing views sought to relate EAS to economic activities (including the accommodation of freight traffic), traffic generating potential and past air service level. The CAB disapproved the specific level of service requested by these communities because (1) the communities historically generated a low level of traffic or (2) the requests were inconsistent either with the limits set by the Board's guidelines (i.e. more than two round trips a day or more than two hubs) or with its policies (i.e. unacceptably distant hub or specific type or size of aircraft).[43]

Further evidence of disagreement with the CAB's EAS rulings is the number of appeals filed by the communities, the local airlines serving them, and state agencies. Appeals were filed in 23 percent of the cases handled in the first year of the program. While many appeals were based on more than one issue, the two most common issues were capacity and the choice and number of hubs.[44] Most of the capacity appeals, however, were on behalf of communities that had received the 160-seat maximum guarantee, and, thus, represent a fundamental disagreement with the EAS guidelines rather than with the CAB's specific determination methodology or process.[45]

In assessing the EAS needs at decertificated points the CAB utilized somewhat different considerations: traffic potential, isolation as measured by distance to the nearest hub, the reliability of previous air service, availability of other public transportation, quality of air service at the nearest hub, recent improvements at the local airport, and the community's potential for supporting either nonsubsidized air service or subsidized air service with reasonable levels of subsidy.[46] Only seven of the decertificated points had qualified for the EAS program by the end of 1981 with nine others under appeal.[47]

The General Accounting Office (GAO) reported on how communities evaluated the CAB's EAS criteria for decertificated points. Of the twenty-nine states that had such points eighteen responded to the GAO's question on the adequacy of these criteria. Eight considered the CAB's criteria as adequate, two did not know, and eight offered suggestions for improving CAB's determinations. The most often mentioned criticisms were that the CAB was too restrictive in interpreting the criteria and that CAB relied too heavily on historic traffic, which may have been depressed due to the poor quality of previous carrier service.[48]

Though the above discussions indicate some dissatisfaction with the CAB's EAS determinations at both certificated and decertificated points, most of the communities that qualified for the EAS program were granted the maximum level of guaranteed seats and had more than the minimum two daily round-trips to the designated hub. As of November 1981 almost 65 percent of the points (196 communities) were guaranteed the maximum 160 seats per day,[49] and as of July 1981 only about 13 percent had the guaranteed minimum of two daily frequencies or fewer (40 communities with two and 1 community with one).[50] These latter 41 communities had generated low-traffic levels in 1978 — 23 of the communities had an average of ten or fewer daily enplanements and only three points had average daily passenger levels above twenty-five.[51] In spite of what appears to be a fairly liberal granting of protection and service guarantees by the CAB, several valid criticisms of the EAS guidelines and determinations have been voiced.

Criticisms

Criticisms of the CAB's implementation of the EAS program can be categorized as criticisms of the general guidelines (including criticisms concerning omission of key factors) and criticisms of the CAB's individual determinations. A discussion of the more frequently cited and more important problems and criticisms follows.

The CAB's general EAS guidelines failed to include a consideration of air cargo service. The CAB rationalized this exclusion.

> Given the statutory limitations and availability of surface transportation in most of the United States, it does not appear permissible or necessary for the board to consider air cargo in deciding what air transportation services we should subsidize. . . . we would note that cargo service has never been required under the certificate authority of carriers at the eligible points, but has generally been available as part of the usual combination passenger/cargo service that carriers provide. We fully expect that carriers providing passenger service meeting essential air service requirements will likewise transport cargo in combination service to the extent they can. Thus, we will not incorporate guidelines for cargo other than for Alaska points.[52]

The assumption that carriers meeting EAS requirements would provide cargo service fails to recognize that many points would likely experience a substitution of commuter aircraft for larger certificated carriers' aircraft after deregulation. The CAB also appears to have dismissed the importance of air cargo service to smaller communities. On the contrary, the availability of local airport air cargo service can be a significant factor in a small community's economic growth. The CAB had some latitude in deviating from the ADA's definition of EAS, but chose not to in this instance.

A criticism levied at Congress more than at the CAB was the failure to include as eligible points some 203 small communities that were receiving air service from noncertificated carriers at the time the ADA was passed. The GAO reported that 102, or 50 percent, of these communities lost all air service between 1978 and 1982.[53] Though the GAO found no evidence that these services were abandoned so that the noncertificated carriers providing the services could serve subsidized communities, it is likely that deregulation provided other more profitable opportunities that at least some of these carriers pursued. Regardless of the reasons for abandonment, a large number of small communities suffered complete loss of commercial air carrier service after deregulation with no federal guarantee of protection.

The CAB's use of historic traffic levels as a major factor in determining a community's EAS needs has been severely criticized. As Addus notes, the reliance upon historic traffic levels (primarily using 1978, a "good" year for air passenger traffic volumes) fails to consider changes in the spatial structure and travel patterns of small communities and would technically exclude emerging new communities (with no traffic history) from EAS eligibility.[54] As regions and communities experience economic growth, passenger transportation demand changes. The availability of quality air transport service, as discussed earlier, may exert a favorable impact on economic growth and, hence, air travel demand. Conversely, since the location decisions of economic activities in small communities were usually based on the air service that existed under the regulatory system prior to the ADA, airline deregulation might disrupt these activities.[55] Obviously, historic traffic data are useful, but traffic potential is a more relevant factor for EAS determinations.

A final significant criticism pertains to the hub designation determinations of the CAB. Frequently the CAB designated the closest hub point, which often was a small hub with limited services available.[56] Thus, travelers might need to make several connections before reaching their destinations. A related complaint against the CAB was its refusal to specify an airport at the hub point. Thus, travelers might need to use surface transportation from a supplementary airport to the major airport at a hub point, potentially adding significant travel time and inconvenience.

Section 419 Subsidy Program

The ADA empowered the CAB to grant federal subsidies, if necessary, to guarantee EAS to eligible points for at least ten years. Through 1986 more than $195 million of subsidy in total had been awarded to carriers providing EAS (see Table 5.3). As of January 1, 1984, there were 104 points in the contiguous forty-eight states receiving $30.4 million in annual 419 subsidy payments or an average of $292,348 per point.[57] As of February 1, 1986, there were 105 points in thirty-five of the forty-eight states receiving an estimated $24.1 million in annual 419 subsidies or an average of $229,144 per point. Table 5.4 provides data on the annual subsidy levels and number of subsidized points on a state-by-state basis.

Table 5.3. Section 419 subsidies, 1979–1986

Fiscal year	Section 419 Subsidy ($000)		
	Hold-in[a]	Normal	Total
1979	1,798	—	1,798
1980	8,264	1,451	9,715
1981	5,548	8,770	14,318
1982	9,622	16,634	26,256
1983	17,009	24,998	42,007
1984	3,727	32,861	36,588
1985	2,058	30,426	32,484
1986 (est)	4,000	28,000	32,000
	52,026	143,140	195,166

Source: Unpublished data, Department of Transportation.

[a]Hold-in subsidies come into effect when a carrier files for deletion from an EAS point. The DOT requires the carrier (i.e., "holds" the carrier) to continue serving that point while negotiations are held with a substitute carrier.

The Section 406 subsidy program was retained until September 30, 1983, in order to provide for a smooth transition to the 419 program. In January 1979 the CAB altered its method of determining Section 406 subsidies in an attempt to match more closely the actual costs of small community service with the subsidies provided the carriers serving these communities and to slow the exit of local service airlines from small community service during the transition period. The CAB instituted the "service incentive payment" program, which heavily penalized carriers that withdrew service from any subsidy-eligible point. A carrier that stopped service to a subsidy-eligible point would have its subsidy payments for service to other subsidized points substantially reduced.[58] In spite of, or perhaps because of, these incentives local service and regional carriers continued to eliminate service to small communities. In

Table 5.4. Section 419 subsidies by state pursuant to CAB/DOT decisions in carrier selection cases with rates in effect on February 1, 1986

State	Annual Subsidy	Subsidized Points	Average Subsidy Per Point
Alabama	$ 111,409	1	$111,409
Arizona	624,339	3	208,113
Arkansas	420,005	2	210,003
California	1,869,554	7	267,079
Georgia	654,273	2	327,137
Idaho	158,705	1	158,705
Illinois	632,384	2	316,192
Indiana	286,907	1	286,907
Iowa	962,776	4	481,388
Kansas[a]	1,898,701	8	237,338
Maine	209,092	1	209,092
Michigan[b]	1,208,104	5	241,621
Minnesota	711,455	4	177,864
Mississippi	114,681	1	114,681
Missouri	424,991	1	424,991
Montana[c]	1,850,000	8	231,250
Nebraska[d]	2,702,170	12	225,181
Nevada	591,457	1	591,457
New Mexico	758,496	6	126,416
New York	1,029,300	5	205,860
North Carolina	294,119	2	147,060
North Dakota	716,003	2	358,002
Oklahoma	676,421	3	225,474
Oregon	317,971	2	158,986
South Dakota	545,498	3	181,833
Tennessee	299,715	1	299,715
Texas	794,427	3	264,809
Utah	396,393	2	198,197
Vermont	155,232	1	155,232
Virginia	518,960	2	259,480
Washington	469,491	3	156,497
West Virginia	1,246,137	5	249,227
Wyoming	410,972	1	410,972
Total	$24,060,138	105	$229,144

Source: Compiled from unpublished data supplied by Department of Transportation. Subsidy levels include some services being provided under interim rates pending the outcome of rate renewal and/or carrier selection cases.

[a]Includes Lamar, Colorado.
[b]Includes Manitowoc and Marinette, Wisconsin.
[c]Includes Williston, North Dakota.
[d]Includes Yankton, South Dakota.

1978 more than 130 points in the forty-eight states received Section 406 subsidized service while as of September 1982 only 37 points were left with such service.[59] Ironically, during much of this time the annual 406 subsidy payments continued to increase.

The Section 419 subsidy program was expected to be more cost efficient than the 406 program. First, the 419 subsidies were to be directly tied to a CAB-determined essential service level. The 406 subsidies, as previously discussed, were not linked to defined objective standards. Carriers had a great deal of freedom in determining the routes to be flown and the scheduling of flights. Also, 406 subsidies were often provided to carriers serving communities that were not eligible for 419 subsidies due to their average daily enplanements exceeding eighty. In 1981, for example, over 44 percent of the 406 subsidies were paid to carriers serving points enplaning more than one hundred passengers per day on average.[60] Second, competitive bidding by carriers wishing to provide EAS was expected to result in lower levels of subsidy. Third, commuter airlines that operated equipment more economically suited to small community service usually replaced the local service and regional airlines in providing EAS.

Various comparisons of the 406 and 419 subsidy programs reveal the 419 program to be less costly (and, thus, more efficient if one assumes the EAS determinations to be adequate). Meyer, Oster, et al., compared the 1981 subsidy levels per passenger for points enplaning fewer than forty passengers per day and for points enplaning between forty and one hundred passengers per day. The 419 subsidy per passenger was $47.38 compared to $69.89 under the 406 program for the under-forty passengers per day group. The 419 program was also less costly: $20.40 versus $28.36 in the forty to one hundred passengers group.[61] The CAB in 1984 reviewed the subsidy levels for sixty-nine points in the lower forty-eight states that had been subsidized under both programs. The maximum annual rate for these communities under Section 406 summed to $32.3 million, whereas they were at that time being served under Section 419 at an annual cost of $19.6 million.[62]

The Section 419 subsidy program has not been without problems, however. Some of the problems were more apparent during the years immediately following deregulation, while others have been more persistent as they are related to the EAS standards or subsidy determination processes.

A problem in the early years of deregulation was the lack of competitive bidding in many of the EAS awards. Through September 1981 only twenty of thirty-eight subsidy awards involved more than one carrier in the final selection process. In five of these cases the low-cost bidder was not selected. Four of these cases occurred in the first six months of the selection process, and the incumbent or more established carrier was chosen in all five cases.[63]

Deviating from the low-cost bidders was not necessarily an inefficient or inappropriate decision as the CAB soon discovered that many of the commuter airlines lacked sophisticated and sound traffic-forecasting skills. In fact, the CAB, in a number of instances, granted greater subsidies than were requested because it was concerned that smaller airlines frequently overestimated their ability to generate traffic and, thus, underestimated their financial shortfalls.[64] Compounding this problem was the basing of EAS levels on 1978 traffic volumes (1978 was a banner year for airline passenger travel) and setting subsidy awards as a fixed amount for the following two years. In 1981 a number of carriers petitioned for subsidy rate increases while in the first year of their two-year contract. Most of their proposals had been based on peak travel levels and had projected annual growth, not reductions, in traffic. A number of these petitions were granted by the CAB.[65]

Having neither the subsidy awards nor the EAS levels responsive to changes in economic conditions is a fundamental problem of the 419 program. It places a large burden of the downside risk on the carriers[66] and during periods of economic downturn can create severe financial problems for the carriers. The economic recession that encompassed 1981 resulted in the forementioned petitions for subsidy rate increases and led to a high carrier turnover rate among the EAS points. Turnovers potentially have an adverse affect on future travel, which further increases the subsidy and financial problems of the carriers.[67]

Having reviewed the Section 419 small community air transport service program, it is time now to take a look at the changes in air service that have occurred in small communities since deregulation.

Small Community Air Service Since Deregulation

Many studies of the changes in air service to small communities since deregulation have been conducted by federal agencies, state agencies, and independent researchers. Most of the studies performed a before and after deregulation analysis of air service levels, comparing service levels in either 1977 or 1978 with service levels in a year subsequent to the ADA. The majority of the studies focused on the service measures (or a subset thereof) employed by the CAB in its EAS guidelines: size of hubs, number of seats available, flight frequency, number of stops, flight schedules, and type of airline equipment. Relatively few studies investigated changes in air fares at small communities.

Though the early studies are interesting in that they provide a view of the changes in service levels over time, one must take into consideration several factors other than deregulation that were affecting demand and costs and, hence, service levels during the years shortly after the ADA. As mentioned previously, economic recessions in 1980 and 1981–1982 curtailed demand for air travel. Additionally, airline industry fuel prices increased 90 percent in constant dollars from 1978 to 1981, and the August 1981 air traffic controllers' strike forced the FAA to allocate limited landing/takeoff slots at affected hub airports.[68] As a result, it is difficult to determine the impact of deregulation alone upon the air service to small communities during these early postderegulation years. Also, it took some time for market adjustments to occur during the transition from a regulated environment to a deregulated environment. For these reasons the early studies will not be reviewed here. Rather, a comparison of the changes in service levels between the time of the ADA and just prior to the sunset of the CAB will be provided. However, the appendix to this chapter contains summaries of the information provided by several of the earlier studies for the interested reader.

Before reviewing the post-ADA air service levels it should be reiterated that small community service levels had been declining for at least ten years prior to the passage of the ADA. As the local service airlines grew in size and began operating larger jet aircraft, they became more suited economically to serving larger communities. The small communities' traffic levels no longer permitted profitable operations without subsidy, and the amounts of subsidy required to attain profitability became unacceptable in many instances to the federal government. Additionally, as has been discussed, the 406 subsidy program often provided incentives to the subsidized carriers to provide a lower quality of service (e.g., multistop service and service during off-peak hours). Consequently, when one makes a comparison of small community service levels at the time of the ADA with those in effect at some subsequent point in time, one must remember that a trend of service level and quality reductions was well established before deregulation. Indeed, a better approach to analyzing service level changes since deregulation would require a comparison of the service changes over some period of time prior to the ADA with changes over the post-ADA time period for a common set of communities. The use of a baseline year (usually 1977 or 1978) for the measure of predetregulation service levels, however, is standard practice.

Two of the more thorough and recent studies of postderegulation service to small communities were performed by the U.S. General Accounting Office (using CAB data) and the Civil Aeronautics Board.[69] These studies provide the basis for the following discussion of air transportation service changes in small communities.

The Results of Selected Studies on Small Community Air Service

An assessment of air service to small communities must reflect both the level or availability of service and the quality of service. Both the GAO and CAB studies investigated the service measures utilized in the CAB's EAS (essential air service) guidelines. Neither study dealt solely with air service to small communities, but rather investigated service to communities of all sizes. Most data presented in the studies are disaggregated on the basis of hub size as defined by the Federal Aviation Administration (FAA). Large hubs are located in the largest metropolitan areas (e.g., Atlanta, Boston, Chicago) and each enplanes 1 percent or more of the nation's total domestic enplanements. Medium hubs (e.g., Albuquerque, Buffalo, Cleveland) each enplane 0.25 percent to 0.99 percent of the nation's total domestic enplanements, and small hubs (e.g., Baton Rouge, Colorado Springs, Des Moines) each enplane 0.05 percent to 0.24 percent. As of December 1983 there were twenty-five large hubs, thirty-three medium hubs and fifty-two small hubs. The remaining 431 airports, each of which enplanes less than 0.05 percent, are defined as nonhubs and generally are comprised of smaller communities than appear in the other three categories. As discussed in Chapter 1, "small" is a relative term, and small communities in the context of air transportation vis-à-vis bus or truck transportation tend to have much larger populations. For comparative purposes both small hubs' and nonhubs' air transport service changes will be reviewed here.

Availability of Scheduled Air Service. The GAO reports that the number of nonhub communities receiving scheduled air service decreased by 91 between October 1978 and October 1984 (23 communities gained service while 114 lost service). Only 4 of the 114 communities that lost all scheduled air service were eligible for protection under the EAS subsidy program. The CAB determined, however, that 3 had no EAS and 1 community agreed to be served via a nearby community.[70] Thus, the predetermination trend of a declining number of communities in the scheduled air service network continued after deregulation despite the existence of Section 419.

Number of Available Seats. The best measure of the quantity or availability of service at airports receiving service is the estimated number of available seats per week. Between October 1977 and October 1984 small hubs as a group experienced approximately a 10 percent gain (from about 1.0 million to 1.1 million) while nonhubs suffered an estimated 8.3 percent loss (from 1.2 million to 1.1 million).[71] Jones's investigation of the number of available seats per week at 104 EAS-subsidized nonhub communities reveals that 83 of the 104 suffered a reduction in the number of available seats between October 1978 and October 1984 (thirty-three of the thirty-seven states with EAS-subsidized communities suffered a net loss).[72] In total the EAS-subsidized points experienced a 47.5 percent reduction in available seats per week. Table 5.5 presents a summary of Jones's findings by state.

Obviously, the EAS-subsidized nonhubs lost more service on average than the nonsubsidized nonhubs. The EAS-subsidized nonhubs' share of total available seats per week for all nonhubs declined from 8.2

Table 5.5. Available seats per week at EAS-subsidized communities, by state, 1978 compared to 1984

State (with number of subsidized points)	Seats Available Per Week (week of October 1)		Absolute change	Percentage change
	1978	1984		
Alabama [1]	360	330	−30	−8.3
Arizona [4]	599	1,610	1,011	168.8
Arkansas [3]	4,052	2,496	−1,556	−38.4
California [7]	15,633	8,995	−6,638	−42.5
Colorado [1]	442	456	14	3.2
Georgia [2]	846	613	−233	−27.5
Idaho [1]	4,261	1,406	−2,855	−67.0
Illinois [1]	1,056	352	−704	−66.7
Indiana [1]	450	96	−354	−78.7
Iowa [4]	6,648	2,230	−4,418	−66.5
Kansas [7]	5,202	4,807	−395	−7.6
Kentucky [1]	1,160	165	−995	−85.8
Maine [1]	456	253	−203	−44.5
Michigan [3]	2,544	852	−1,692	−66.5
Minnesota [4]	4,636	1,462	−3,174	−68.5
Mississippi [3]	1,221	918	−303	−24.8
Missouri [1]	270	96	−174	−64.4
Montana [7]	1,725	1,606	−119	−6.9
Nebraska [8]	7,940	4,009	−3,931	−49.5
Nevada [1]	1,477	798	−679	−46.0
New Mexico [6]	6,163	3,172	−2,991	−48.5
New York [5]	4,009	1,903	−2,106	−52.5
North Carolina [1]	1,566	360	−1,206	−77.0
North Dakota [3]	1,242	1,382	140	11.3
Oklahoma [4]	2,316	1,140	−1,176	−50.8
Oregon [4]	7,081	3,757	−3,324	−46.9
Pennsylvania [1]	684	342	−342	−50.0
South Dakota [4]	4,896	1,380	−3,516	−71.8
Tennessee [1]	528	121	−407	−77.1
Texas [3]	1,096	1,065	−31	−2.8
Utah [2]	891	1,058	167	18.7
Vermont [1]	703	437	−266	−37.8
Virginia [1]	1,624	180	−1,444	−88.9
Washington [3]	825	207	−618	−74.9
West Virginia [1]	429	342	−87	−20.3
Wisconsin [2]	2,256	1,084	−1,172	−52.0
Wyoming [1]	950	132	−818	−86.1
Total	98,237	51,612	−46,625	−47.5

Source: Compiled from data presented in J. Richard Jones, "The Trade-Offs Involved in the Elimination of the Essential Air Service Subsidy," *Proceedings of the Annual Meeting of the Transportation Research Forum,* Vol. 26, No. 1 (1985): pp. 345–346.

percent in October 1978 to 4.7 percent in October 1984. More than half of the reduction in available seats per week for all nonhubs during this period occurred at the subsidized nonhubs.

Weekly Departures between Hub Types. One measure of the quality of air service is the frequency of flights as measured by the number of departures per week. The GAO reports that between October 1977 and October 1984 the number of weekly departures increased from about 11,200 to 14,700 (or 31.3 percent) at the small hubs and from about 29,000 to 34,800 (or 20.0 percent) at the nonhubs.[73] In addition to the increase in quality of service as measured by overall changes in flight frequency, both small hubs and nonhubs experienced an increase in quality of service as measured by flight frequency to medium and large hubs where passengers are better connected to the national air transportation system. Table 5.6 summarizes the changes in the number of flights per week between the relevant (for this study) hub types. Small hubs as a group gained 7,200 flights per week to and from large and medium hubs (for an approximate 23.2 percent increase) while nonhubs gained 6,200 flights per week (for an approximate increase of 11.4 percent).

Table 5.6. Weekly flights between hub categories (in thousands)

Between	Flights Per Week		Absolute Change[a]	Percentage Change[b]
	Week of 10/1/77	Week of 10/1/84		
Large and small	22.4	27.4	5.0	22.2
Large and nonhub	41.2	47.3	6.0	14.7
Medium and small	8.7	10.9	2.2	25.5
Medium and nonhub	13.3	13.5	0.2	1.2
Small and small	2.8	2.7	−0.1	−2.9
Small and nonhub	9.6	8.0	−1.6	−16.9
Nonhub and nonhub	18.8	17.5	−1.3	−6.9

Source: General Accounting Office, *Deregulation: Increased Competition Is Making Airlines More Efficient and Responsive to Consumers,* GAO/RCED-86-26 (Washington, DC: November 6, 1985), p. 79.

[a]Difference between 1977 and 1984 figures are rounded to nearest 0.1 thousand based on actual date.

[b]Percentage change is calculated from actual data.

Type of Equipment. As projected before deregulation, smaller aircraft replaced larger aircraft in many of the short haul, light density markets. While this may be viewed as a decrease in the quality of service in these markets as most passengers prefer the larger aircraft, one must remember that the CAB did impose certain requirements (e.g., two engines, two pilots, pressurized and air-conditioned cabin if necessary to provide usable air service), which were intended to insure a minimal quality of equipment. Also, the substitution of smaller aircraft for larger equipment resulted in improvements in flight frequency.

The GAO reports a decrease in seats per departure between October 1977 and October 1984 for both small hubs and nonhubs. Seats per departure dropped from 89.3 to 74.8 for small hubs and from 41.4 to 31.6 for nonhubs.[74] Not only were smaller aircraft deployed to these communities, but frequently smaller airlines replaced larger airlines in providing service to small hubs and nonhubs. Table 5.7 provides data on scheduled weekly flight departures by state at communities where larger airlines were replaced by smaller airlines. EAS-subsidized communities as a group enjoyed a 27.9 percent increase in the number of weekly flight departures, and nonsubsidized communities benefited from a 50.8 percent increase.

Number of Stops.   Recalling that the CAB permitted a maximum of two stops between an EAS point and its hub, another pertinent measure of the change in quality of air service since deregulation would be the number of communities experiencing an increase or reduction in the number of stops in transit to hub airports. The CAB collected data on changes in nonstop service by hub size. Tables 5.8 and 5.9 summarize the number of markets losing all nonstop service and the markets gaining new nonstop service, by all aircraft and by jet aircraft, respectively. Markets involving nonhubs experienced a net gain of nonstop service between 1978 and 1983 when all aircraft are included but experienced a significant reduction of jet nonstop service. Small hubs suffered a reduction of nonstop service on both accounts.

Table 5.10 measures service on the basis of the percentage of passengers receiving single carrier (i.e., on-line) and single plane service by market category. As the CAB notes,

> Although passengers prefer single-plane service, in its absence they exhibit a strong preference for single-carrier service. By not having to change airlines, passengers reduce the chance of missing a connecting flight or losing their baggage. They also avoid long walks between terminals at large airports. By developing hub-and-spoke operations, a carrier provides passengers with numerous convenient online connecting opportunities and increases the number of markets in which it provides single carrier service.[75]

In general, passengers flying between nonhub and hub airports enjoyed an increase in both single plane and single carrier service from 1978 to 1983, the lone exception being a decrease in single carrier service

Table 5.7. Scheduled weekly flight departures at communities where smaller airlines replaced larger airlines, by state

State	EAS-Subsidized Communities Week of 10/1/77	10/1/84	Percentage change	Nonsubsidized Communities Week of 10/1/77	10/1/84	Percentage change
Alabama	21	30	42.8	140	135	−3.6
Arizona	—	—	—	89	258	189.9
Arkansas	28	47	67.8	405	551	36.0
California	226	318	40.7	315	540	71.4
Colorado	—	—	—	189	282	49.2
Connecticut	—	—	—	208	502	141.3
Georgia	41	57	39.0	—	—	—
Idaho	47	61	29.7	141	345	144.7
Illinois	24	36	50.0	273	466	70.7
Iowa	82	135	64.6	145	217	49.7
Kansas	—	—	—	193	296	53.4
Kentucky	20	16	−20.0	65	151	132.3
Louisiana	—	—	—	187	297	58.8
Maine	19	22	15.7	255	180	−29.4
Massachusetts	—	—	—	707	1,503	112.6
Michigan	89	71	−20.2	358	530	48.0
Minnesota	102	113	10.8	—	—	—
Mississippi	47	35	−25.5	43	69	60.4
Missouri	—	—	—	146	82	−43.8
Montana	95	136	43.2	—	—	—
Nebraska	262	403	53.8	—	—	—
Nevada	14	42	200.0	14	42	200.0
New Hampshire	—	—	—	294	440	49.7
New Jersey	—	—	—	74	255	244.5
New Mexico	139	223	60.4	150	255	70.0
New York	—	—	—	88	81	−7.9
North Carolina	115	44	−61.7	136	111	−18.4
North Dakota	51	110	115.7	—	—	—
Oklahoma	36	48	33.3	95	80	−15.7
Oregon	94	81	−13.8	67	67	0.0
Pennsylvania	—	—	—	152	91	−40.1
South Carolina	—	—	—	69	133	92.7
South Dakota	102	114	11.8	—	—	—
Tennessee	12	17	41.6	60	32	−46.6
Texas	—	—	—	249	317	27.3
Utah	—	—	—	38	31	−18.4
Vermont	43	18	−58.1	—	—	—
Virginia	49	56	14.3	138	147	6.5
Washington	—	—	—	150	227	51.3
West Virginia	—	—	—	398	328	−17.6
Wisconsin	19	36	89.5	21	153	628.6
Wyoming	14	22	57.1	288	369	28.1
Total	1,791	2,291	27.9	6,340	9,563	50.8

Source: General Accounting Office, *Deregulation: Increased Competition Is Making Airlines More Efficient and Responsive to Consumers*, GAO/RECD-86-26 (Washington, DC: November 6, 1985). Compiled from data provided on pages 71–73.

Table 5.8. Number of markets with nonstop service

	July 1978 Markets	Markets Losing All Nonstop Service	Markets Gaining New Nonstop Service	July 1983 Markets	Change 1978–1983
Between nonhubs and					
Large hubs	217	54	56	219	+2
Medium hubs	122	33	43	132	+10
Small hubs	146	47	47	146	+0
Nonhubs	250	79	91	262	+12
Total	735	213	237	759	+24
Between small hubs and					
Large hubs	237	54	48	231	−6
Medium hubs	139	38	34	135	−4
Small hubs	57	19	17	55	−2
Total	433	111	99	421	−12

Source: General Accounting Office, *Deregulation: Increased Competition Is Making Airlines More Efficient and Responsive to Consumers,* GAO/RCED-86-26 (Washington, DC: November 6, 1985), p. 68.

Table 5.9. Number of markets with jet nonstop service

	July 1978 Markets	Markets Losing All Jet Nonstop Service	Markets Gaining New Jet Nonstop Service	July 1983 Markets	Change 1978–1983
Between nonhubs and					
Large hubs	147	66	33	114	−33
Medium hubs	66	31	29	64	−2
Small hubs	90	43	20	67	−23
Nonhubs	86	48	24	62	−24
Total	389	188	106	307	−82
Between small hubs and					
Large hubs	226	65	45	206	−20
Medium hubs	125	51	27	101	−24
Small hubs	49	23	17	43	−6
Total	400	139	89	350	−50

Source: General Accounting Office, *Deregulation: Increased Competition Is Making Airlines More Efficient and Responsive to Consumers,* GAO/RCED-86-26 (Washington, DC: November 6, 1985), p. 69.

Table 5.10. Share of passengers receiving single carrier and single plane service, by market category

	2nd Quarter 1978		2nd Quarter 1983	
	On-line share (%)	Single plane share (%)	On-line share (%)	Single plane share (%)
Between nonhubs and				
Large hubs	70.3	53.2	88.0	61.0
Medium hubs	72.7	49.9	81.2	58.2
Small hubs	95.2	83.8	91.5	89.2
Between small hubs and				
Large hubs	81.7	55.2	93.8	56.5
Medium hubs	70.4	31.9	87.6	36.9
Small hubs	71.1	28.7	77.3	38.7

Source: Civil Aeronautics Board, *Implementation of the Provisions of the Airline Deregulation Act of 1978,* report to Congress, January 31, 1984, p. 35.

between nonhubs and small hubs over this time period. The percentages of passengers receiving single carrier and single plane service between small hubs and other hubs increased in all market categories. The CAB also reports that the average number of carriers providing nonstop service at small hubs and nonhubs increased rather substantially.[76] Thus, passengers at these communities had a wider array of carriers to choose from.

Time of Flights. Though the CAB did not establish specific EAS guidelines for scheduled flights times at small communities, it was concerned about this aspect of service quality. An analysis of changes in service convenience in the various hub markets between June 1978 and June 1981 was performed by the CAB. Service convenience was measured on two dimensions—how close to a passenger's preferred time of day a flight was scheduled to arrive and flight duration (i.e., shorter flights are more convenient, and the number of stops and plane changes affect the duration of a flight).[77] A passenger's preferred time of day depends on whether travel is local (i.e., hub is the final destination point) or through (i.e., passenger connects with another flight at the hub) in nature. The CAB utilized published flight schedules and, thus, projected flight durations rather than actual flying times. Consequently, flight delays were not considered in the convenience measure. Also, due to data limitations the CAB could not include the probability of obtaining a seat on one's desired flight as a measure of convenience.

The CAB discovered that service convenience worsened slightly between small and medium hubs and between small hubs. On the other hand, a significant improvement in service convenience occurred for travel between small and large hubs. The only nonhub markets in the CAB's sample were markets in which one city was a nonhub and the other was New York, Chicago, or Los Angeles. Service convenience in these markets declined slightly overall but improved somewhat in those markets where trunk and local service carriers had been replaced by commuter airlines.[78]

Deterioration of service convenience over this time period was not an unexpected result because the number of flight departures and available seats decreased from 1978 to 1981. Typically, greater flight frequency results in a greater likelihood of having flights scheduled at the preferred times. Thus, the CAB was somewhat surprised to find improvements in service convenience in some markets during a period of decreasing flight frequencies.

Though the frequency of flights increased between 1981 and 1984, the decrease in the number of air traffic controllers after the Professional

Air Traffic Controllers Organization (PATCO) strike and the propensity of airlines to schedule a large number of flights during peak travel hours created severe congestion problems at some major airports. As a result, it is likely that service convenience as measured by the number of flights scheduled at preferred times increased during this period, but the increased number of flight delays arising from airport congestion likely increased the duration of flights (and lessened service convenience). The CAB did not perform an analysis of service convenience over this time period.

Air Fares. The GAO requested the CAB to conduct a study of the change in air fares in small communities' air transport markets since deregulation. The CAB compared average 1983 fares in these markets to the fares that would have resulted had the CAB's 1974 formula for setting air fares (adjusted for air transport cost changes in the interim) been in effect. The underlying assumption here is that had regulation continued, the fare-setting formula used by the CAB from 1974 to 1977 would have remained in effect. The CAB required strict adherence by the airlines to the 1974 formula through early 1977 but began granting the airlines increasing fare flexibility from February 1977 until the ADA was passed in October 1978.[79] Thus, it seems that formula-based fare levels provide a reasonable benchmark against which to compare the post-deregulation 1983 fare levels.

The CAB data base used in the fare analysis consisted of all 1,552 markets in the forty-eight contiguous states and the District of Columbia that were over fifty miles apart and had nonstop service. Markets that had too few passengers to calculate an average fare level were excluded from the study. Within the nonstop markets, the fare formula was applied to all passengers, whether or not they were traveling nonstop.[80] The GAO used hub size to approximate community size and created new market categories for the purpose of analyzing fare changes by community size and distance between origin and destination. The GAO grouped together flights between small hubs, between small hubs and nonhubs, and between nonhubs and used these flights to represent travel between small communities. Flights between large and small hubs, between large and nonhubs, between medium and small hubs, and between medium and nonhubs were grouped together to represent travel between small and large/medium communities. The sample was also divided on the basis of short-distance markets (50 to 400 miles; 648 markets), medium-distance markets (401 to 1,200 miles; 704 markets) and long-distance markets (more than 1,200 miles; 200 markets).[81]

The CAB discovered that 1983 air fares on the average in markets involving small communities were lower than the 1974 formula (adjusted to 1983 cost levels) would have required. Actual 1983 average fares between small and large/medium communities were 93 percent of the formula fare for short-distance markets, 96 percent for the medium-distance markets, and 73 percent for the long-distance markets. Actual 1983 fares for flights between small communities were 92 percent of the formula fare for short-distance markets. The average fare level for medium-distance markets with small communities as the origin and destination was higher than the formula fare by 6 percent, but there were only four markets in this category (compared to at least twenty-eight markets in each of the other market categories) and less than 0.1 percent of all passengers in all categories. There were no markets in the long-distance small community to small community category.[82]

As is the case with the other measures of service quality, there was substantial variation in average fare levels among the small community markets. There are obviously winners and losers among the small communities affected by the changes facilitated by airline deregulation. The GAO reports, for example, that twenty-eight of the fifty-two markets between small communities, representing about 48 percent of the passengers in that category, incurred average fares above the formula level.[83]

The GAO concluded that the overall air fare level in 1983 was lower than what it would have been had regulation continued. It also concluded that the number of passengers traveling in a market has more effect on fares than does community size.[84] Interestingly, average fares in the medium-distance markets were higher, relative to the formula, than fares in the short-distance markets. This is somewhat surprising since it was generally believed that the formula frequently set fares below costs in the short-distance markets prior to deregulation. Perhaps the move toward smaller aircraft and new, lower-cost airlines serving these markets has resulted in decreased costs of service.

Passenger Traffic at EAS Points

Though Congress established and the CAB implemented policy to ensure adequate air service to small communities, and service levels by most measures increased at many small communities, air passenger traffic at these communities has generally declined since deregulation. Tables 5.11 and 5.12 provide data on revenue passenger enplanements at nonsubsidized and subsidized (i.e., receiving subsidy as of January 1986) EAS points, respectively. Unfortunately, similar data for years preceding 1979 are not available. Thus, it is not possible to compare preregulation and postderegulation traffic volumes. However, as 1979 was the year

Table 5.11. Revenue-enplaned passengers activity since deregulation for non-subsidized EAS points, by state

	1979	1985	Percentage Change (−)
Alabama			
Anniston	20,404	11,796	(42.2)
Dothan	72,498	57,024	(21.3)
Muscle Shoals/Florence/	22,251	13,023	(41.5)
Sheffield/Tuscumbia			
Tuscaloosa	30,800	11,204	(63.6)
Total	145,953	93,047	(36.2)
Arizona			
Flagstaff	10,620	21,616	103.5
Grand Canyon	197,997	214,835	8.5
Prescott	598	8,333	1,293.5
Yuma	27,236	46,473	70.6
Total	236,451	291,257	23.2
Arkansas			
Fort Smith	96,182	61,233	(36.3)
Hot Springs	18,965	2,304	(87.9)
Texarkana	33,601	28,066	(16.5)
Total	148,748	91,603	(38.4)
California			
Bakersfield	95,289	113,174	18.8
Chico	16,061	15,378	(4.3)
El Centro	10,419	0	(100.0)
Eureka/Arcata	81,251	63,853	(21.4)
Inyokern	10,763	11,739	9.1
Lake Tahoe	162,243	76,900	(52.6)
Santa Ana	548	195	(64.4)
Oxnard/Ventura	48,430	19,096	(60.6)
Palmdale/Lancaster	0	2,112	—
Red Bluff/Redding	8,120	46,799	476.3
Salinas/Monterey	262,325	188,233	(28.2)
San Luis Obispo	65,669	50,730	(22.7)
Santa Barbara	229,623	284,065	23.7
Santa Maria	52,845	53,376	1.0
Total	1,043,586	925,650	(11.3)
Colorado			
Alamosa	15,029	9,643	(35.8)
Aspen	137,291	178,965	30.4
Cortez	11,684	7,080	(39.4)
Durango	66,206	89,922	35.8
Gunnison	27,340	19,738	(27.8)
Montrose/Delta	32,074	19,871	(38.0)
Pueblo	36,103	19,916	(44.8)
Steamboat Springs/Hyden/Craig	29,945	38,430	28.3
Total	355,672	383,565	7.8

Table 5.11. (*continued*)

	1979	1985	Percentage Change (−)
Connecticut			
Bridgeport	14,529	47,356	225.9
New Haven	73,497	84,161	14.5
New London/Groton	99,204	60,881	(38.6)
Total	187,230	192,398	2.8
Florida			
Elgin AFB, Valparaiso	115,260	126,615	9.9
Gainesville	181,600	157,294	(13.4)
Key West	30,890	94,505	205.9
Lakeland	1,825	109	(94.0)
Melbourne	204,273	265,205	29.8
Panama City	73,623	91,730	24.6
Total	607,471	735,458	21.1
Georgia			
Albany	69,061	50,295	(27.2)
Augusta	16	1,037	638.1
Brunswick	0	11,018	—
Columbus	151,597	107,866	(28.8)
Macon	103,269	53,879	(47.8)
Valdosta	28,884	15,085	(47.8)
Waycross	220	8	(96.4)
Total	353,047	239,188	(32.3)
Idaho			
Lewiston/Clarkston	42,125	27,314	(35.2)
Pocatello	72,316	41,311	(42.9)
Sun Valley/Hailey/Ketchum	22,800	29,024	27.3
Total	137,241	97,649	(28.8)
Illinois			
Bloomington	33,381	31,921	(4.4)
Champaign-Urbana	112,636	165,338	46.8
Danville	15,048	5,930	(60.6)
Decatur	41,760	40,221	(3.7)
Galesburg	10,343	6,818	(34.1)
Marion/Herrin	12,840	17,066	32.9
Mattoon/Charleston	5,152	4,935	(4.2)
Quincy/Hannibal	25,417	17,465	(31.3)
Rockford	14,164	19,394	36.9
Springfield	129,450	115,432	(10.8)
Total	400,191	424,520	6.1
Indiana			
Bloomington	23,519	10.147	(55.7)
Elkhart	47,553	26,974	(43.3)
Lafayette	62,430	24,072	(61.4)
Muncie/Anderson/ New Castle	19,611	7,816	(60.1)
Terre Haute	33,613	20,247	(39.8)
Total	186,726	89,256	(52.2)

Table 5.11. (*continued*)

	1979	1985	Percentage Change (−)
Iowa			
Burlington	29,287	25,407	(13.2)
Dubuque	21,972	34,675	57.8
Waterloo	89,028	58,077	(34.8)
Total	140,287	118,159	(15.8)
Kansas			
Liberal/Guyman, OK	14,845	5,782	(61.1)
Manhattan/Junction City/ Ft. Riley	40,052	42,574	6.3
Salina	25,954	7,353	(71.7)
Topeka	64,057	31,502	(50.8)
Total	144,908	87,211	(39.8)
Kentucky			
London/Corbin	1,785	195	(89.1)
Owensboro	5,686	8,650	52.1
Paducah	46,875	35,855	(23.5)
Total	54,346	44,700	(17.7)
Louisiana			
Alexandria	80,116	38,302	(52.2)
Lafayette	145,299	138,644	(4.6)
Lake Charles	59,359	36,761	(38.1)
Shreveport	467,371	354,137	(24.2)
Total	752,145	567,844	(24.5)
Maine			
Augusta/Waterville	22,590	12,546	(44.5)
Bangor	248,073	208,678	(15.9)
Bar Harbor	11,265	9,273	(17.7)
Portland	286,268	519,866	81.6
Presque Isle/Houlton	43,887	28,678	(34.7)
Rockland	10,563	7,103	(32.8)
Total	622,646	786,144	26.3
Maryland			
Hagerstown/Martinsburg, WV	30,683	29,374	(4.3)
Salisbury	53,296	53,318	0.0
Total	83,979	82,692	(1.5)
Massachusetts			
Hyannis	160,371	82,972	(48.3)
Martha's Vineyard	29,189	64,109	119.6
Nantucket	183,998	63,580	(65.4)
New Bedford/Fall River	6,593	48,942	642.3
Worchester	37,711	31,948	(15.3)
Total	417,862	291,551	(30.2)

Table 5.11. (*continued*)

	1979	1985	Percentage Change (−)
Michigan			
Alpena	13,880	7,429	(46.5)
Battle Creek	42,800	17,161	(59.9)
Benton Harbor/St. Joseph	37,594	11,638	(69.0)
Escanaba	21,928	11,187	(49.0)
Flint	124,396	135,410	8.9
Hancock/Houghton	30,101	21,571	(28.3)
Iron Mountain/Kingsford	18,116	8,966	(50.5)
Ironwood/Ashland, WI	11,813	2.949	(75.0)
Kalamazoo	142,741	169,202	18.5
Marquette	47,615	39,758	(16.5)
Muskegon	85,395	45,207	(47.1)
Pellston	32,743	15,383	(53.0)
Traverse City	99,098	75,983	(23.3)
Total	708,220	561,844	(20.7)
Minnesota			
Bemidji	21,599	23,843	10.4
Brainerd	16,036	21,510	34.1
Chisholm/Hibbing	31,620	22,452	(29.0)
Duluth/Superior, WI	143,691	102,155	(28.9)
International Falls	12,624	16,720	32.4
Winona	808	32	(96.0)
Total	226,378	186,712	(17.5)
Mississippi			
Columbus	50,511	45,118	(10.7)
Greenville	31,464	20,028	(38.3)
Greenwood	1,604	269	(83.2)
Gulfport/Biloxi	85,212	57,601	(32.4)
Jackson/Vicksburg	445,267	380,211	(14.6)
Laurel/Hattiesburg	24,951	9,459	(62.1)
Meridian	33,228	23,610	(28.9)
Tupelo	11,059	7,803	(29.4)
University/Oxford	1,111	782	(29.6)
Total	684,407	544,881	(20.4)
Missouri			
Cape Girardeau/Sikestown	12,958	11,639	(10.2)
Columbia/Jefferson City	54,810	57,587	5.1
Ft. Leonard Wood	11,070	5,126	(53.7)
Springfield	115,136	201,531	29.9
Total	233,974	275,883	17.9
Montana			
West Yellowstone	11,281	2,660	(76.4)
Total	11,281	2,660	(76.4)
Nebraska			
Grand Island	53,817	25,013	(53.5)
North Platte	26,879	11,445	(57.4)
Scottsbluff	31,324	21,254	(32.2)
Total	112,020	57,712	(48.5)

Table 5.11. (*continued*)

	1979	1985	Percentage Change (−)
Nevada			
Elko	12,171	13,198	8.4
Total	12,171	13,198	8.4
New Hampshire			
Berlin	0	3	—[a]
Keene	12,793	9,480	(25.9)
Laconia	9,649	2,767	(71.3)
Lebanon/White River Jct., VT	36,438	38,129	4.6
Manchester/Concord	69,710	58,575	(16.0)
Total	128,590	108,951	(15.3)
New Jersey			
Atlantic City[b]	47,012	221,415	371.0
Cape May	n/a[c]	n/a	n/a
Teterboro	2,286	6,469	183.0
Trenton	48,389	28,100	(41.9)
Total	97,687	255,984	162.0
New Mexico			
Clovis	5,741	5,195	(9.5)
Farmington	50,825	59,138	16.4
Roswell	23,109	25,773	11.5
Total	79,675	90,106	13.1
New York			
Binghamton/Endicott/ Johnson City	127,161	170,126	33.8
Elmira/Corning	84,805	85,142	0.4
Glens Falls	2,169	193	(91.1)
Islip	139,514	422,571	202.9
Ithaca/Cortland	n/a	n/a	n/a
Jamestown	43,157	27,297	(36.7)
Liberty/Monticello	2,798	17	(99.4)
Poughkeepsie	33,371	33,757	1.2
Rockville Center	n/a	n/a	n/a
Utica/Rome	35,867	34,925	(2.6)
White Plains	55,922	200,320	258.2
Total	524,764	974,348	85.7
North Carolina			
Asheville	186,069	189,500	1.8
Fayetteville	159,145	205,156	28.9
Hickory	19,331	13,874	(28.2)
Jacksonville/Camp Lejeune	47,493	97,570	105.4
Kinston/Goldsboro	57,402	88,821	54.7
New Bern/Morehead City/ Beaufort	21,906	15,597	(28.8)
Wilmington	88,693	148,055	66.9
Total	580,039	758,573	30.8

Table 5.11. (*continued*)

	1979	1985	Percentage Change (−)
Ohio			
Akron/Canton	221,280	208,667	(5.7)
Mansfield	13,525	2,380	(82.4)
Youngstown	109,224	65,181	(40.3)
Zanesville/Cambridge	0	40	—
Total	344,049	276,268	(19.7)
Oklahoma			
Lawton/Ft. Sill	70,831	60,275	(14.9)
Stillwater	0	1,343	—
Total	70,831	61,618	(13.0)
Oregon			
Albany/Corvalis	309	366	18.4
Astoria/Seaside	1,035	272	(73.7)
Bend/Redmond	21,601	24,166	11.9
Klamath Falls	30,734	14,664	(52.3)
Medford	117,639	120,596	2.5
North Bend/Coos Bay	15,118	10,099	(33.2)
Total	186,436	170,163	(8.7)
Pennsylvania			
Altoona	26,203	18,213	(30.5)
Bradford	24,489	10,385	(57.6)
Clearfield/Philipsburg/ Bellefonte/State College	5,424	49,901	820.0
Du Bois	20,962	20,145	(3.9)
Erie	152,265	133,069	(12.6)
Hazelton	31	11	(64.5)
Johnston	23,863	17,439	(26.9)
Lancaster	37,195	43,764	17.7
Oil City/Franklin	12,816	8,225	(35.8)
Reading	49,982	57,211	14.5
Williamsport	52,721	39,829	(24.5)
Total	405,951	398,192	(1.9)
South Carolina			
Florence	30,756	26,926	(12.5)
Greenville/Spartanburg	693	161	(76.8)
Myrtle Beach	112,071	196,672	75.5
Total	143,520	223,759	55.9
South Dakota			
Aberdeen	40,201	24,398	(39.3)
Pierre	39,928	12,011	(69.9)
Watertown	16,486	12,182	(26.1)
Total	96,615	48,591	(49.7)

Table 5.11. (*continued*)

	1979	1985	Percentage Change (−)
Tennessee			
Jackson	12,989	3,600	(72.3)
Total	12,989	3,600	(72.3)
Texas			
Abilene	80,876	65,957	(18.4)
Beaumont/Port Arthur	101,202	68,825	(32.0)
Brownsville	99,442	68,787	(30.8)
College Station	37,209	42,171	13.3
Harlingen/San Benito	312,021	371,770	19.1
Laredo	37,035	28,594	(22.8)
Longview/Kilgore/Gladwater	21,321	23,989	12.5
Mission/McAllen	130,969	195,208	49.0
San Angelo	69,759	44,474	(36.2)
Tyler	30,429	33,128	(8.9)
Victoria	14,354	15,007	(4.5)
Waco	43,124	26,403	(38.8)
Wichita Falls	77,533	64,490	(16.8)
Total	1,055,274	1,048,803	(0.6)
Utah			
Vernal	9,371	4,004	(56.8)
Total	9,371	4,004	(56.8)
Vermont			
Newport	0	0	0.0
Rutland	5,757	6,196	7.6
Total	5,757	6,196	7.6
Virginia			
Charlottesville	64,245	96,658	50.5
Lynchburg	50,219	66,804	33.0
Newport News/Hampton/ Williamsburg/Yorktown	135,835	61,868	(54.5)
Roanoke	455,641	311,051	(31.7)
Staunton	19,636	12,270	(37.5)
Total	725,576	548,651	(24.4)
Washington			
Pasco/Kennewick/Richland	144,099	147,721	2.5
Pullman/Moscow, ID	28,834	23,811	(17.4)
Walla Walla	22,473	20,202	(10.1)
Wenatchee	13,871	16,018	15.5
Yakima	68,478	59,143	(13.6)
Total	277,755	266,895	(3.9)

Table 5.11. (*continued*)

	1979	1985	Percentage Change (−)
West Virginia			
Greenbrier/White Sulphur Springs	41	520	1,168.3
Parkersburg/Marietta, OH	48,308	42,216	(12.6)
Total	48,349	42,736	(11.6)
Wisconsin			
Appleton	97,587	105,906	8.5
Beloit/Janesville	6,946	30	(99.6)
Eau Claire	46,032	34,156	(25.8)
Green Bay/Clintonville	351,837	224,510	(36.2)
La Crosse	77,401	74,698	(3.5)
Oshkosh	70,706	23,930	(66.2)
Rhinelander/Land O'Lakes	29,803	15,421	(48.3)
Wausau/Stevens Point	6	284	4,633.3
Total	680,318	478,935	(29.6)
Wyoming			
Cheyenne	42,746	25,539	(40.3)
Jackson	51,017	67,124	31.6
Laramie	17,016	8,216	(51.7)
Lovell/Powell/Cody	14,428	6,209	(57.0)
Riverton/Lander	22,174	8,237	(62.9)
Rock Springs	29,870	16,096	(46.1)
Sheridan	21,450	10,864	(49.4)
Total	198,701	142,285	(28.4)

Source: Unpublished data provided by U.S. Department of Transportation.

[a]Passenger level was zero so change cannot be computed.

[b]Passenger data reflects activity at two airports in Atlantic City, Pomona Field and Bader Field.

[c]Data not available.

Table 5.12. Revenue-enplaned passengers activity since deregulation for subsidized EAS points, by state

State/Point	1979	1985	Percentage Change (−)
Alabama			
Gadsden	3,683	1,205	(67.3)
Total	3,683	1,205	(67.3)
Arizona			
Kingman	384	3,199	733.1
Page	1,432	4,425	209.0
Winslow	490	640	30.6
Total	2,306	8,264	258.4
Arkansas			
El Dorado/Camden	5,557	2,573	(53.7)
Harrison	11,618	2,130	(81.7)
Jonesboro	7,054	2,816	(60.1)
Total	24,229	7,519	(69.0)
California			
Blythe	556	1,182	112.6
Crescent City	3,454	1,755	(49.2)
Merced	6,825	7,197	5.5
Modesto	31,147	21,909	(29.7)
Santa Rosa	6,742	3,741	(44.5)
Stockton	162,243	81,509	(49.8)
Visalia	17,119	10,960	(36.0)
Total	228,086	128,253	(43.8)
Colorado			
Lamar	2,259	2,403	6.4
Total	2,259	2,403	6.4
Georgia			
Athens	11,264	9,357	(16.9)
Moultrie/Thomasville	2,941	715	(75.7)
Total	14,205	10,072	(29.1)
Idaho			
Twin Falls	40,140	26,117	(34.9)
Total	40,140	26,117	(34.9)
Illinois			
Mount Vernon	5,026	5,247	4.4
Sterling/Rock Falls	7,929	3,415	(56.9)
Total	12,955	8,662	(33.1)
Indiana			
Kokomo/Logansport/Peru	576	1,579	174.1
Total	576	1,579	174.1

Table 5.12. (*continued*)

State/Point	1979	1985	Percentage Change (−)
Iowa			
Clinton	6,519	741	(88.6)
Fort Dodge	8,779	5,278	(39.9)
Mason City	14,062	6,611	(53.0)
Ottumwa	4,687	467	(90.0)
Total	34,047	13,097	(61.5)
Kansas			
Dodge City	7,562	4,246	(43.9)
Garden City	7,500	7,335	(2.2)
Goodland	2,924	1,540	(47.3)
Great Bend	4,834	3,219	(33.4)
Hays	9,263	6,583	(28.9)
Hutchinson	1,646	770	(53.2)
Independence/Parsons/Coffeyville	0	798	—[a]
Total	33,729	24,491	(27.4)
Maine			
Lewiston/Auburn	1,307	931	(28.8)
Total	1,307	931	(28.8)
Michigan			
Jackson	1,380	8,791	537.0
Manistee/Ludington	2,908	197	(93.2)
Marinette, WI/Menominee	11,034	1,300	(88.2)
Sault Ste. Marie	13,529	5,609	(58.5)
Total	28,851	15,897	(44.9)
Minnesota			
Fairmont	6,083	2,383	(60.8)
Mankato	6,877	1,423	(79.3)
Thief River Falls	13,778	4,824	(65.0)
Worthington	3,283	1,019	(69.0)
Total	30,021	9,649	(67.9)
Mississippi			
Natchez	2,731	3,185	16.6
Total	2,731	3,185	16.6
Missouri			
Kirksville	2,772	1,669	(39.8)
Total	2,772	1,669	(39.8)

153

Table 5.12. (*continued*)

State/Point	1979	1985	Percentage Change (−)
Montana			
Glasgow	2,805	2,876	2.5
Glendive	981	1,621	65.2
Havre	924	1,137	23.1
Lewiston	503	565	12.3
Miles City	917	1,288	40.5
Sidney	1,839	4,885	165.6
Wolf Point	1,745	2,222	27.3
Total	9,714	14,594	50.2
Nebraska			
Alliance	3,259	337	(89.7)
Chadron	2,963	599	(72.5)
Columbus	2,102	735	(65.0)
Hastings	3,888	958	(75.4)
Kearney	6,475	3,467	(46.5)
McCook	3,718	1,110	(70.1)
Norfolk	7,799	2,807	(64.0)
Sidney	1,948	612	(68.6)
Total	32,152	10,625	(67.0)
Nevada			
Ely	5,584	2,759	(50.6)
Total	5,584	2,759	(50.6)
New Mexico			
Alamogordo/Holloman AFB	12,273	4,094	(66.6)
Carlsbad	4,767	15,958	234.8
Gallup	11,534	2,692	(76.7)
Hobbs	5,893	5,239	(11.1)
Santa Fe	3,750	1,759	(53.1)
Silver City/Hurley/Deming	5,988	2,769	(53.8)
Total	44,205	32,511	(26.5)
New York			
Massena	5,277	3,617	(31.5)
Ogdensburg	4,247	3,182	(25.1)
Plattsburgh	13,712	7,114	(48.1)
Saranac Lake/Lake Placid	8,951	5,600	(37.4)
Watertown	4,482	5,077	13.3
Total	36,669	24,590	(32.9)
North Carolina			
Rocky Mount/Wilson	5,453	1,291	(76.3)
Winston-Salem	46,703	4,436	(90.5)
Total	52,156	5,727	(89.0)

Table 5.12. (*continued*)

State/Point	1979	1985	Percentage Change (−)
North Dakota			
Devils Lake	6,687	3,125	(53.3)
Jamestown	14,087	3,865	(72.6)
Williston	10,223	7,450	(27.1)
Total	30,997	14,440	(53.4)
Oklahoma			
Enid	6,043	2,751	(54.5)
McAlester	699	641	(8.3)
Ponca City	1,691	1,432	(15.3)
Total	8,433	4,824	(42.8)
Oregon			
Pendleton	36,804	10,211	(72.3)
Salem	13,477	2,272	(83.1)
Total	50,281	12,483	(75.2)
South Dakota			
Brookings	2,740	3,224	17.7
Huron	7,164	2,884	(59.7)
Mitchell	4,536	1,300	(71.3)
Yankton	6,316	993	(84.3)
Total	20,756	8,401	(59.5)
Tennessee			
Clarksville/Ft. Campbell/ Hopkinville, KY	1,948	424	(78.2)
Total	1,948	424	(78.2)
Texas			
Brownwood	5,878	2,395	(59.3)
Paris	2,912	1,089	(62.6)
Temple	15,258	7,313	(52.1)
Total	24,048	10,797	(55.1)
Utah			
Cedar City	2,457	7,483	204.6
Moab	2,358	552	(76.6)
Total	4,815	8,035	66.9
Vermont			
Montpelier/Barre	7,562	882	(88.3)
Total	7,562	882	(88.3)

Table 5.12. (*continued*)

	1979	1985	Percentage Change (−)
Virginia			
Danville	2,375	2,435	2.5
Hot Springs	1,832	2,134	16.5
Total	4,207	4,569	8.6
Washington			
Ephrata/Moses Lake	3,720	3,987	7.2
Total	3,720	3,987	7.2
West Virginia			
Beckley	15,994	6,124	(61.7)
Clarksburg/Fairmont	35,469	19,446	(45.2)
Elkins	2,739	1,297	(52.6)
Morgantown	28,860	18,110	(37.2)
Princeton/Bluefield	20,164	2,826	(86.0)
Total	103,226	47,803	(53.7)
Wisconsin			
Manitowoc	7,575	594	(92.2)
Total	7,575	594	(92.2)
Wyoming			
Worland	8,067	3,188	(60.5)
Total	8,067	3,188	(60.5)

Source: Unpublished data provided by U.S. Department of Transportation.
[a]Passenger level was zero so change cannot be computed.

the CAB established general guidelines for determining individual EAS levels, a comparison of 1979 and 1985 passenger enplanements reflects the trends in passenger activity since federal establishment of minimum service levels.

Of the 231 nonsubsidized EAS points listed in Table 5.11, 152 have experienced a decrease in annual passenger enplanements while 79 have maintained or increased their volumes. Of the 152 communities that have suffered decreased traffic volumes, 110 have incurred annual reductions of 25 percent or more, and 48 of these have had reductions of 50 percent or more. Of the forty-five states with nonsubsidized EAS points, thirty-one have experienced reductions with fourteen of these having reductions of at least 25 percent. In total, passenger enplanements decreased from 13,679,186 in 1979 to 13,093,480 in 1985, a 4.28 percent decrease. Obviously, there were many big winners as well as big losers among the nonsubsidized EAS communities.

The subsidized EAS points have seen their passenger volumes decline significantly over the time period 1979 to 1985. Of the 101 communities listed in Table 5.12, 76 have suffered a decrease in annual enplanements with 71 experiencing a reduction of 25 percent or more and 53 experiencing a reduction of 50 percent or more. Of the thirty-five states with subsidized EAS points, twenty-seven have had reductions in passenger traffic with all twenty-seven suffering a decline of 25 percent or more. In total, passenger enplanements decreased from 918,012 in 1979 to 474,226 in 1985, a 48.34 percent decrease. Federal subsidy, which was intended to attain the minimum essential service levels, has not reversed the preregulation trend of declining passenger levels at these communities.

Though the traffic losses at subsidized EAS points have been substantial, nearly one-half (i.e., 49 of 101) of these communities are located within one hundred miles of a hub airport where alternative air service is available. Table 5.13 lists these communities and the percentage change in annual enplanements, 1979 versus 1985, for each. The 21

Table 5.13. Changes in traffic (revenue-enplaned passengers) at subsidized EAS points, by distance from alternative service at a hub airport, 1979–1985

0–60 miles	% change (−)	61–100 miles	% change (−)
Gadsden, AL	(67.3)	Kingman, AZ	733.1
Merced, CA	5.5	El Dorado/Camden, AR	(53.7)
Stockton, CA	(49.8)	Jonesboro, AR	(60.1)
Visalia, CA	(36.0)	Modesto, CA	(29.7)
Moultrie, GA	(75.7)	Santa Rosa, CA	(44.5)
Kokomo, IN	174.1	Athens, GA	(16.9)
Clinton, IA	(88.6)	Mt. Vernon, IL	4.4
Lewiston/Auburn, ME	(28.8)	Fort Dodge, IA	(39.9)
Jackson, MI	537.0	Ottumwa, IA	(53.0)
Mankato, MN	(79.3)	Great Bend, KS	(33.4)
Worthington, MN	(69.0)	Thief River Falls, MN	(65.0)
Santa Fe, NM	(53.1)	Natchez, MS	16.6
Plattsburgh, NY	(48.1)	Lewiston, MT	12.3
Saranac Lake, NY	(37.4)	Chadron, NE	(72.5)
Salem, OR	(83.1)	Columbus, NE	(65.0)
Brookings, SD	17.7	Norfolk, NE	(64.0)
Yankton, SD	(84.3)	Alamogordo, NM	(66.6)
Clarksville, TN	(78.2)	Hobbs, NM	(11.1)
Montpelier, VT	(88.3)	Massena, NY	(31.5)
Danville, VA	2.5	Watertown NY	13.3
Manitowoc, WI	(92.2)	Jamestown, ND	(72.6)
		Enid, OK	(54.5)
		Ponca City, OK	(15.3)
		Huron, SD	(59.7)
		Mitchell, SD	(71.3)
		Temple, TX	(52.1)
		Hot Springs, VA	16.5
		Ephrata/Moses Lake, WA	7.2

Source: Percentage changes taken from Table 5.11 and 5.12.

points located within sixty miles of a hub airport accounted for 30.63 percent (281,159) of 1979 passenger enplanements at all subsidized EAS points and 31.50 percent (139,792) of the decrease in volumes for 1985. The 28 points located between sixty-one and one hundred miles from a hub airport accounted for 21.53 percent (197,606) of 1979 enplanements at all subsidized EAS points and 18.79 percent (83,392) of the decrease in volumes for 1985. Thus, approximately one-half of the passengers departing from the subsidized EAS points in 1979 had alternative, superior air service available within one hundred miles of the EAS community.

Summary and Conclusion. On the basis of aggregate air service measures, service to small hubs and nonhubs has generally improved since deregulation. Flight frequency as measured by weekly departures has increased significantly for both small hubs (31.3 percent) and nonhubs (20.0 percent), and the number of carriers providing service at these points has also increased. A CAB study concluded that air fares are now lower at small communities as well.

The results of changes on other service dimensions are mixed. The availability of air service as measured by the number of available seats has increased at small hubs but decreased at nonhubs. In general, smaller aircraft have replaced larger aircraft at both small hubs and nonhubs, but the greater increase in flight frequency at small hubs has resulted in their increase in the number of available seats. Quality of service as measured by the number of nonstop flights by all types of aircraft has improved at nonhubs but worsened at small hubs, but jet nonstop service has decreased at both. Service convenience (i.e., time of flights) has improved for flights between small and large hubs but has declined between small and medium hubs and for flights between small hubs.

In aggregate, the number of passenger enplanements at the nonhub EAS points has declined since the CAB established individual EAS levels in 1979. The decline in annual enplanements at subsidized EAS points, the smallest communities receiving scheduled air service, was nearly 50 percent between 1979 and 1985. Nonsubsidized EAS points experienced an aggregate annual decline of less than 5 percent. Of course, many subsidized and nonsubsidized EAS points have benefited from substantial growth in passenger traffic. Additionally, one-half of the subsidized EAS points that have suffered declines in passenger volumes are located within one hundred miles of a hub airport (with 21 percent located within sixty miles of a hub airport), and thus have fairly good access to the national air transportation system.

Though the federal government has been able to retain scheduled air service (at minimum EAS levels) in many small communities that likely would have lost such service without government intervention, and though air service since deregulation has improved overall in small communities, the trend of decreasing passenger volumes at these points, which was evident before deregulation, has continued. It is likely that market forces beyond those in the transportation realm have been more influential in determining air passenger activity at these communities.

On the other hand, a number of small communities have experienced substantial growth in passenger enplanements. It is likely that deregulation has played a more significant role in this development by removing the institutional barriers to commuter airline entry to these markets. The current service levels provided by commuter airlines operating smaller, propeller-driven aircraft are generally better than those offered by the regional airlines before deregulation. The Section 419 subsidy program has also removed many of the Section 406 incentives that produced lower service levels. Thus, it is safe to say that deregulation has *facilitated* the growth in passenger volumes in some communities. However, it is not appropriate to attribute the decline in passenger activity in other communities to air transport deregulation. One could argue that the EAS levels established by Congress and the CAB are not sufficient, but the actual granting of entry and exit and pricing freedoms to the airlines has not *caused* the declines in passenger volumes.

Future Trends and Strategies That May Impact on Service at Small Communities

The future availability and quality of air transport service at many small communities is contingent upon carrier and government trends and strategies. Of particular importance to all nonhub EAS points is the financial and operating performance of the commuter airline industry. Future service levels at these points are inextricably tied to the commuter airlines' ability to generate sufficient returns on their investments, to finance aircraft acquisition, and to gain or retain access to the hub points. Future service levels at EAS points and other small communities will also be affected by the federal legislation that extends and amends the Small Community Air Service program contained in Section 419 of the Airline Deregulation Act of 1978. The Airport and Airway Safety and Capacity Expansion Act of 1987 makes significant changes in the definition of essential air service, in the eligibility requirements, and in the funding requirements for subsidized service. The following two sections will identify and discuss the key trends and strategies in the private and public sectors that are likely to affect future service to small communities.

Commuter Airline Industry

The role of the commuter airline industry in small community air service since deregulation has already been discussed. The relaxation of CAB entry restrictions and the substitution of the Section 419 subsidy program for the Section 406 program provided opportunities and incentives for commuter lines to expand their operations. The industry aggressively seized these opportunities and achieved phenomenal growth rates of 131 percent in passengers (from 11.3 million to 26.1 million) and 206.6 percent in revenue passenger miles (from 1.36 billion to 4.17 billion) over the period 1978 to 1984. The commuters have also achieved increases in traffic density and average length of haul, and improved utilization of aircraft.[85] These operating achievements have not, however, always produced improvements in financial performance. A recent study by Molloy and Sarathy reveals that between 1978 and 1985, 271 commuter airlines ceased operations (and 257 new start-ups occurred) in the forty-eight contiguous states. Additionally, capital spending by publicly held commuter airlines over a three-year period ending in 1983 exceeded total cash generated from internal sources by $100 million. The carriers financed this shortfall through both long-term debt and equity offerings with the result being a high average debt to equity ratio for these firms.[86]

To date the commuter airlines have been able to finance their fleet expansions and acquisitions through a variety of innovative financial arrangements, including greater use of aircraft manufacturer financing, the use of operating leases, and off-balance sheet debt financing.[87] Between October 1978 and October 1983 commuters also had access to federal equipment loan guarantees established by the ADA. Sixteen commuters providing passenger service to small communities were granted approximately $46.5 million of guarantees while this program was in effect. Nine of these airlines were ranked among the largest fifty commuters (on the basis of 1984 passenger traffic), and two were among the largest ten.[88]

The potential expiration of Section 419 operating subsidies, the substantial decline in passenger enplanements at many EAS points, the termination of the federal equipment loan guarantees in 1983, and the high industry turnover since deregulation raise serious questions about the ability of the commuter airlines to continue to attract the capital necessary to provide the existing or expanded levels of service to small communities. One potentially positive development in this regard is the establishment of marketing and operating alliances between many of the major and national airlines and commuters.

The Changing Relationship between the Commuters and Jet Carriers.
Commuter airlines have enjoyed a close working relationship with the larger carriers for some time. As Oster and Pickrell note, "Throughout the 1970's and early 1980's, commuters and jet carriers routinely coordinated their schedules to facilitate connections, shared adjacent gate space on the jet carrier's concourse, engaged in joint advertising and promotional fares, interlined baggage and tickets, and cooperated in many other ways."[89] Recently, however, the relationship has changed as a result of code-sharing agreements and major carrier purchases of commuter lines.

As of January 1, 1985, only seventeen code-sharing agreements were in effect in the forty-eight contiguous states. (Most of these were part of the Allegheny Commuter System, an alliance between Allegheny Airlines [now USAir] and the commuter airlines that flew replacement service on the routes abandoned by Allegheny.) By mid-1986 there were nearly sixty commuter carriers representing almost 75 percent of the industry's capacity involved in such agreements with all twelve major airlines and four national carriers.[90] With code-sharing, commuter flights are identified by the two-letter designator code of the larger carrier on the computer reservations systems (CRS). As such, the commuter-jet carrier interline is treated as an on-line (i.e., one carrier) flight on the CRS. The advantage of this to commuters is that on-line flights have priority over interline flights in the listing of alternative flights on the CRS. Thus, a commuter with a code-sharing agreement will have its flights listed before those competitors who have no such agreement. This is a very important competitive advantage given that 70 percent of airline tickets are sold by travel agents, and up to 90 percent of the flights are booked from the first screen called up.[91]

Additional benefits of the recent marketing alliances between commuters and jet carriers include personnel training by the larger carrier, bulk purchase discounts on fuel, quantity discounts on the purchase of standardized aircraft, and services provided by the jet carrier such as handling of commuters' reservations and ground services at the hub airport.[92] These same benefits accrue to commuters who are acquired by major carriers. Many such acquisitions have occurred since deregulation—ten in 1986 alone involving the larger commuters.[93] The major carriers benefit from code-sharing and mergers as they help the commuter feed traffic to a particular carrier. Without the code-sharing agreement or merged operation a commuter airlines' traffic would be accessible to all competing jet carriers at the hub.

There are, of course, potential pitfalls for the commuter in code-sharing arrangements. The commuter's fortunes may become very dependent upon the fortunes of the larger partner, and the commuter loses some independence as the major carrier may exert some influence on the commuter's operations.[94] For example, commuters are often required to provide high-frequency service to meet the major airlines' connecting banks. As noted in one business periodical, this has had a downward effect on the size of commuter aircraft and stimulated a resurgence in the operation of the nineteen-seater.[95] Another problem has developed in the pricing area. The commuters' partnerships with the majors sometimes result in lower fare levels for the commuters as their flights become involved in the fare-discounting wars of the major carriers.[96]

Small community travelers gain some benefits from the cooperative ventures of the commuters and their major carrier partners, but code-sharing and mergers in and of themselves provide no added benefits. Indeed, Oster and Pickrell have identified reduced roles for independent commuter airlines and increased barriers to entry for small, low-cost airlines into hub markets as potential disadvantages of the new relationships between commuter and jet carriers for small communities.[97]

Many of the small communities receiving scheduled air service generate passenger volumes sufficient to support only one commuter carrier. An independent carrier is more likely to offer flights that provide convenient connections with a number of jet carriers at the hub. A commuter allied with a jet carrier is likely to schedule its flights to connect with only its partner's connecting banks. Additionally, as Oster and Pickrell explain, "the cost of connecting with a different jet carrier may increase if the commuter offers joint fares only with its marketing alliance partner. Prior to the spread of code-sharing marketing alliances, commuter airlines typically were able to offer joint fares with all the jet carriers with whom they connected. More recently, however, several jet carriers have withdrawn joint fares from all commuters other than their marketing alliance partners."[98]

Code-sharing arrangements may also serve to lessen the ability of small, low-cost jet carriers to enter less dense markets by denying these potential competitors equal access to commuter feed traffic. Thus, small community passengers may suffer from lessened competition at the small hub airports to which they have access. Competition, and the benefits derived therefrom, may also be reduced at hub airports as a result of other major carrier activities, as the next section details.

Carrier Concentration at Hub Airports.   With the advent of economic deregulation the large jet carriers have increased their use of the hub-and-spoke route network strategy. This operating strategy permits the large airlines to retain more passengers on-line and to attain more efficient use of aircraft and personnel. The consolidation of operations at a hub airport allows the carrier to increase its load factor on most flights into and out of the hub, to often use larger aircraft with lower unit costs, and to increase the frequency of its service. Air travelers benefit to the extent that the hub-and-spoke strategy provides on-line service in lieu of interline service that might otherwise exist.[99]

A potentially harmful consequence of the hub-and-spoke strategy for air travelers is the increased carrier concentration levels that have resulted at certain hub airports. A study by Phillips discovered that two-firm concentration levels based on passenger enplanements increased by 5 percentage points or more at ten large hub airports between 1977 and 1984 while decreasing by 5 percentage points or more at eight large hubs. Measured in terms of departures, the two-firm concentration levels increased 5 percentage points or more at eleven large hubs and declined at six. Phillips also discovered that the dominant firm's share of total enplanements increased 5 percentage points or more at six large hubs between 1977 and 1984 and declined at only two large hubs.[100]

Since 1984 the airline industry has undergone additional major restructuring as a result of several mergers among the major and national carriers. In 1986 alone, Texas Air — which already controlled Continental Airlines and New York Air — added Eastern, Frontier, and People Express to its family of airlines; Trans World Airlines merged with Ozark Air Lines; Northwest Airlines purchased Republic Airlines; and Delta Air Lines acquired Western. American Airlines and USAir joined the merger mania with their purchases of Air Cal and Pacific Southwest Airlines, respectively. More mergers involving the nation's largest air carriers have been proposed. The result of these combinations has been an even greater increase in carrier concentration levels at some airports.

There is evidence to support the contention that air fare levels increase as carrier concentration levels increase.[101] This is likely true not only for flights originating at the hub airport, but for flights captive to that hub airport as well. Given that most nonhub EAS points have service to only one or a few hub airports, passengers from these small communities will suffer higher fares as the concentration levels increase at their hubs.

The increased use of the hub-and-spoke strategy by the large jet carriers since deregulation has created another potential concern for small communities: commuter carrier access to some hub airports.

Commuter Airlines' Access to Hub Airports.   Commuter airlines' access to hub airports may be limited due to either airspace or airport space congestion problems, both of which are affected by the tremendous growth in airline service at major hubs since deregulation. The Federal Aviation Administration (FAA) estimated that ten commercial airports were experiencing airspace congestion problems in 1986, and a 1984 report by the U.S. Office of Technology Assessment predicted that the number of congested airports could increase to sixty-one by the year 2000.[102]

In response to chronic congestion problems that have plagued New York's Kennedy and La Guardia airports, Chicago's O'Hare, and Washington's National, the FAA has allocated hourly reservations (i.e., "slots") among the principal users of these airports. Slot constraints were also imposed on a temporary basis at twenty-two airports following the 1981 air traffic controllers' strike. In 1985 the U.S. Department of Transportation (DOT) began allowing airlines to buy and sell slots at the four capacity-controlled airports.[103] Though this practice has not been approved at other airports with airspace congestion, there are advocates of this market-oriented approach to slot allocation.

The commuter airline industry opposes slot restrictions and slot allocations since they effectively serve to limit competition in specific markets. Proposals to auction slots to the highest bidder are particularly disconcerting to commuters.[104] Commuter flights from small communities to hub airports generally do not generate the profit levels that would enable commuters to outbid larger carriers with more lucrative routes. Unless special efforts are made by the federal government to ensure slot availability to commuters serving nonhub EAS points or to small communities directly rather than to carriers, many small communities could lose scheduled air service if airspace capacity problems continue to spread to other hub airports.

Airport space congestion may also hinder commuter service to hub airports. As Mergel has observed,

> Terminal access is still a problem facing the industry in many larger airports. Commuters are generally given last priority in terms of access to counter and gate space. Another problem is that the space allocated is often that scheduled for renovation. Thus commuters are often forced to move from one area to another within the terminal complex at the discretion of the airport management. For the smaller carriers, the related problem of signage (the ability to identify themselves within the terminal complex) is also important, since many airports provide little or no location information on small carriers. Commuter airlines generally feel that they are discriminated against in terms of their ability to get more desirable, permanent and well identified locations in the airport terminal complex.[105]

With so many uncertainties, potential problems, and issues of concern related to the provision of scheduled air service to small communities, many have looked to the public sector for assistance. The next section identifies the potential roles of the various levels of government.

Government Involvement in Small Community Air Service

Each level of government—federal, state, and local—has played a role in retaining or developing small community air service. To date the federal government has been the most active and significant participant. Economic regulation (e.g., common carrier obligations and cross subsidization), operating subsidies (i.e., the 406 and 419 subsidy programs) and equipment loan guarantees for EAS carriers, the collection and allocation of funds for airport development, and airport slot allocations are among the various actions taken by the federal government over the years. State and local government activities have predominantly involved promotion, preparation of studies for hearings at the DOT, attracting and working with air carriers, and lobbying efforts in Washington, D.C.[106] These levels of government have also funded airport development and provided financial incentives or benefits to commuter airlines in some cases (e.g., exemption from state fuel taxes).[107] In general, however, state and local governments have not provided direct subsidies to EAS carriers. A study by the General Accounting Office (GAO) in 1983 reported most states were opposed to state administration and funding of the EAS program. A few states even had laws prohibiting the payment of state subsidies to private businesses.[108]

It is quite possible that the level of federal EAS subsidies will be reduced in the near future. The Reagan administration proposed the elimination of the EAS program in its 1986 and 1987 fiscal budget submissions but failed to gain the congressional support necessary to terminate the program.[109] There was strong sentiment in Congress, however, for changing the program to eliminate wasteful subsidies. A DOT report to Congress identified some of the more questionable subsidies paid in 1985. For example,

- A $515 subsidy for one passenger a day on flights between Manitowoc, Wisconsin, and Chicago. The fare at Manitowoc was $89 while a subsidy-free flight with an $85 fare was available thirty-nine miles away at Green Bay, Wisconsin.

- A subsidy of $236 per passenger for the two to three daily passengers making the seventy-four-mile flight from Jackson, Michigan, to Detroit. Alternate subsidy-free service was available at Lansing, Michigan, a thirty-nine-mile drive from Jackson.

• A subsidy of $274 per passenger for a daily average of two passengers flying from Clinton, Iowa, to Chicago. Subsidy-free air service was available at the Quad Cities, a thirty-five-mile drive from Clinton.

• A subsidy of $167 per flight for the one passenger daily on the forty-eight-mile flight between Nashville and Clarksville, Tennessee.[110]

Additionally, the GAO study concluded, and the CAB agreed, that most of the communities receiving EAS subsidies in 1982 were not making progress toward attaining self-sustaining service in a free market environment.[111] The EAS subsidy program was intended to provide small communities sufficient time to adjust to the new deregulated environment. With the expiration of the Section 419 program scheduled to occur in October 1988, federal policy makers were faced with the decision of whether or not to extend the program, knowing full well that the end of federal subsidies would likely mean the end of scheduled air service at several of the EAS points.

Airport and Airway Safety and Capacity Expansion Act of 1987. In December 1987 Congress passed the Airport and Airway Safety and Capacity Expansion Act. This legislation continues the small community essential air service program but includes significant changes in the definition of essential air service, eligibility requirements, and funding.

BASIC ESSENTIAL AIR SERVICE. Basic essential air service (basic EAS) is defined as scheduled air transportation of persons and cargo to a hub airport that has convenient connecting or single plane air service to a substantial number of destinations beyond such airport. A hub airport is defined as an airport that annually generates 0.25 percent or more of the total annual enplanements in the United States (i.e., a large- or medium-hub airport). Basic EAS includes, at least, the following elements:

1. two daily round-trips six days per week with not more than one intermediate stop on each flight
2. flights at reasonable times taking into account the needs of passengers with connecting flights at the hub airport and at rates, fares, and charges that are not excessive when compared to the generally prevailing fares of other air carriers for like service between similar pairs of points
3. service provided in an aircraft with an effective capacity of at least fifteen passengers if the average daily enplanements at the eligible point in any calendar year beginning after December 31, 1975, and end-

ing on or before December 31, 1986, exceeded eleven passengers (except when requiring such service would require subsidy to an eligible point that had not previously received a subsidy for EAS, or when a community agrees in writing to the use of smaller aircraft)

4. service which accommodates the estimated passenger and cargo traffic at an average load factor of not greater than 50 percent or, in any case in which such service is being provided with aircraft with fifteen passenger seats or more, sixty percent

5. service provided in an aircraft with at least two engines and using two pilots, unless scheduled air transportation in such aircraft had not been provided on each of sixty consecutive operating days at any time since October 31, 1978, and

6. in the case of service that regularly exceeds eight thousand feet in altitude, service provided with pressurized aircraft

Eligible points under this section of the act include those points that were determined to be eligible for EAS determinations under the ADA of 1978 and that had received scheduled air service at any time during the twelve-month period ending October 1, 1988. Additionally, only points that are located forty-five highway miles or more from the nearest hub airport (i.e., large or medium hub) are eligible to receive guaranteed basic EAS.

Whenever the secretary of the DOT determines that basic EAS will not be provided without subsidy, air carriers may apply to provide subsidized service. In selecting a carrier, the DOT will consider the applicant's demonstrated reliability in providing scheduled air service; the contractual, marketing, and interline arrangements that the applicant has made with larger air carriers that will ensure service beyond the hub airport to passengers and cargo; and the preferences of actual and potential users of air transportation at the eligible point.

These changes in the small community air transportation service policy address many of the problems and concerns that were identified and discussed earlier. Particularly noteworthy are the new definition of the term "hub" and the exclusion of points within forty-five highway miles of a hub airport.

Redefining hub to include only large- and medium-hub airports provides eligible points greater access to the national air transportation system. Previously, many of the EAS points were guaranteed air service to small hubs where the number of carriers and the frequency of flights were not nearly as great as one finds at large and medium hubs. As a result, small community passengers often encountered multiple connections in route to their final destinations and long (from a time perspective) flights. Quality of air service as measured by these two dimensions of service should improve with the guarantee of service to large and medium hubs with no more than one intermediate stop on each flight. Including the marketing and interline arrangements between applicant commuter airlines and larger carriers as a criterion in selecting carriers should also favorably affect the quality of service at subsidized points (though, as noted earlier, there are potential problems inherent to such arrangements as well). Additionally, the act protects an EAS point's access to an airport at which the FAA limits the number of takeoffs and landings by, in essence, placing such operating authority with the community rather than with a specific carrier.[112]

The exclusion from eligibility of points within forty-five highway miles of a hub airport indicates that Congress understands that surface transportation to a hub airport is often a viable, less costly means of accessing the national air transportation system. Indeed, many small communities in the EAS subsidy program have reported losing a significant number of passengers to nearby hub airports where better service and scheduling, larger airplanes, and lower fares are available.[113] The data presented in Table 5.13 support this contention. Rather than utilizing air transportation to provide access to the national air transportation system, many small communities may be better served with public surface transportation to hub points. The adoption of a multimodal or intermodal approach to providing essential transportation service to small communities will be discussed in Chapter 6.

ENHANCED ESSENTIAL AIR SERVICE.   A state or local government may submit a proposal for enhanced essential air service (i.e., scheduled air transportation of a higher level or quality than basic EAS) to an eligible point at which basic EAS is being provided. The proposal must include an agreement relating to compensation for the proposed enhanced essential air service. Two alternative subsidy plans are available. One plan requires the state or local government to pay 50 percent of the subsidy with the federal government share also set at 50 percent. The second plan involves the federal government providing 100 percent of the required subsidy but conditions the continued receipt of such subsidy on the success of the proposed service. If the proposed service is not successful in terms of increasing passenger usage of the airport facilities and reducing the amount of subsidy provided by the DOT, the eligible point loses all federal subsidy for enhanced EAS. The subsidized service must show success in terms of objective criteria to be established by the DOT for not less than a two-year period in order to continue to receive federal subsidy for enhanced EAS.

Allowing the state and local governments greater participation in the determination of air service needs and in the subsidization of enhanced service makes a great deal of sense. State and local governments are in a much better position vis-à-vis the federal government to gauge the air service needs of the eligible points. One complaint concerning the federal government's determinations of individual EAS levels was its almost exclusive reliance on historic passenger volume data rather than passenger volume potential. Planning for air transportation service should occur within the context of an overall integrated economic plan. Thus, states should have greater knowledge of the future economic activities at various communities.

An argument can be made that a more realistic assessment of a community's air service needs will result if the local (and/or state) government is sharing the costs involved in attracting or retaining scheduled service. Cost-sharing provides an incentive at the local and state levels for the most efficient and effective means of meeting air service needs. Cost-sharing may also be deemed appropriate given that the benefits of the scheduled service at EAS points are largely local in nature. Certainly the impacts of scheduled air service upon economic development are more significant at the local and state levels than at the federal level.

SUBSIDY FOR SERVICE TO OTHER SMALL COMMUNITIES.   The act expands the number of small communities that may obtain some federal funding of air transportation. Any point that is not eligible for basic (and, thus, enhanced) EAS determinations and subsidy may submit a proposal to the DOT for subsidized air service. The DOT will approve such a proposal and designate such point as eligible for federal subsidy:

1. if, at any time before October 23, 1978, the point was served by an air carrier that held a certificate issued under Section 401
2. if the point is more than 50 miles from the nearest small hub airport or an eligible point
3. if the point is more than 150 miles from the nearest hub airport, and
4. if the state or local government submitting the proposal or any other person is willing and able to pay 25 percent of the cost of providing the proposed compensated air transportation

Points not meeting the above eligibility criteria may submit proposals and may receive federal subsidy equal to 50 percent of the required subsidy if the DOT determines that the proposal is reasonable. In determining whether a proposal is reasonable the DOT will consider, among other factors, the traffic generating potential of the point, the cost to the federal government of providing the proposed service, and the distance of the point from the closest hub airport. Federal subsidy may be withdrawn after two years if the DOT determines that withdrawal would be in the public interest.

Other Considerations and Recommendations.   It is apparent that states and communities will be required to take a more active role in funding and planning air transportation service in the future. It is also apparent that one of the more difficult problems to be resolved concerns providing access to the national air transport system to rural, small communities since these communities often generate insufficient passenger volumes to support nonsubsidized air service, and their geographic isolation makes surface transportation to hub airports a less viable alternative. A regional planning approach rather than the traditional local approach seems to be more appropriate for addressing rural transportation problems.

A regional approach would emphasize the development of fewer but larger and more centrally located airports that would each serve a wider geographic area and larger population base. Potential passengers in the service area have fewer transportation alternatives—the geographic isolation of their communities prevents them from diverting to hub airports for air service and makes surface transportation service to destination points less attractive. Ideally, the regional airport would thus be able to attract enough passengers to support nonsubsidized (or, at least, less subsidized) air service and a higher quality of service than would exist if each small, rural community maintained its own facilities and scheduled service.

Unquestionably, there are many obstacles to overcome in order for a regional planning approach to work. There is usually strong resistance from the individual communities to surrendering their local air service. Besides the obvious loss of convenience to local passengers, communities perceive a loss of status and decline in their attractiveness to business firms relative to the regional center. It may be difficult to attain cooperation, particularly in cost-sharing, from these communities. The states must take the initiative in promoting regional planning. The states can mandate or direct the regional approach by their allocations of subsidy monies to designated regional centers. Such an approach by itself, however, will not foster the attitude of cooperation among the affected communities that is necessary to make the regional approach an effective one. The states must educate the communities on the benefits of regional cooperation and should provide support or assistance to help communities without local air service to access the regional airports. The concept of transport "linkages" is developed and discussed in detail in the next chapter.

In addition to the federal government's role in the EAS program, many other federal policies and actions have a significant, if indirect, impact upon air service to small communities. Two key issues of concern to small community interests are the availability of federal funds for airport development and commuter airline access to hub airports. The federal government has been duly (and widely) criticized for its unwillingness to apportion money for airport development and for improvement and expansion of the air traffic control system from the Airport and Airways Trust Fund. This trust fund, which receives its revenues from a variety of user charges, had an uncommitted balance of $5.6 billion as of September 1987.[114] The withholding of these funds could impede the establishment of regional airports to serve small, rural communities. Also, given the problems with airport and airspace congestion at several large hubs, many have argued that the withholding of these funds has contributed to the air traffic control system's capacity problems. The potential ramifications for small communities of free market approaches to allocating airport terminal and landing slots have already been discussed. If the federal government is truly committed to providing access to the national air transportation system for small communities, it must take steps to assure that hub airport and airspace capacity constraints do not limit access by these communities.

All indicators point to significant changes in small community air service in the near future. The incentive for greater involvement of the state and local governments provides both challenges and opportunities—the challenges of funding and promoting regional cooperation to effectively and efficiently link small communities with the national air transportation system and the opportunity to determine the most appropriate levels of service within the context of the states' and regions' overall economic plans. The federal government, in addition to continuing the EAS program, will affect the quality of small community air service through its involvement with the airport and airspace congestion problem.

Conclusion

This chapter provided a review of several studies of air transportation service at small communities before and after deregulation, presented data on passenger volumes at these communities, and identified several key issues and concerns yet to be resolved. Generally, according to most studies, service levels have improved, fares are lower than they would have been had economic regulation continued, and the 419 subsidy program is more efficient and effective than its predecessor. On the other hand, many states and communities have expressed dissatisfaction with the federal government's EAS determinations (though most EAS points receive service levels greater than the minimum requirements[115]), and most subsidized EAS points have not made progress toward generating passenger volumes sufficient to support nonsubsidized service. Small communities are concerned about the financial stability and operating independence of their commuter airlines and potential barriers to hub airport access. The legislated changes in the EAS program appear to address some but not all of the problems and concerns with the small community air service program. There is also an opportunity for more communities to seek subsidized scheduled air transportation.

While the changes that have occurred since deregulation have been thoroughly explored, the relative impact or influence of economic regulation/deregulation vis-à-vis other factors (e.g., changing fuel prices, general economic conditions, and local economic activity) has not. As was noted earlier in the chapter, air service levels and quality had decreased at many small communities before deregulation occurred. Indeed, a large number of communities had lost all certificated carrier service prior to deregulation. The establishment of a more effective subsidy program and guaranteed minimum service standards has not arrested the decline in service levels and passenger emplanements at many small communities. Conversely, many EAS points have enjoyed significantly improved air service since deregulation. A better understanding of the various factors influencing air transport service at small communities is needed. Evidence of the need to further explore the relationships among political, economic, demographic, and geographic influences on air service at small communities is provided by two recent studies that challenge conventional wisdom.

Jones and Cocke employed discriminant analysis to determine if certain community characteristics would distinguish between those non-hubs that had service improvements and those that experienced reduced service over the time period 1978–1983. Their study investigated the influence of geographic factors (i.e., distance from large-, medium-, and small-hub airports) and demographic and economic factors (i.e., population, buying power, and value added by manufacturing). The results of their analyses led them to conclude that the two community groups are more similar than different.[116]

Morrison and Winston attempted to determine the portion of net service loss to small communities that could be attributed to deregulation. They first estimated a time series regression (with quarterly observations from the third quarter 1979 through the first quarter 1984) that specified the number of points served under deregulation by air carriers as a function of macroeconomic variables, fuel price, and a time trend. They then applied the results of this analysis to predict the number of points that would have been served during 1975–1977 had the airlines not been regulated. A comparison with the actual number of points being served during 1975–1977 led them to conclude that, holding other influences constant, more points would have been served during this time period if the airlines had not been regulated. They obtain the same result with different specifications and regulatory periods.[117] Morrison and Winston note, "Although the quantitative significance of this finding should be viewed with caution, the strong qualitative implication is that deregulation is not responsible for short-run net losses in service to small communities. It appears that these losses are largely explained by the increase in fuel prices and by cyclical macroeconomic conditions as temporarily better profit opportunities appeared elsewhere."[118]

As conventional wisdom on the relative roles of government regulation and economic, demographic, and geographic factors has been questioned, there is also a need to question the traditional approach to essential air service planning and funding. The next chapter provides the basis of a nontraditional approach to small community transportation service.

Appendix

Summaries of Selected Studies Analyzing Changes in Air Service to Small Communities since Deregulation

Four elements are included in the format of each summary: (1) Author(s) and/or organization performing study,* (2) latest year's data included in study, (3) population or sample of communities in study, (4) service measures and levels of aggregation utilized in analysis.

1. (1) Oster (1980). (2) 1979. (3) 505 nonhub and 86 small hub airports in forty-eight contiguous states. (4) Number of weekly flight departures to all points, and number of weekly flight departures to each airport type (i.e., large, medium, small, and nonhub airports) from all nonhubs (as a group) and all small hubs (as a group), and from all airports experiencing termination of certificated carrier service. Number of weekly flights (in total) and weekly flights during commuting hours to main hub from nonhubs (as a group) and from small hubs (as a group).

---

*Please see references for bibliographical citation for each study summarized in this appendix.

2. (1) Vellenga and Allen. (2) 1980. (3) Small communities in Indiana, Iowa, Kansas, Minnesota, Missouri, and Nebraska. (4) Number of weekly flights, carrier types (i.e., majors, nationals, large regionals, small regionals, commuters) and aircraft types by city (available data varied from state to state).

3. (1) Stephenson and Beier. (2) 1980. (3) 102 small communities in forty-eight contiguous states identified in a 1976 U.S. DOT study as likely to incur reduction in or loss of certificated air carrier service after deregulation if subsidies were removed. (4) Level of aggregation: communities grouped into five sets on bases of size of population and labor force; service levels determined for each set separately and compared across sets. Measures: number of communities receiving certificated carrier service, weekly nonstop flights by certificated carriers, market share (as percentage of total weekly flight departures) of certificated carriers vis-à-vis commuters, availability of jet service, weekly available seats, average number of direct city connections, average number of hubs connected by direct service, number of carriers providing service, price leadership by certificated and commuter airlines, air fares to small communities compared to overall growth in fares for domestic air carriers as authorized by CAB.

4. (1) General Accounting Office (Report: GAO/RCED–83–179). (2) 1982. (3) 518 nonhub and 62 small-hub airports located in forty-eight contiguous states. (4) Number of flight departures and seats available per week by airport type and for each state. Number of flight departures per week by hub market (i.e., between airport types: for instance, between small hubs and nonhubs, between nonhubs and nonhubs). Changes in weekly aircraft departures at each community where small carriers replaced larger certificated carriers since deregulation.

5. (1) Ming, Tolliver, and Zink. (2) 1982. (3) Seven nonhub airports in North Dakota. (4) Number of daily arrival and departure flights and available seats per day for all nonhubs in study. Weekly flight frequencies and seats available for communities that lost certificated carrier service. Air fare changes (adjusted for inflation) from Bismarck and Fargo compared to nearest hub airport's (Minneapolis) fare changes. Bismarck's and Fargo's air fare per passenger-mile and discount fares compared to those of four large hub airports.

6. (1) Warren. (2) 1982. (3) Two small hub airports (Evansville, IN-Henderson, KY; and Davenport, IA-Rock Island, IL-Moline, IL) and one nonhub airport (Springfield, IL). (4) Number of passenger enplanements at each airport. Frequency of daily weekday flight departures by carrier type (i.e., major, national, large regional, small regional, commuter) for every destination city served from airports in study.

7. (1) Molloy. (2) 1982. (3) 541 nonhub and 65 small-hub airports in forty-eight contiguous states. (4) Percentage change in passenger enplanements, weekly aircraft departures by schedules, airlines, and number of destinations per flight; weekly aircraft departures by commuter airlines; and weekly available seats for nonhubs (as a group) and small hubs (as a group). Daily flight frequencies, daily passenger enplanements, guaranteed daily seats, number of daily flights to hub airports, air service termination and reductions of service by airline type, and changes in coach fares for essential air service (EAS) points (as a group).

8. (1) Civil Aeronautics Board (1984). (2) 1983. (3) Hub and nonhub airports in forty-eight contiguous states (numbers not specified). (4) Average number of carriers providing nonstop service, number of city pairs with nonstop jet service, number of city pairs with nonstop service (regardless of aircraft type), net entry and exit of carriers, percentage of passengers receiving single carrier and single plane service, weekly frequency of nonstop flights, and changes in certificated carrier service at nonhub communities: by market type (i.e., between airport types; for instance, between small hubs and nonhubs, between nonhubs and nonhubs) for each measure. Total weekly flight departures and available seats at EAS (as a group) and non-EAS (as a group) nonhubs. Number of weekly flight departures and available seats, and annual and daily passenger enplanements at each nonhub airport and at each small hub airport.

9. (1) Jones and Cocke. (2) 1983. (3) 503 nonhub communities in forty-eight contiguous states. (4) Frequency of daily flights and available seats by time of day, changes in scheduling of flights and available seats by time of day, and number of carriers by carrier type providing service at the nonhubs (as a group). Number of weekly flights and available seats by state.

10. (1) General Accounting Office (1985). (2) 1984. (3) 52 small hubs and 431 nonhubs in forty-eight contiguous states. (4) Actual air fares as a percentage of Domestic Passenger Fare Investigation (DPFI) formula fares by size of origin and destination communities and distance between them. Number of markets with nonstop jet service, seats per departure, flight departures per week, available seats per week, and service convenience (CAB index based on time of day and flight duration) by market (hub) type. Seats per departure, weekly flight departures, and weekly available seats by hub type. Weekly flight departures at each community where smaller airlines replaced larger airlines. Percentage changes in weekly flight departures and available seats by state.

Notes

1. The regulatory agency was first called the Civil Aeronautics Authority. It became the Civil Aeronautics Board in 1940.

2. Ivor P. Morgan, "Government and the Industry's Early Development," in *Airline Deregulation: The Early Experience,* ed. John R. Meyer and Clinton V. Oster. (Boston: Auburn House Publishing Company, 1981), pp. 17–19.

3. Civil Aeronautics Board, *Implementation of the Provisions of the Airline Deregulation Act of 1978,* Report to Congress, January 31, 1984, pp. 7–8.

4. James F. Molloy, Jr., *The U.S. Commuter Airline Industry: Policy Alternatives* (Lexington, MA: Lexington Books, 1985), pp. 7–9.

5. *Ibid.,* p. 9.

6. John R. Meyer, Clinton V. Oster, Jr., et al., *Deregulation and the New Airline Entrepreneurs,* (Cambridge, MA: The MIT Press, 1984), pp. 11–12.

7. Jonathan D. Mayer, "Local and Commuter Airlines in the United States," *Traffic Quarterly,* Vol. 31, No. 2 (April 1977): p. 336.

8. Meyer, Oster, et al., p. 12.

9. Meyer, Oster, et al. point out that the CAB deviated from the every-stop requirement when trunk airlines were involved in feeder service (see p. 13).

10. Mayer, pp. 339–40.

11. Meyer, Oster, et al., p. 12.

12. Morgan, p. 21.

13. See Mayer, pp. 337–40; Morgan, pp. 28–30; and Molloy, pp. 11–12 for a more thorough discussion of these actions.

14. A more in-depth discussion of the locals' responses to these route-strengthening policies may be found in Mayer, pp. 340–42; Morgan, pp. 30–31; and Molloy, pp. 10–13.

15. Molloy, p. 12.

16. Mayer, p. 341.

17. Meyer, Oster, et al., p. 18.

18. The Civil Aeronautics Act of 1938 did not address the regulatory status of those airlines that had been operating on a nonscheduled basis. However, CAB Regulation 400-1, decided on October 18, 1938, exempted these carriers from economic regulation.

19. Meyer, Oster, et al., p. 19.

20. Molloy, pp. 9–10; and Meyer, Oster, et al., pp. 18–20.

21. Molloy, p. 14.

22. *Ibid.,* pp. 14–15.

23. Meyer, Oster, et al., p. 20.

24. *Ibid.*

25. *Ibid.*

26. Molloy, p. 65.

27. *Ibid.,* p. 67.

28. The interested reader is referred to Molloy, pp. 67–69; and Meyer, Oster, et al., pp. 14–16, for a more detailed discussion of these problems with the individual carrier-based subsidy program.

29. Molloy, p. 69.

30. *Ibid.,* p. 70.

31. Meyer, Oster, et al., p. 17.

32. David R. Graham and Daniel P. Kaplan, *Competition and the Airlines: An Evaluation of Deregulation,* Staff Report, Office of Economic Analysis, Civil Aeronautics Board, December 1982, p. 140.

33. Meyer, Oster, et al., p. 17.

34. Also assisting the local service carriers in their fleet modernization was the Government Guaranty of Equipment Loans Act, which in 1957 authorized the CAB to guarantee equipment loans for local service airlines.

35. Meyer, Oster, et al., p. 17.

36. See Molloy, pp. 75–76, for one such example.

37. Civil Aeronautics Board, *Implementation of the Provisions of the Airline Deregulation Act of 1978,* Report to Congress, January 31, 1984, p. 47.

38. Civil Aeronautics Board, Bureau of Pricing and Domestic Aviation, *List of Eligible Points,* January 1979.

39. Civil Aeronautics Board, "Guidelines for Individual Determinations of

Essential Air Transportation," 14 CFR Part 398, *Federal Register,* Vol. 44, No. 175 (September 7, 1979): p. 52646.

40. Abdussalam A. Addus, "Essential Air Service Determination for Small Communities," *Transportation Quarterly,* Vol. 38, No. 4 (October 1984), p. 563.

41. *Ibid.,* pp. 564–65.

42. *Ibid.,* p. 565.

43. *Ibid.,* p. 566.

44. Meyer, Oster, et al., p. 190.

45. *Ibid.*

46. *Ibid.,* p. 191.

47. *Ibid.*

48. General Accounting Office, *More Flexible Eligibility Criteria Could Enhance the Small Communities Essential Air Service Subsidy Program,* GAO/RCED–83–97 (Washington, D.C., May 18, 1983), p. 18.

49. Meyer, Oster, et al., p. 189.

50. Molloy, pp. 51–53.

51. *Ibid.,* p. 51.

52. Civil Aeronautics Board, "Guidelines for Individual Determinations of Essential Air Transportation," p. 52656.

53. General Accounting Office, *More Flexible Eligibility Criteria,* p. 16.

54. Addus, "Essential Air Service," p. 569.

55. *Ibid.*

56. Molloy, p. 53.

57. *Ibid.,* p. 77.

58. Meyer, Oster, et al., pp. 194–95.

59. Molloy, p. 71.

60. Meyer, Oster, et al., p. 197.

61. *Ibid.*

62. Civil Aeronautics Board, *Implementation of the Provisions of the Airline Deregulation Act of 1978,* p. 51.

63. Meyer, Oster, et al., p. 192.

64. Molloy, p. 82.

65. *Ibid.*

66. Meyer, Oster, et al., p. 199.

67. Molloy, p. 83.

68. General Accounting Office, *Deregulation: Increased Competition Is Making Airlines More Efficient and Responsive to Consumers,* GAO/RCED–86–26 (Washington, D.C., November 6, 1985), pp. 42–43.

69. General Accounting Office, *Deregulation,* pp. 42–43; Civil Aeronautics Board, *List of Eligible Points.*

70. General Accounting Office, *Deregulation,* p. 29.

71. *Ibid.,* p. 74.

72. J. Richard Jones, "The Trade-Offs Involved in the Elimination of the Essential Air Service Subsidy," *Proceedings of the Annual Meeting of the Transportation Research Forum,* Vol. 26, No. 1 (1985): pp. 345–46.

73. General Accounting Office, *Deregulation,* p. 74.

74. *Ibid.*, p. 70.

75. Civil Aeronautics Board, *Implementation of the Provisions of the Airline Deregulation Act of 1978,* p. 34.

76. *Ibid.*, p. 14.

77. General Accounting Office, *Deregulation,* p. 36.

78. *Ibid.*, p. 37.

79. *Ibid.*, p. 65.

80. *Ibid.*, p. 63.

81. *Ibid.*, pp. 63–64.

82. *Ibid.*, p. 67.

83. *Ibid.*, p. 26.

84. *Ibid.*

85. James F. Molloy, Jr., and Ravi Sarathy, "Staying in the Race: Growth and Survival at Commuter Airlines," *Transportation Journal,* Vol. 25, No. 4 (Summer 1986): pp. 31–33.

86. *Ibid.*, pp. 31–32.

87. *Ibid.*, p. 33.

88. Kenneth C. Williamson, David J. Bloomberg, and Roger A. Peterson, "Commuter Air Carriers and Federal Equipment Loan Guarantees," *The Logistics and Transportation Review,* Vol. 22, No. 3 (1986): pp. 246–47.

89. Clinton V. Oster, Jr., and Don H. Pickrell, "Marketing Alliances and Competitive Strategy in the Airline Industry," *The Logistics and Transportation Review,* Vol. 22, No. 4 (1986): pp. 374–75.

90. *Ibid.*, pp. 374–83.

91. Mark Ivey and Pete Engardio, "Commuter Airlines: The Days of Flying Solo Are Over," *Business Week,* August 11, 1986, p. 75.

92. Oster and Pickrell, pp. 372–73.

93. Ivey and Engardio, p. 75.

94. Oster and Pickrell, p. 383.

95. Craig Jenks, "Commuter Airlines Face Turbulence," *Journal of Commerce,* April 3, 1987, p. 6A.

96. *Ibid.*

97. Oster and Pickrell, p. 385.

98. *Ibid.*

99. Laurence T. Phillips, "Structural Change in the Airline Industry: Carrier Concentration at Large Hub Airports and Its Implication for Competitive Behavior," *Transportation Journal,* Vol. 25, No. 2 (Winter 1985): p. 19.

100. *Ibid.*, pp. 21–24.

101. Phillips; and Dipendra Sinha, "The Theory of Contestable Markets and U.S. Airline Deregulation: A Survey," *The Logistics and Transportation Review,* Vol. 22, No. 4 (December 1986): pp. 405–19. Phillips and Sinha identify and discuss the results of studies on the relationship between fare levels and carrier concentration levels.

102. John W. Fischer, *Airlines under Deregulation at Mid-Decade: Trends and Policy Implications,* Report No. 86–67 E, Congressional Research Service, The Library of Congress, April 1986, p. 18.

103. *Ibid.,* pp. 18–19.

104. Joseph Mergel, *An Analysis of the Commuter Airline Industry under Deregulation,* Staff Study, U.S. Department of Transportation, Research and Special Programs Administration, July 1984, pp. 50–51.

105. *Ibid.,* pp. 49–50.

106. See for examples David B. Vellenga and Daniel R. Vellenga, "Essential Airline Service Since Deregulation: Selected States in the Northwestern and Southwestern U.S.," *The Logistics and Transportation Review,* Vol. 22, No. 4 (1986): pp. 339–70.

107. *Ibid.,* p. 365.

108. General Accounting Office, *More Flexible Eligibility Criteria,* p. 28.

109. Fischer, *Airlines,* p. 16.

110. "Some Airports Likely to Lose Commuter Subsidy Pay-outs," *Journal of Commerce,* July 7, 1987, p.5B.

111. General Accounting Office, *More Flexible Eligibility Criteria,* pp. 6–7.

112. If an air carrier that is providing basic EAS between an eligible point and an airport at which the FAA limits the number of takeoffs and landings provides notice of its intention to suspend, terminate, or reduce such service, the DOT shall require the operating authority to be transferred to the replacement carrier unless the replacement carrier does not need such authority or such authority is being used to provide air service with respect to more than one eligible point (Section 419(b)(7) as amended by Airport and Airway Safety and Capacity Expansion Act of 1987).

113. General Accounting Office, *More Flexible Eligibility Criteria,* pp. 8 and 22; and Fischer, p. 16.

114. James C. Miller III, "Airport Woes and Trust Fund's Surpluses," *Wall Street Journal,* September 15, 1987, p. 32.

115. Abdussalam A. Addus, "Subsidizing Commuter Airlines," *Transportation Quarterly,* Vol. 41, No. 2 (April 1987): p. 169.

116. J. Richard Jones and Sheila I. Cocke, "Deregulation and Non-Hub Airports: Discriminant Analysis of Economic, Demographic and Geographic Factors," *Proceedings of the Annual Meeting of the Transportation Research Forum,* Vol. 25, No. 1 (1984): pp. 251–57.

117. Steven Morrison and Clifford Winston, *The Economic Effects of Airline Deregulation* (Washington, DC: The Brookings Institution, 1986), pp. 49–50.

118. *Ibid.,* p. 50.

Strategies for Adequate Transportation Service to Small Communities

The preceding chapters provided an in-depth review of the changes in transportation service to small, rural communities since economic deregulation of the air, bus, rail, and truck transportation industries. The results of deregulation have been mixed. Bus and rail deregulation produced an exodus of carriers from rural communities to the extent that a large number of these communities no longer have bus or rail service. An overwhelming majority of surveyed rural communities reported either neutral or positive effects of trucking deregulation. Airline deregulation led to an aggregate increase in the quality and level of service to small communities, but many of the smaller points have experienced substantial declines in passenger enplanements and could not support nonsubsidized air service. Also, a substantial number of communities lost all scheduled air service prior to deregulation.

The extent and nature of federal, state, and local government involvement in preserving rural community transportation have varied widely by mode across the nation. Since deregulation, the federal government has been most active in subsidizing and establishing minimum service standards for airline service, but has adopted a laissez-faire attitude with respect to trucking service. The states and communities have, in general, put forth little effort to affect transportation service by these modes through subsidies. Conversely, the federal government has provided only limited subsidies for the preservation of rail and bus transportation to rural areas. Several states and communities have, however, been active in purchasing rail track and providing rehabilitation funds, operating subsidies, and technical advice to shippers and entrepreneurs who seek to take over lines. Ten states reported having subsidy programs for intercity bus transportation, and a few of these have established other programs to increase bus ridership by addressing safety, scheduling, and promotion problems.

Though the extent and nature of government involvement in rural transportation have changed over time and varied from mode to mode, there is one element of consistency to the involvement. All levels of government have elected to address transportation issues and problems on a modal basis or from a modal perspective. Transportation planning, economic regulation, and subsidy programs have been implemented in the context of a modal approach rather than an integrated transportation system approach. In doing so, cost and service trade-offs inherent in the substitutability of certain modes have been ignored. Similarly, potential cost and service benefits from promoting the coordination of intermodal movements have been missed.

The purpose of this chapter is to propose a global, or integrated, transportation system approach to rural community transportation. The next section provides an overview of the proposed approach and the assumptions and guiding principles underlying the recommendation for such an approach.

Overview of the Global Approach

Global strategies would include both substitution strategies, that is, facilitating substitution of another mode more suited for the particular volume of traffic for the mode currently serving the community, and intermodal strategies, for example, facilitating the linking of two modes to complete the transportation service. Both the substitution and intermodal strategies have the same impact on the transportation service to small communities — the mode that has the cost and operating characteristics that match up most closely with the levels of traffic generated by the community would provide the service.

These strategies are based upon several assumptions about the future regulatory and promotional policies of the federal government. One assumption is that the amount of federal economic regulation of transportation will not increase from what it is today and is likely to be reduced in certain areas such as trucking. Intrastate trucking regulation will also likely be reduced either by legislative action at the state level or by federal preemption. State regulation of bus operations, railroads, and air is already very limited given the amount of federal preemption that has taken place in the last several years.[1] A second assumption is that the level of federal funding to prop up transportation service through subsidy is likely to diminish. Though subsidies to airlines serving smaller communities were extended beyond the scheduled 1988 expiration date, there is no guarantee that the level of subsidy will increase. Indeed, given the size of the federal deficit, there is pressure to limit spending in many areas. To the degree that the strategies suggested below require financial assistance from government, it is assumed that the funding will have to come primarily from state or regional agencies.

Changes in federal regulatory and promotional policies have made the problem of inadequate transportation service for rural communities clearly a community problem — not a problem for the carriers. The carriers can now more easily drop service points that are not profitable or less profitable to serve. The strategies to help rural communities must focus on the types of transportation needs of the community and not on the retention of certain modes.

In addition to the focus on a transportation solution, the strategies proposed here are based upon the policy change reflected in the regulatory reform federal legislation that greater reliance should be placed on market forces in determining the quantity, quality, and cost of transportation services. The implicit property rights that communities had under strict economic regulation no longer exist. The reduction, if not the elimination, of the common carrier service obligations for transportation firms reflects this changing policy. If there is to be government financial involvement in supporting transportation services jeopardized by the elimination of cross subsidization because of regulatory reform, the level of government involved should depend upon the distribution of the externalities of maintaining the service. Thus, if externalities are local in nature, local government should be involved; if externalities are national in scope, the federal government should be involved if government intervention is decided.

The conceptual and operational aspects of the basic strategies will be discussed for passenger service and freight service separately. There are fundamental differences between passenger service and freight service that affect the feasibility of certain strategies for small community transportation services. First, it is much more feasible to hold freight in inventory than to "accumulate" passengers in inventory to achieve a certain minimum volume of traffic. Although much freight is very time sensitive, in many cases it is economically and commercially possible to accumulate freight so that carriers can provide less frequent but profitable service. Bunching passengers over a substantial time period is less feasible. Passengers, of course, do not have complete control over departure time when using a for-hire carrier. In fact, the primary advantage of the automobile over the for-hire passenger sector is that people can leave when they want to leave. A second difference is the ease with which freight can be gathered and funneled into a hub and then moved in quantity in the line-haul portion of the movement. Although the airlines have adopted this strategy, that is, developing hub-spoke networks, on a much larger scale since deregulation, the ability to transport people by bus or even by bus-air with a hub-spoke arrangement is limited given the increase in travel time that such an arrangement would create.

The four guiding principles of the strategies discussed below are (1) government should not subsidize a particular mode for performing a certain type of service to rural areas, for example, small-package service, if a carrier from another mode can provide adequate service at a reasonable cost at a profit; (2) government should facilitate the matching of modes with the threshold volume requirements (i.e., traffic volumes required to support nonsubsidized service); (3) government should facilitate a community's efforts to generate a level of demand to meet required thresholds, for example, assisting shippers' agents in establishing truckload shipments for communities in a certain area if the alternative is no for-hire transportation or substantially less economical transportation; and (4) the level of government involved, federal, state, or local, should depend upon the distribution of the externalities from the program.

Before addressing the applicability of the global approach to rural passenger and freight transportation, the conduciveness of the current regulatory environment to such an approach should be discussed. While the previous chapter reviewed economic regulation from the modal perspectives, the following section will discuss and analyze the regulatory reform impacts on intermodal transportation.

Current Regulatory Environment for Proposed Global Strategies

The legislation that has caused concern about transportation services to rural communities has also improved the regulatory environment for developing and implementing global transportation strategies. Both general policy statements and specific references to substitution and intermodal responses to rural community transportation problems can be found in most of the regulatory reform legislation.

With respect to passenger transportation, congressional support of substitution strategies is clearly seen in Section 6 of the Bus Regulatory Reform Act of 1982. In that section, easier market entry standards for bus companies are established for the ICC to follow in cases where interstate transportation service will be a substitute for discontinued rail or commercial-air passenger service to a community with no remaining passenger service.[2]

A person issued a certificate under this provision would only have to meet the requirements of safety fitness and proof of minimum financial responsibility. Section 5 of the act explicitly makes the promotion of intermodal transportation part of the national transportation policy—a policy that applies to both freight and passenger transportation. In Section 26 of the act, Congress mandated that the ICC conduct a study on bus terminals that would examine a number of issues, including the desirability of intermodal terminals.

The 1978 Airline Deregulation Act (ADA) did not include any provisions per se that would facilitate or encourage the substitution of bus for air or additional use of intermodal transportation, such as private auto—air or bus-air transportation. To some degree the act inhibited the development of substitution and intermodal strategies through its guaranteed essential air service provision that provided for subsidized air service to essential air points for ten years. This ten-year transition to an unregulated period hopefully provided community planners sufficient lead time to at least develop transportation alternatives for the direct air service that many communities will likely lose when the subsidies are removed or reduced. Although the 1978 act did not address intermodal transportation, Section 7 of the Motor Carrier Act of 1980 (MCA of 1980) exempts from economic regulation transportation of passengers by motor vehicle incidental to transportation by aircraft.

With respect to freight transportation, both the Staggers Rail Act and the MCA of 1980 provided for an environment that supports both the substitution of one mode for another and the use of intermodal transportation. The Staggers Rail Act added to the Rail Transportation Policy section the phrase "to ensure effective competition and coordination between rail carriers and other modes,"[3] and the MCA of 1980 added the provision to the National Transportation Policy, which stated that its goal was "to promote intermodal transportation."[4]

Section 5 of the MCA of 1980 eased the entry requirements for motor carriers submitting an application for transportation services that would be a direct substitute for abandoned rail service to a community if such abandonment results in the community not having any rail service. The carrier in this situation would only have to pass the less demanding "fit, willing and able" entry test.

Other provisions provided additional opportunities for intermodal freight movements. For example, the ICC used the exemption provision of the Staggers Rail Act to exempt from economic regulation transportation that is provided by rail carrier as part of a continuous intermodal movement. The exemption decision by the ICC has been credited as the primary reason for the rapid growth in piggyback movements in the United States in the last several years. Likewise, the MCA of 1980 exempted from regulation "transportation of property by motor vehicle as part of a continuous movement, which, prior or subsequent to such part of the continuous movement, has been or will be transported by an air carrier."[5] The CAB had previously specified a thirty-five-mile radius limit around airport cities for surface pickup-and-delivery services as part of air transport movement and amended its regulations in October 1981 as the result of this provision.[6]

In addition to these legislative changes, recent ICC decisions with respect to formation of transportation companies should increase the use of both types of strategies by carriers. The ICC used the general regulatory reform provisions of the acts passed in 1980 to defend its decisions in rulemaking to facilitate and stimulate rail ownership of trucklines and its decision to permit the Norfolk Southern Railway to purchase North American Van Lines.[7] Subsequently, the Burlington Northern and the Union Pacific railroads acquired trucklines to supplement their transportation offerings. The railroads can use their trucklines in any manner they want in order to serve their customers in this new regulatory environment. The impact of a 1986 court decision, which placed restrictions on how the railroads could use their recently acquired trucklines, will need to be examined. An amendment was attached to the 1986 antidrug law, which exempted the recent rail-truck mergers from this court decision.[8] This new intermodal policy position by the ICC is also indicated by its approval of the acquisition of American Commercial Barge Lines, Inc., one of the largest barge lines in the country, by the CSX, one of the country's largest railroads.

In sum, as a result of the regulatory reform movement in the last several years, there are more opportunities for carriers of different modes to coordinate their operations to provide intermodal movements more effectively and the freedom for carriers of one mode to enter markets abandoned by other modes. In a recent study of intermodal operations in the United States, Mahoney argued that these regulatory reform actions have made intermodality more feasible. Furthermore, he notes that in the history of U.S. transportation legislation, there has not been a single unifying statute enforcing or promoting intermodality. Although some benefits might be generated with such a statute, Mahoney conjectures that in the long run, intermodality might suffer under such a statute because it would not allow the freedom and flexibility necessary for carriers of different modes to enter into intermodal agreements.[9]

Economic deregulation has thus created an environment conducive to the substitution of one mode for another and better coordination of service among the modes. The next two sections outline the global approach for passenger and freight transportation, respectively, to rural areas.

Global Strategies for Passenger Transportation

The intramodal strategy in the intercity bus area of easing entry requirements to allow other, smaller bus lines to take the place of service abandoned by the larger carriers clearly is not adequate. There is no clear evidence that a small bus company can run more profitably in the low-density areas than the larger companies. The downward adjustment of costs both by the larger carriers serving light-density areas or smaller companies is matched by the downward adjustment of revenues. This point was demonstrated in Figure 4.1 of Chapter 4, which used available 1981 data to demonstrate the differential in average costs and revenues for entire intercity bus systems and for the portions of each system running through Iowa. As is apparent, the operating costs are somewhat lower for the Iowa portion of these routes than for each system as a whole, but revenues were also generally less.

For the airlines, on the other hand, the difference in cost structures between the large certificated carriers predominantly using jet aircraft and commuters using turbo props is more significant. Even in the regulated era, commuter airlines were well on their way to replacing jet operations in many light-density, short haul markets. Nationally, those small communities where commuters have replaced jets have had a 25 percent increase in flights on the average and a corresponding increase in convenience. On the other hand, small communities that retained jet service have had a deterioration of service: reduced frequency of departures and higher costs for the traveler. Commuter airlines have a number of cost advantages. In many short haul markets fuel costs have made jet service increasingly uneconomical. Turbo props' operations use only about three gallons of fuel for each available seat on a hundred-mile flight as compared with four gallons per seat available on a jet. In general, commuters have not been encumbered by extensive long-term debt with substantial interest payments (though commuter airlines' debt levels have been increasing as noted in Chapter 5) or even by expensive labor packages that plague some major carriers.[10]

Nevertheless, although these cost differentials provided opportunity for commuters in small markets, they cannot assure success since that depends on the individual carrier's ability to optimize the relationship among the various elements.[11] The potential for failure among commuters that enter the market with only minimal marginal profitability is apparent in the rapid turnover among commuter airlines serving small cities. It is clear that not all small cities that have enjoyed air transportation in the past can support it in a deregulated environment with no federal subsidies. Clues such as turnovers in commuter airlines and gaps in service, enplanements of less than twenty-five a day, and substantially higher fares cannot be overlooked. They are indicative of communities with insufficient demand for air service. This demand has been further eroded as many potential travelers have opted to travel to larger hubs where they can be assured of more reliable, less costly air service.

The evidence on the impacts of deregulated passenger service indicates that replacement service for points abandoned by larger carriers has either been inconsistent or unreliable. What is needed is a broad-based, intermodal approach to service allocation, one responsive to both levels of demand and operating costs.

The model in Figure 6.1 suggests a reallocation of mode of intercity passenger service based on community size and travel demand.[12] It proposes an air sector for the urbanized and larger rural places and a connecting role for intercity buses for the smaller large-sized rural places and larger medium-sized rural places. Rural public transit and automobile transportation are economically better suited for connecting smaller places with the intercity bus hubs.

Intercity bus service could be used effectively to link small nonhub cities to small hubs if service were convenient and cost little more than the auto trip plus parking. Express bus service operated by Greyhound has increased considerably since deregulation. During the year 1985–1986 alone there was a 37 percent increase in this type of service, including service to a number of additional medium-size hubs in the Midwest.[13] In the same year, however, express service was dropped to three airports. Unfortunately, the listing of the service does not necessarily indicate frequent convenient service—only connections which link up with buses going to the airport. For example, in Iowa, the town of Newton is listed as having express bus service to the Des Moines airport, but that only reflects an opportunity for a timely transfer in downtown Des Moines. Other towns that are about as close to Des Moines and on Greyhound routes are not listed.[14] Far more work is needed both in scheduling and advertising to provide a viable connecting service. Some small bus lines have also begun to include airport connections, but far more effort is needed to improve efficiency and inspire confidence in this type of serv-

Fig. 6.1. Integrated intermodal system.

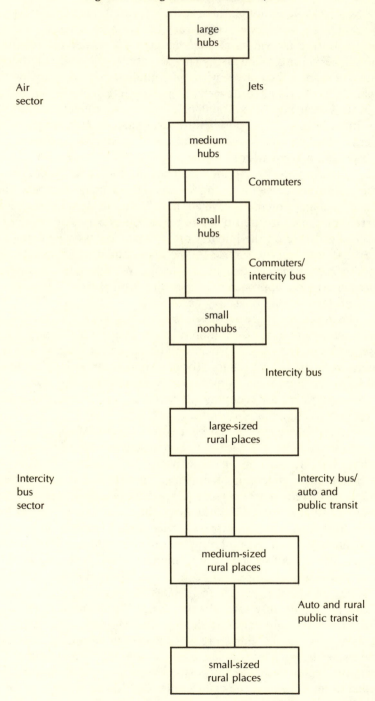

ice. In addition, dedicated airport buses from a single small city to an air hub would certainly not generate sufficient ridership to produce a financially viable service.

Within the air sector commuter hub-and-spoke efforts have proved and will continue to prove viable for connecting small hubs and some nonhubs (with at least twenty-five daily enplanements) to medium and large hubs. Certificated carriers with jet service will operate primarily in medium and large hubs, although some stand-alone small hubs in the less densely populated areas of the Midwest and West may also be able to support a limited amount of jet service.

At the opposite end of the spectrum the model suggests that the smaller rural places be served by rural public transit systems that will serve as feeders to intercity bus lines at stops in midsize towns. Such linkages have been effectively developed in California and Pennsylvania. The experiment in Iowa would have had much more chance of succeeding if transfers were at a regularly designated terminal in midsize towns rather than at various highway stops and gas stations. This approach of relying on public transit in the least dense areas has the benefit of allocating subsidies to the lowest cost operations, operations that cannot be viable for carriers in the private sector. The demand for rural public transit would need to be demonstrated in individual communities before investments were made in this type of system. The alternative in this population class is frequently private auto or shared ride, which may well meet the needs of travel to midsize towns or small cities.

Consistent with the objective of providing a transportation solution, this type of linkage system minimizes the traditional differences among passengers using bus and airline service. Already these distinctions have frequently been blurred as airline discount fares have at times underpriced the lowest fare offered by bus operators. For example, in February 1986 the fare from Des Moines to Denver was twenty-nine dollars one way by air but fifty-nine dollars one way by bus. This is, of course, an extreme case but the differentials are often minimal. The system does leave in place the most common use for intercity bus travel—the short trip connection between medium-sized towns and small cities.

If this strategy were to be applied in Iowa, the result would be to phase out air service at airports with minimal enplanements such as Burlington and Clinton while at the same time emphasizing their importance as intercity bus centers. Both currently have at least five scheduled bus stops a day and are transfer and rest-stop locations. Des Moines, a small, stand-alone hub, would retain jet service while other Iowa cities with daily enplanements over twenty-five would emphasize commuter air service to their nearest major hub or to Des Moines.

The fundamental policy underlying the strategy proposed here is that although it might be a desirable objective of government to provide a person or shipper/receiver in a rural community with access to transportation at a reasonable cost, the person does not have a right to be provided transportation service by a particular mode. Thus, a person living in a rural community may expect some type of passenger transportation service after the last commercial scheduled airline service abandons the community, but the person does not have the right to continued air service. Adequate bus service to the closest small or nonhub airport or direct bus service for shorter distances would be considered as adequately meeting transportation service needs of a small community. This policy of a transportation solution instead of a modal solution is a much more cost-effective way of guaranteeing a minimum level of transportation. Such a multimodal approach allows a more rational restructuring of the transportation industry in the small community area and is much more consistent with present-day regulatory policies.

This strategy is by no means prescriptive, but it does offer a logical base for developing a systematic response to demands for passenger travel, one that responds to both the constraints and opportunities inherent in the current deregulated environment. Obviously, community size is but one determinant of potential passenger demand. Some places with smaller populations may be able to support a better quality and level of service than their location in the hierarchy depicted in Figure 6.1 would indicate. It is also acknowledged that the strong preference many persons have for air over bus service may hinder the implementation of this policy. The question remains, what role is appropriate for the government to play in the establishment of this strategy.

Global Strategies for Freight Transportation

The forces of competition and commercial pressures have forced and the new regulatory environment has allowed the carriers involved in the movement of freight to practice both the substitution and intermodal strategies. Much of the rail service, like air passenger and freight service, involves another carrier in the pick-up or delivery stage of the movement and is, therefore, already an intermodal movement. The hub-spoke technique used by air passenger service and air freight service has been used to an increasing extent in both intramodal and intermodal movements on the freight side. The unregulated piggyback component of the freight transportation sector, which is an example of a hub-spoke intermodal freight movement, has been the fastest growing component for the railroads. Thus, a strategy that encourages and increases rail-truck intermodal movements should be viewed more as evolutionary than revolutionary.

Generally speaking, the rural community freight transportation service needs can be broken down into small package, general commodity, and bulk commodity service. Table 6.1 contains a matrix that incorporates the spectrum of transportation services and size of rural communities. The movement up and down a particular column relates to the financial viability threshold for each type of transportation service. Of course, the relationship between size of community and volume of traffic needed for viability for a particular type of carrier depends upon the degree of isolation from major traffic lanes, nature of the economic activities in the community, and other factors.

Table 6.1. For-hire freight transportation service viability thresholds

Size of Rural Community[a]	Small Package	General Freight	Bulk Commodities
<5,000	UPS	Truck	Truck
5,000–25,000	Bus, UPS, truck	Rail, truck	Rail, truck
25,000–50,000	Bus, UPS, air, truck	Rail, truck	Rail, truck

[a]Based on International Business Services, Inc., *Intercity Bus, Rail and Air Service for Residents of Rural Areas*, U.S. Department of Transportation, Report No. DOT-P-10-80-18, January 1980, p. 2-2.

The quality of small community transportation service differs with respect to each of these three service areas in the postderegulation era and so does the feasibility of substitution and intermodal strategies. It should be noted that the intermodal strategies should not necessarily preempt an existing modal strategy such as state financial support of a short-line railroad. For certain products, an all-rail movement is the only economically viable method of transportation. In addition, the abandonment of a rail line is not easily reversible. These global strategies can either supplant or supplement existing modal strategies. An optimal mix of modal and global strategies should be the objective of the private sector and government.

The evidence on the amount and cost of transportation service for small package freight to and from small communities indicates that regulatory reform has had little impact on this transportation market. UPS was consistently rated as providing high quality service at a reasonable cost before deregulation and remains ranked high. As Table 6.1 indicates, UPS can profitably provide service in the smallest of communities. Some substitution between bus small package service and UPS has taken place—UPS for small package service by bus. Although UPS serves almost all communities in the United States, certain shippers apparently were dependent upon the available bus service to provide Saturday small package express service, which UPS does not provide to many small communities. It should be noted that the MCA of 1980 made entry relatively easy for carriers providing transportation of shipments weighing one hundred pounds or less. The very time-sensitive small package freight requiring air service will not be affected — most small airports that will lose air service when the subsidies are terminated are not major air freight terminals. For example, Federal Express provides air freight service to only a relatively small number of airports now. The busiest airport in Iowa, the Des Moines airport, is not used by Federal Express. The truck portion of the intermodal truck-air movement will simply become longer in many situations.

The general commodity transportation needs are apparently being adequately met in the unregulated environment. The truckload (TL) trucking sector has had a large influx of new firms, and thus shippers involved in truckload movements have benefited from the reduced entry controls on trucking. The less-than-truckload (LTL) sector is becoming more concentrated but the quality and cost of service have not suffered as a result of this concentration. The larger trucking lines in the LTL sector have implemented the strategy of opening new terminals in the less densely populated areas. For example, Yellow Freight Inc. has a terminal in Harlan, Iowa, a community of about five thousand. Yellow Freight serves a number of even smaller towns out of this terminal.

The rapid development of rail piggyback service over the last several years is an example of the use of an intermodal strategy nurtured by the easing of the regulatory controls. Much of the lost less-than-carload (LCL) rail traffic and more recently the rapidly declining boxcar business of the railroads have shifted toward rail piggyback.[15] The most recent significant development in the piggyback industry is the strategy of a few railroads like the Burlington Northern and the Santa Fe of reducing the number of piggyback terminals by developing piggyback hubs. For example, the number of piggyback ramps in the state of Iowa declined from twenty-two in 1982 to thirteen in 1985.[16] The hub strategy is designed to allow the railroads to compete with trucks in some markets and in other markets to permit the railroads to abandon low-volume branch lines that lose money but maintain their general commodity traffic by substituting truck hauls for that portion of the movement.[17] The hub centers are designed, equipped, and operated to minimize the intermodal transfer time and expense, which will make rail-truck intermodal transportation via piggyback more competitive with trucking. These hubs are fully mechanized intermodal terminals that collect and distribute via truck within about a two hundred mile radius.[18] Although this reduction in the number of piggyback terminals has its disadvantages, the efficiencies gained in the use of the larger hubs outweigh the losses. It is unlikely that many rural communities lie outside a two hundred-mile radius of a rail-truck hub.

The regulatory reform that stimulated the growth of the piggyback form of intermodality also created a favorable environment and need for transportation intermediaries. These intermediaries, for example, freight forwarders, freight brokers, shippers' agents, and shippers' associations, have experienced tremendous growth during the last several years. Although they perform a number of functions unrelated to intermodal transportation, one of their main contributions is arranging rail-truck intermodal transportation. As noted by Mahoney,

> Middlemen play an important role in intermodality. They serve both shipper and carrier by consolidating small shipments into larger consignments; they palletize or containerize shipments for intermodal movement, issue their own documents for the through intermodal haul, take legal responsibility for the goods being moved, provide through rates, perform pickup and delivery service, and render other useful functions to simplify the intermodal process and move freight expeditiously.[19]

Not all types of middlemen perform all of these functions but some do. With almost complete deregulation of the intermediaries as the result of freight forwarders being deregulated in the fall of 1986, the distinctions between these various types of intermediaries are becoming blurred.

The important point is that these middlemen perform services that are key to the facilitation of intermodal movements and particularly so for shippers located in rural communities who may be less knowledgeable about transportation alternatives than shippers located in urban areas. In addition to performing the basic functions of consolidation and handling most of the necessary transactions, which reduce the costs to the shipper of using intermodal transportation, these intermediaries play an important role of providing competition for the large LTL carriers in small towns. This role will become more important in the future as the LTL trucking industry grows more concentrated.

These intermediaries thus play a role both in the substitution strategy, if one views these intermediaries as firms of a different mode,[20] and in the intermodal strategy. In addition, the consolidation role played by intermediaries essentially increases the volume of traffic, which may allow a community to meet the threshold requirement of a particular mode that it could otherwise not meet. In two recent, independent studies of the freight broker industry, the overwhelming majority of brokers were found to provide trucking service to small, isolated communities with very little trouble in most cases.[21]

The bulk commodity transportation needs of a community are not as easily addressed in the context of either the substitution or intermodal strategy. As noted above, the recent changes made by the regulatory reform legislation have made it easier for trucks to be substituted for abandoned rail service and for the use of intermodal transportation. In contrast to the situation involving small-package freight and general commodities, however, the economics and technology surrounding bulk commodity transportation reduce the feasibility of these strategies. The economics pertain to the fact that railroads can haul certain bulk commodities at much less cost per ton-mile. In addition the service advantages of trucking over railroads are not as meaningful to shippers given the lower value per unit and thus less shipper concern about inventory and other logistical costs. The technological limitations pertain primarily to the intermodal strategy, which will be discussed below.

The possibilities of substituting trucking for rail service is not as limiting as once thought, however. In 1978 the staff of the Association of American Railroads conducted a study that attempted to estimate the likely costs of replacing rail transportation with truck transportation for all rail traffic in the United States. This study, which apparently understated the cost advantage of rail transportation to a certain degree, indicates that railroads enjoy a significant cost advantage on only four commodities—coal, chemicals, minerals, and petroleum.[22] The completion of the Interstate Highway System (the forty-two-thousand-mile system created in 1956) has reduced the cost of lost rail service.[23] The problem remains, however, in cases where a community shipping or receiving large quantities of any of these four bulk commodities loses rail service. In these cases the state or local government could work to maintain rail service with the use of a short-line railroad, as discussed in Chapter 2, or examine the possibilities for the intermodal rail-truck transportation of bulk commodities.

The possibilities of effective use of intermodal truck-rail transportation for bulk commodities are somewhat limited but expanding. At the present time a wide variety of product lines are handled in rail-truck intermodal transfers. Dry bulk products include sand, potash, flour, coal, grains, bauxite, sulfur, phosphate, salt, limestone, iron, and plastic pellets. Liquid bulk products include a variety of product petroleum lines, fertilizer, and chemicals.[24] Although the overall volume of intermodal rail-truck bulk movements is not large, it is expected to grow, with piggyback moving further into the movement of bulk commodities.[25]

The two methods of making bulk transfer between rail and truck are loose bulk transfer and the transfer of bulk commodities in containers, which is a more recent development. The carriage of bulk commodities in containers has been characterized as the frontier of advancement and one of the two fastest areas of growth in containerization.[26] Currently shippers of liquid chemicals have received the greatest benefit from containerization of bulk commodity transportation. Apparently dry bulk containers are not yet operationally feasible for intermodal rail-truck transportation, but they are being used in other types of intermodal movements and are soon expected for rail-truck intermodal movements.[27] A promising development for bulk commodity shippers in small communities is the increasing use of both flexible and rigid types of the intermediate bulk container (IBC). Most of the IBCs are the flexible type and are essentially big bags that hold one-ton payloads. The greatest use of the flexible IBC is by shippers of fertilizer and other farm aids, but it also has been used by chemical food products shippers.[28]

In short, the increasing use of containers for bulk movements shows some promise as a solution to transportation problems for small community rail shippers of bulk commodities in communities losing rail service. Certain limitations still exist to widespread use of containerized bulk movements, including the requirement of expensive lifting equipment at the transfer point and at either the origin or destination or both. In addition, special trailer chassis are required to haul bulk containers over the road.

The Role of Government in Facilitating the Global Strategies

Given that there is a desire to have adequate transportation service available to rural areas at a reasonable cost to taxpayers and that a global approach is more rational and efficient than the traditional approach, a key question arises: what role or roles should the government (local, state, or national) play in facilitating the global strategies proposed here?

The federal government has already taken important steps to enhance the substitution strategy. Reduced regulations have allowed carriers more freedom to make commercial decisions to enter and leave particular markets in response to market forces. Some level of government still has the opportunity, and possibly the responsibility, to subsidize the last type of transportation service to a particular community if a legitimate need exists and no carrier from any mode is willing to replace the service being abandoned. As noted above, this is likely to be some form of public transit for passenger transportation and rail service for bulk commodities on the freight side. The other two types of freight categories, small package and general commodities, require services that apparently can be provided to rural communities profitably by a carrier in one of the modes. In the case of a subsidy, or outright government ownership, the service should be designed to feed into the national network as cost effectively as possible.

An active role of government in facilitating intermodal transportation to help resolve rural community transportation problems appears to be more challenging but also to have more potential. The government will have to walk the thin line between doing too much, and thus interfering with the efficiencies of the marketplace, and doing too little and allowing decisions by carriers that produce outcomes that are possibly not optimal from society's point of view. Government can facilitate intermodal transportation for both passengers and freight by taking a more active role in reducing the transaction costs and subsidizing part of the transfer costs—the basic costs that inhibit additional use of intermodal transportation.

Transaction costs can be grouped into three categories. Search costs are costs to the shipper or traveler of shopping for the service desired and then selecting among the suppliers. Negotiation costs are costs of establishing the price and nonprice terms of the transactions. The cost of coordinating schedules and routing to minimize idling of equipment and wait time would be a negotiation cost. The cost of assuring that the transaction is carried out to completion under the negotiated terms of the agreement is the final type of cost—enforcement costs. The latter two types of transaction costs are more relevant to freight movements.

For passenger travel these transfer costs are more subtle but nonetheless real. They take the form of wait time for passengers as well as schedule adjustment costs on the part of carriers. Rarely is there an out-of-pocket charge for the transfers, but passengers must be assured of efficiency and convenience in order to even consider what is consistently noted on modal ridership surveys as the least desirable service option. Intramodal transfers themselves require careful scheduling coordination. For intermodal transfers the complexity increases measurably. Assuring public transit to intercity bus and air connections provides major challenges for minimizing transfer costs.

In major metropolitan areas passengers can be assured of relative convenience in using airport express buses or airport limousines. The inconvenience of the intermodal transfer is minimized either by checking bags through at the point of origin or by boarding at home or hotel and avoiding airport parking problems. Relatively short headways can be guaranteed. Providing similar compensation for the inconvenience of transfer is all but impossible in rural areas, given a scattered population base. Nevertheless coordinated schedules are essential if passengers from a community with abandoned air service are to be assured that an intercity bus to the nearest remaining airport will enable them to meet their flight. Similarly passengers must be assured that a public transit vehicle will be able to connect successfully with a convenient intercity bus stop on the interstate both on the way out and on the return.

The costs of coordinating schedules and assuring their efficient and reasonably frequent operation are not costs that the respective carriers will wish to incur in a deregulated environment. The actual number of passengers to be benefited is too small to affect a profit margin, and independent scheduling is certainly easier to operate.

One answer to retaining some form of intercity passenger service for a small city in danger of losing air service would be to contract with an intercity bus company to transport passengers to the next closest airport. This would mirror the earlier train contracts with bus companies for services the railroad could no longer provide. Since deregulation has all but removed the public service requirement, to continue operation in small towns subsidy for this contract would need to flow from the relevant local government or governments. After all, far more benefits would flow to the city being served than to the airline company, which would barely notice the small reduction in passengers. Certainly such subsidies would be far less costly than maintaining an underutilized airport.

Freight transaction costs, which obviously exist even when only one carrier of one mode is used, are likely to increase when intermodal transportation is used because of a number of reasons. For example, due to the increased number of parties involved in the movement, more arrangements will have to be made that increase search, negotiation, and enforcement costs. Particularly troublesome to the small shipper in a rural community is the cost associated with the issue of loss and/or damaged goods. Shippers tend to have more problems when using two carriers of the same mode in collecting loss and damage claims. The time and costs associated with processing and collecting claims are greater when using intermodal transportation due to the likely increase in the number of participants, for example, the transfer terminal operator, and due to the differing liability rules and responsibilities among modes.

What role should and can the government play in reducing transaction costs to travelers, shippers, receivers, and carriers? Some believe that government should not intervene at all based upon the argument that the best intentioned government program creates more problems and inefficiencies than benefits by creating distortions in the market. Others argue that the additional transaction costs associated with intermodal movement are true costs and should be considered by shippers and travelers when making decisions. The position taken here is that in many cases there is a legitimate role for government to play in facilitating intermodal transportation by reducing transaction costs for both carriers and shippers.

The government can reduce transaction costs involved in intermodal transportation in two basic ways. First, it can provide a regulatory environment that fosters the growth of intermediaries who provide essential information and other services for shippers, particularly shippers in rural communities, who want to use intermodal transportation. A largely unregulated environment appears to be most appropriate both in allowing the necessary flexibility in pricing and service offerings for the intermediary industry, and thus intermodal transportation, to thrive. A contrary view is that the intermediary industry, particularly the freight broker sector of the industry, needs regulation to prevent abuses of shippers who are not aware of all the pitfalls of using carriers of different modes in one move. A recent effort by a motor common carrier to have the ICC regulate certain aspects of the industry was not adopted by the ICC.[29]

Second, in addition to the passive role of not overregulating the intermediaries, the government can take an active role in reducing the transaction costs by helping establish intermodal moves. For example, the state of Iowa helped to negotiate and publicize the joint rail-barge tariff involving the Milwaukee Railroad and Alter Bargelines that was established in the late 1970s. The Iowa DOT arranged meetings between the carriers and shippers, publicized the tariff through distribution of news releases to newspapers, radio and television stations, and wire services and sponsored a seminar, "Export Grain Marketing with Intermodal Transportation."[30] Although some of these actions would not be feasible in many situations involving small communities, they do illustrate what has and can be done. On the passenger side, the state can become more involved in advertising existing bus-air intermodal services and become more involved in the establishment of such services.

A particularly troublesome issue affecting transaction costs of shippers involved in intermodal movements is the issue of collecting claims for loss and damage. One factor that apparently inhibits the use of intermodal transportation is the increased uncertainty with respect to loss and damage liability when two or more modes of transportation are involved. Deregulation of both the various modes of transportation and the intermediaries has added to the uncertainty related to intermodal liability issues.[31] The shipper in a small community may find it difficult and costly to ascertain what liability rules apply for a particular intermodal movement.

The Shippers National Freight Claim Council recently proposed to separate the liability issue from the other transportation issues and to reregulate with respect to liability rules in order to protect the shipper. The council apparently supported the other aspects of deregulation.[32] Uniform conditions and limitations for each mode in a through movement have been argued to be desirable.[33] The argument by deregulationists that it is more cost effective for shippers to take out their own insurance for the specific type of cargo movement required is not as persuasive when small shippers in rural areas are involved. A less intrusive governmental approach would be to simply disseminate more information for shippers in small communities about the problems and possible solutions with respect to loss and damage liability when using intermodal transportation.

One additional type of transaction cost results from the lack of interest by a carrier from one of the modes in participating in an intermodal movement because of potential competition. In many cases the carriers that would jointly provide service can also be competitors on the same or similar move. What the proper role of the government should be in this situation is not clear. Should the government require an unwilling carrier of one mode to participate with a carrier of another mode? Existing legislation allows the ICC to require carriers of different modes to establish joint rates under certain circumstances such as rail-barge traffic when the participating barge line is a common carrier. This authority was most recently expanded by the MCA of 1980, which allowed the ICC to require the establishment of joint-rates between water common carriers and motor common carriers under certain circumstances. A potential anomalous development of increasing regulatory oversight to help make deregulation work was noted by Mahoney. "However, even in a deregulated environment it may be necessary to devise provisions to deal with instances where a long-haul carrier refuses to cooperate with an interline or intermodal partner in order to keep the long haul for itself."[34]

The history of the administration of the authority to force railroads to establish joint rates with water common carriers, however, strongly suggests that such a policy may have limited effectiveness. Although anticompetitive problems may develop, the establishment of a regulatory environment that facilitates the creation of integrated multimodal transportation firms is probably the most effective way to achieve a higher level of intermodal usage. Any anticompetitive practices by an integrated transportation company in this deregulated environment could be addressed by an effective antitrust policy.

The question concerning the government's role with respect to the transshipment of freight is: what can the government do to reduce the costs and time of transferring freight from one mode to another? For passenger transportation, the question is: what can be done to reduce the costs and inconvenience of transferring from one mode to another for a passenger using intermodal transportation? Apparently, there is a lack of cross-modal terminals in both the freight area—particularly in the bulk commodity area—and in the passenger area.[35] The most intrusive but possibly the most effective role of government is to develop through outright ownership or subsidization the development of cross-modal terminals. These cross-modal terminals would be viewed as part of the transportation infrastructure in the same manner as highways, airways, and other types of terminals such as airports and seaports. The coordination of the decisions in the private sector with the decisions in the public sector might prove to be difficult.

In addition to the outright investment in intermodal or cross-modal freight terminals, the government could play a meaningful role by funding research projects addressing engineering and economic issues related to the design, operation, and location of intermodal terminals. Research in the area of rail-barge intermodal transportation of coal and grain indicates that the location of the transshipment facility and the nature of the transshipment terminal can greatly affect the total logistical costs of the shipper.[36]

On the passenger side, the government role must be that of a facilitator, providing incentives for coordination. There is no longer federal government encouragement to provide coordinated regional rural transit systems. The current Section 18 rural transit program as implemented in most states provides no specific encouragement for intermodal or rural intercity bus coordination. Efforts along this line are dependent upon local initiative. Current federal government incentives for cross-modal coordination are nonexistent.

Nevertheless, in California, state user-side subsidies have become the vehicle for furthering intermodal coordination between the intercity bus and a passenger train and for linking public and private bus service. Unfortunately, similar train-bus coordination is only possible in the relatively small numbers of rural communities still served by rail. Contracts for transporting the elderly and handicapped are awarded intercity bus companies in California and Pennsylvania, among others.

Regional coordination is the key to encouraging rural public transit—intercity bus linkage. The limited number of riders makes stops off the main highway infeasible in a deregulated environment; but rural public transportation linkage with the bus at well-defined transfer points might well provide for the needs of those without access to private vehicles and others who wish to travel by intercity bus. User-side subsidies for the handicapped and elderly such as those provided in Pennsylvania and West Virginia might well offer the stimulant necessary to pursue this type of arrangement. There are, however, examples of private enterprise; one small operator in Michigan operates a regular route service connecting his town, which recently lost bus service, with the continuing stop on the interstate. The role of the local or state government would be to facilitate such arrangements and to assure the provision of adequate, reliable, transfer points. The state of Vermont, for example, is using some Section 18 money to encourage linkage between vans from small towns and Vermont transit. A common ticket agent sells through tickets. Rural terminals need not be dedicated facilities but they should provide clean, reliable waiting areas and be equipped with travel information.

There are few intermodal terminals on the passenger side. In a recent study that attempted to estimate the number of terminals that accommodated both intercity buses and at least one other mode, it was found that less than 4 percent of all such facilities in the United States were intermodal.[37] The number of bus terminals identified as having rail and/or airline service at the terminal or within one block was found to be small. Eighty-two facilities have intercity rail services, and only thirty-seven facilities have airline service at or within one block of the facility.[38] The small number of intermodal terminals may have more to do with the limited service points of the other modes than the unattractiveness of intermodal facilities.[39]

The bus terminal study mandated by the Bus Regulatory Reform Act of 1982 (BRRA) found that government intervention, both in the planning and funding areas, is the key to the successful development and operation of an intermodal terminal. Agencies involved in funding and organizing intermodal terminal projects include cities, regional authorities, state and federal agencies, and private interests. This diverse set of interests with different motives and perspectives suggests the necessity of a state or regional agency to coordinate the project. Public funding can be justified to aid the development of a terminal where the individual modes' private benefits, which would not justify an investment, are less than the total benefits because of the existence of public benefits. In the two states (Michigan and California) having successful intermodal programs, statewide plans exist to guide the process of funding and design. It is possible, because of the competitive nature of the modes involved, that the private interests would not participate in the development of the intermodal terminal because of the legitimate concern of diversion of traffic to the other mode. A subsidy by some level of government might be sufficient for the carrier to participate financially in the project.

Rural Transportation Subsidy

There is a role for government in the provision of transportation service to specific communities or focus groups that need but cannot support nonsubsidized transportation service. Subsidization is justifiable when the expected social benefits, both economic and noneconomic, exceed the expected social costs, including the subsidy. Federal, state, and local governments are already involved in subsidizing the users of publicly provided transportation facilities and infrastructure to the extent that user charges do not cover the cost of maintaining and operating these public assets in the air, bus, and trucking transport sectors. Some states and local governments have become heavily involved in purchasing, rehabilitating, and maintaining railroad infrastructure since the federal government has generally withdrawn from providing such support.

As has been covered in earlier chapters, there is presently a trend toward greater reliance upon state and local provision of operating subsidies for air, bus, and rail service. Although some federal money may be available for such purposes, state and local governments will in all likelihood be expected to bear a much greater share of the costs than they have in the past. This trend is not likely to be reversed in the foreseeable future due to the huge federal deficit. Notwithstanding the federal government's desire to reduce its spending, more cost sharing by the state and local governments is supportable on other grounds. First, as previously noted, most of the benefits accrue to the state and the immediately affected area. Second, the transportation needs are better known at the state-local level. Third, more realistic and reasonable requests for federal subsidy are likely to result when the state and local governments are also providing public funds. Thus, better investment of public monies and a better matching of the distribution of social costs and benefits are likely to occur with state-local participation in the funding of transportation service to rural areas.

In order to implement the global approach or strategy it is also necessary to alter the traditional approach to establishing subsidy programs. Rather than appropriating and earmarking monies for specific mode investments and operations, a rural transportation fund should be established. Ideally the federal government would determine the amount of rural transportation funding it wants to provide each state and tender the monies to the states for general transportation projects involving service to rural areas. The states and communities would be required to provide matching funds. Transportation projects would be identified at the community or regional level and formal applications for state appropriations would be submitted. The states would then appropriate the federal and state monies to the highest priority projects. This approach is currently being used by a number of states in allocating Section 18 funds. Unfortunately, to date, when funds have become available for allocation to rural transit, a complex of federal regulations have inhibited expenditures according to state and regional priorities. For example, the state legislature of Iowa proposed allocation of $1.7 million of oil overcharge money as subsidy for rural public transit in 1986–1987. Although state priorities were developed and local proposals were submitted, conflicting federal regulations have made such funds very difficult to access and use.

The only hope that many sparsely populated areas have for attracting and sustaining good transportation service, with or without subsidy, is to increase their transportation leverage by organizing or cooperating on a regional basis. The establishment of regional transportation centers or hubs to which both freight and passengers will be funneled from other rural communities within each region is consistent with the models depicted in Figure 6.1 and Table 6.1. A regional center though having a relatively small population of its own would be able to generate a larger intercity traffic volume, which might put it above the threshold volume requirements of a higher quality mode of transport. Of course, the residents of the regional centers would benefit more than the residents in the outlying areas. However, the latter group will benefit to the extent that the regional center reduces the distance they or their freight must travel to connect with better quality and/or lower cost transportation. The improvement in transportation service to the region may also produce other benefits such as attracting new businesses to the region and increasing land values.

The recommendation for a regional approach to the rural transportation problems may pose challenges in the subsidy area. It may be difficult to persuade those communities or counties that will not serve as the regional transportation center to participate in a multicommunity or multicounty project. The state could, of course, utilize the power of the public purse to mandate or force the regional approach by refusing to subsidize any services that are not consistent with an approved regional plan. Such an approach has been well instituted in Iowa where all funding for rural public transportation flows through regional transportation coordinators. Regional cooperation is not likely to be fostered by such a policy unless all participants are educated on the benefits of a regional approach, share in the responsibilities of planning, and contribute a level of funding commensurate with the quality of service (and other benefits) they receive.

An analysis of the many alternative ways to grant subsidies is beyond the scope of this book. There are, however, two pertinent and critical concerns that warrant discussion. One problem with subsidized service in the past has been the high turnover rate among carriers, particularly in the air and bus transport industries. High turnover not only creates immediate but short-lived disruptions in service, but also has a longer-term impact as it turns many potential travelers against using the service. It is imperative that the carrier selection process involve a thorough investigation of the business acumen and financial stability of the candidate carriers and that the subsidy levels provided enable the carriers to earn adequate profits while giving an incentive to operate efficiently.

A second concern is prompted by a lesson learned from the generally ineffective and costly 406 air subsidy program. The *primary* focus of this program was on preserving the financial well-being of the airlines rather than assuring adequate service for subsidized communities. Air transport service standards were very broadly defined and poorly monitored. As discussed in Chapter 5, the end result was a deterioration or loss of service to many small communities while subsidy levels increased. The lesson learned is that subsidies should be tied to community-specific service standards. It is difficult if not impossible to construct a subsidy program with incentives that will guide carriers' behaviors to the accomplishment of desired service levels at every affected point. The surest approach to obtaining desired service levels is to specify them and require the subsidized carrier to meet them.

Conclusion

The purpose of this chapter is to outline or describe a better approach to the solution of the rural transportation problem. The existing transportation regulatory environment and federal government attitude favoring more state and local participation in planning and funding, plus the failures or weaknesses of traditional approaches, have created both a need for and an environment conducive to the recommended approach.

Specifically, the authors advocate the adoption of a global approach to transportation policy decisions by all levels of government and increased participation by the states and communities in planning, facilitating, and funding rural transportation service on a regional basis.

The increased financial burden on states and local governments will, of course, present some significant challenges as many of these government units are also encountering budget problems. The substitution and intermodal strategies advocated by the authors have the potential to reduce overall transportation costs and, thus, the need for subsidy. However, the state and local governments are being pressured by other constituencies since transportation is not the only area where the federal government is reducing or eliminating its support.

The global approach will also present challenges to the states' DOTs as they, like their federal counterpart, still tend to address transportation issues and problems from modal perspectives. Most states established DOTs in order to promote an integrated transportation system perspective by placing all transportation agencies (each with a modal focus) in one organization. However, many states still allocate funds to their

DOTs for specific modal programs and projects, and many DOTs have not been able to foster the global perspective throughout their ranks and achieve the efficiencies to be gained from the substitution and intermodal strategies discussed in this chapter.

It is hoped that this review of the changes in transportation service to small rural communities since deregulation and the general recommendations for addressing the rural transportation problem will prove beneficial to those who have an interest in this important transportation policy issue.

Notes

1. Kevin H. Horn, "Federal Preemption of State Transportation Economic Regulation: Conflict Versus Coordination," *Transportation Journal,* Vol. 23, No. 2 (Winter 1983): pp. 28–46.

2. Public Law 97–261, Section 6, Motor Carrier of Passengers Entry Policy.

3. Public Law 96–448, Section 101, Rail Transportation Policy.

4. Public Law 96–296, Section 4, National Transportation Policy.

5. Public Law 96–296, Section 7, Exemptions.

6. John H. Mahoney, *Intermodal Freight Transportation* (Westport, CT: Eno Foundation for Transportation, Inc., 1985), p. 36.

7. See Michael R. Crum and Benjamin J. Allen, "U.S. Transportation Merger Policy: Evolution, Current Status, and Antitrust Considerations," *International Journal of Transport Economics,* Vol. 13 (February 1986): pp. 41–75, for a discussion of the current ICC policies on multimodal transportation companies.

8. Lee Coney, "Major Transportation Legislation Was Passed by the 99th Congress," *Traffic World,* Vol. 208 (November 3, 1986): p. 84.

9. Mahoney, pp. 27–28.

10. Melvin A. Benner et al., *Airline Deregulation* (Westport, CT: Eno Foundation for Transportation, Inc., 1985), pp. 56–57.

11. *Ibid.,* p. 57.

12. The definitions of the various sizes of rural places in Table 6.1 are those contained in U.S. DOT Report No. DOT–P–10–80–18 as discussed in Chapter 1.

13. *Russell's Official National Motor Coach Guide for U.S., Canada, Mexico and Central America,* August 1986 as compared with *Russell's Guide,* June 1985.

14. *Russell's Guide,* August 1986.

15. Iowa Department of Transportation, *1985 Iowa Railroad Analysis Update* (Ames: June 1986), p. 61.

16. *Ibid.,* p. 61.

17. Mahoney, p. 47.

18. Iowa Department of Transportation, *1985 Iowa Railroad Analysis Update,* p. 61.

19. Mahoney, p. 19.

20. See Terence A. Brown, "Freight Brokers and General Commodity Trucking," *Transportation Journal,* Vol. 24 (Winter 1984): p. 4.

21. *Ibid.,* p. 13; and Michael R. Crum, "The Expanded Role of Motor Freight Brokers in the Wake of Regulatory Reform," *Transportation Journal,* Vol. 24, No. 4 (Summer 1985): p. 13.

22. Theodore E. Keeler, *Railroads, Freight, and Public Policy* (Washington, DC: The Brookings Institution, 1983), p. 74.

23. *Ibid.,* p. 143.

24. William T. Fullam, "Intermodal Movement of Bulk Commodities," *Transportation Quarterly,* Vol. 40 (January 1986): p. 90.

25. Mahoney, p. 172.

26. *Ibid.,* p. 108.

27. Fullam, p. 93.

28. Mahoney, p. 109.

29. See "ICC Denies Rulemaking on Brokers' Pricing and Payment Practices," *Traffic World,* Vol. 208 (December 8, 1986), p. 28, for additional discussion of the ICC's position on this issue.

30. Benjamin J. Allen, "Rail-Barge Coordination: An Example and Evaluation of Its Potential," *ICC Practitioners' Journal,* Vol. 50 (March-April 1983): p. 309.

31. Mahoney, p. 75.

32. *Ibid.,* p. 38.

33. *Ibid.,* p. 39.

34. *Ibid.,* p. 131.

35. William T. Coleman, "A Statement of National Transportation Policy," (Washington, DC: U.S. Government Printing Office, September 1977), p. 21.

36. See Benjamin J. Allen and Roy Dale Voorhees, "An Assessment of Rail-Barge Movements," report for the U.S. Department of Transportation under contract DTRS5683–C–00037, September 20, 1985, for a detailed discussion on importance of the transshipment facility.

37. U.S. Department of Transportation and Interstate Commerce Commission, *The Intercity Bus Terminal Study,* December 1984, p. 89.

38. *Ibid.,* p. 90.

39. *Ibid.*

References

Addus, Abdussalam A. "Essential Air Service Determination for Small Communities." *Transportation Quarterly,* Vol. 38, No. 4 (October 1984): pp. 559–74.

_____. "Subsidizing Commuter Airlines." *Transportation Quarterly,* Vol. 41, No. 2 (April 1987): pp. 161–75.

Allen, Benjamin J. "Rail-Barge Coordination: An Explanation and Evaluation of Its Potential." *ICC Practitioners' Journal,* Vol 50 (March-April 1983): pp. 286–309.

Allen, Benjamin J., and Denis A. Breen. "The Nature of Common Carrier Service Obligations." *ICC Practitioners' Journal,* Vol. 46, No. 4 (May-June 1979): pp. 526–49.

Allen, Benjamin J., and John F. Due. "Railway Abandonment: Effects Upon the Communities Served." *Growth and Change,* Vol. 8, No. 2 (April, 1977): pp. 8–14.

Allen, Benjamin J., and Roy Dale Voorhees. "An Assessment of Rail-Barge Movements." Report for the U.S. Department of Transportation, September 20, 1985.

American Trucking Associations, Inc. *American Trucking Trends—1986.* Washington, DC: American Trucking Associations, Inc., 1986.

_____. *Small Town Blues.* Washington, DC: American Trucking Associations, Inc., 1976.

Association of American Railroads. *Statistics of Regional and Small Railroads.* Washington, DC: Association of American Railroads, 1988.

Association of American Railroads. *Yearbook of Railroad Facts.* Washington, DC, Association of American Railroads, various years.

Banks, R. L., and Associates, Inc. *Economic Analysis and Regulatory Implications of Motor Common Carrier Service to Predominantly Rural Communities.* Washington, DC: U.S. Department of Transportation, June 1976.

_____. *Economic Study of Light Density Rail Line Operations.* Washington, DC: U.S. Department of Transportation, 1973.

Beilock, Richard, and James Freeman. "Deregulated Motor Carrier Service." *Transportation Journal,* Vol. 23, No. 4 (Summer 1984): pp. 71–82.

207

———. "Motor Carrier Perceptions of Intrastate Motor Carrier Regulations and Regulators." *ICC Practitioners' Journal,* Vol. 51, No. 3 (March-April 1984): pp 275–85.

Benner, Melvin A., James Oheet, and Elihu Schott. *Airline Deregulation.* Westport, CT: Eno Foundation for Transportation, Inc., 1985.

Borlaug, Karen L. "The Impact of Deregulation on Small Community Trucking Service." Paper presented at Eastern Economic Association, Philadelphia, April 1981.

———. *A One-Year Assessment of the Motor Carrier Act of 1980: Small Community Trucking Service in Nevada and Oregon.* Washington, DC: U.S. Department of Transportation, 1981.

Borlaug, Karen, et al. *A Study of Trucking Service in Six Rural Communities.* Washington, DC: U.S. Department of Transportation, November 1979.

Breen, Denis A., and Benjamin J. Allen. *Common Carrier Obligations and the Provisions of Motor Carrier Service to Small Rural Communities.* Washington, DC: Department of Transportation, 1979.

Brooks-Scanlon Co. v. *Railroad Commission,* 251 U.S. 396 (1920).

Brown, Terence A. "Freight Brokers and General Commodity Trucking." *Transportation Journal,* Vol. 24 (Winter 1984): pp. 4–14.

Charney, Alberta, Nancy Sidhu, and John F. Due. "Short Run Cost Functions for Class II Railroads." *Logistics and Transportation Review,* Vol. 13, No. 4 (1977): pp. 345–60.

Cherington, C. R. *The Regulation of Railroad Abandonments.* Cambridge, MA: Harvard University Press, 1948.

Civil Aeronautics Board. "Guidelines for Individual Determinations of Essential Air Transportation." 14 CFR Part 398, *Federal Register,* Vol. 44, No. 175 (September 7, 1979): pp. 52646–52665.

———. *Implementation of the Provisions of the Airline Deregulation Act of 1978.* Report to Congress, January 31, 1984.

Civil Aeronautics Board. Bureau of Pricing and Domestic Aviation. *List of Eligible Points.* January 1979.

Coleman, William T. "A Statement of National Transportation Policy." Washington, DC: U.S. Government Printing Office, September 1977.

Colorado and Southern Railway Abandonment, 166 ICC 470 (1930).

Conant, Michael. *Railroad Mergers and Abandonment.* Berkeley, CA: University of California Press, 1964.

Coney, Lee. "Major Transportation Legislation Was Passed by the 99th Congress." *Traffic World,* Vol. 208 (November 3, 1986): pp. 82–85.

Congressional Budget Office. *The Impact of Trucking Deregulation on Small Communities: A Review of Recent Studies.* Staff Working Paper. Washington, DC, February 1980.

Consolidated Freightways Corporation of Delaware, et al. Pooling, 109 M.C.C. 596,607 (1971).

Crum, Michael R. "The Expanded Role at Motor Freight Brokers in the Wake of Regulatory Reform." *Transportation Journal,* Vol. 24, No. 4 (Summer 1985): pp. 5–15.

Crum, Michael R., and Benjamin Allen. "U.S. Transportation Merger Policy: Evolution, Current Status, and Antitrust Considerations." *International Journal of Transport Economics,* Vol. 13 (February 1986) pp. 41–75.

Dais, Tricia Marie. "A Study of the Essential Air Service Program in the State of Iowa: Past Implications and Future Directions." Unpublished student paper prepared for the Iowa Department of Transportation, April 25, 1987.

Denver Intermountain and Summit Acquisition, 193 ICC 707 (1933).

Derthick, Martha, and Paul J. Quirk. *The Politics of Deregulation.* Washington, DC: The Brookings Institution, 1985.

Due, John F. *The Causes of Failure of Small and Regional Railroads.* Paper No. 21, Caterpillar Tractor Co. working paper series, Bureau of Economic and Business Research, University of Illinois, Champaign-Urbana, October 1987.

――――. *The Nationwide Experience with New Small Railroads Formed to Take Over Abandoned Lines, 1971–84.* Paper No. 7, Caterpillar Tractor Co. working paper series. Bureau of Economic and Business Research, University of Illinois, Champaign-Urbana, May 1984.

――――. "New Railroad Companies Formed to Take Over Abandoned or Spun Off Lines." *Transportation Journal,* Vol. 24 (Fall 1984): pp. 30–50.

――――. "State Rail Plans and Program." *Quarterly Review of Economics and Business,* Vol. 19, No. 2 (Summer 1979): pp. 109–30.

――――. "The Surprising Role of the State and Local Governments in Preserving Rail Freight Services." *State Government,* Vol. 58, No. 1 (Spring 1985): pp. 7–13.

――――. *Update as of October 1986 on New Railroads Formed to Take Over Lines Abandoned or Spun Off by Major Railroads,* paper No. 18, Caterpillar Tractor Co. working paper series, Bureau of Economic and Business Research, University of Illinois, Champaign-Urbana, November 1986.

Elimination of Certificates as the Measure of "Holding Out." Ex Parte No. MC-77 (Sub-3), January 27, 1981.

Fischer, John W. *Airlines under Deregulation at Mid-Decade: Trends and Policy Implications.* Report No. 86–67 E. Congressional Research Service, The Library of Congress, April 1986.

Fisher, Peter S., and Michael F. Sheehan. *Possibilities for Local, Public, and Cooperative Ownership of Short Line Railroads.* Iowa City: Institute of Urban and Regional Research, University of Iowa, 1980.

Francois, Francis. American Association of State Highway and Transportation Officials. Statement for Submittal to the Subcommittee on Surface Transportation, Senate Committee on Commerce, Science and Transportation Relating to Oversight of the Bus Regulatory Reform Act of 1982. November 1983, November 1984.

Fravel, Fred. "Intercity Bus Service Changes Following the Bus Regulatory Reform Act of 1982." Paper presented at the annual meeting of the Transportation Research Board. January 1985.

――――. "Returns to Scale in the U.S. Intercity Bus Industry." *Transportation Research Forum,* Vol. 19 (1978): pp. 551–60.

Fravel, Fred, Helen Tauchen, and Gorman Gilbert. *Economies of Scale in the U.S.*

Intercity Bus Industry. DOT-RC-92025. Washington, DC: Department of Transportation, July 1980.

Frey, N. Gail, Reuben H. Krolick, Leone Nidiffer, and Jay L. Tronta. "Effects of Deregulation of the California Intrastate Trucking Industry." *Transportation Journal,* Vol. 24, No. 3 (Spring 1985): pp. 4–17.

Friedlaender, Ann, and Robert Simpson. *Alternative Scenarios for Federal Transportation Policy: Freight Policy Models, Volume 1.* Washington, DC: Department of Transportation, December 1978.

Fullam, William T. "Intermodal Movement of Bulk Commodities." *Transportation Quarterly,* Vol. 40 (January 1986): pp. 89–96.

General Accounting Office. *Deregulation: Increased Competition Is Making Airlines More Efficient and Responsive to Consumers.* GAO/RCED–86–26. Washington, DC: November 6, 1985.

_____. *More Flexible Eligibility Criteria Could Enhance the Small Communities Essential Air Service Subsidy Program.* GAO/RCED–83–97. Washington, DC: May 18, 1983.

_____. *Report.* GAO/RCED–83–179. Washington, DC: 1982.

Gordon, Beryl. Statement before the Senate Committee on Commerce, Science, and Transportation Analysis, on oversight of the Motor Carrier Act of 1980, 98th Cong., 1st sess., December 15, 1983.

Graham, David R., and Daniel P. Kaplan. *Competition and the Airlines: An Evaluation of Deregulation.* Staff Report, Office of Economic Analysis, Civil Aeronautics Board, December 1982.

Greyhound Lines, Inc. "Greyhound Shuttle Service Program Manual." Dallas: Greyhound Lines, Inc., April 1988.

Greyhound System Franchise Agreement Packet. Phoenix: Greyhound Lines, Inc., 1985.

Harper, Donald. "Consequences of Reform of Federal Economic Regulation of the Motor Trucking Industry." *Transportation Journal,* Vol. 21, No. 4 (Summer 1982): pp. 35–58.

_____. *Economic Regulation of the Motor Trucking Industry by the States.* Urbana: The University of Illinois Press, 1959.

Horn, Kevin H. "Federal Preemption of State Transportation Economic Regulation: Conflict Versus Coordination." *Transportation Journal,* Vol. 23, No. 2 (Winter 1983): pp. 28–46.

Hulet, John, and Gordon P. Fisher. "An Isolation-Usage Index for Rational Allocation of Air Service to Small Communities." *Proceedings of the Annual Meeting of the Transportation Research Forum,* Vol. 13, No. 1 (1981): pp. 239–47.

"ICC Denies Rulemaking on Brokers' Pricing and Payment Practices." *Traffic World,* Vol. 208 (December 8, 1986): p. 28.

Illinois Department of Transportation. *1987 Illinois Rail Plan.* Springfield: Illinois Department of Transportation, 1987.

Intercity Bus Industry. *Office of Transportation Analysis.* Interstate Commerce Commission. January 1984.

Intercity Bus Study. Study Report, Washington, Oregon, Idaho. Washington, DC: Department of Transportation, January 1982.

International Business Services, Inc. *Intercity Bus, Rail, and Air Service for Residents of Rural Areas.* U.S. Department of Transportation, Report No. DOT–P–10–80–18, January 1980.

Interstate Commerce Commission. *Annual Reports.* Washington, DC: U.S. Government Printing Office.

_____. *Before You Start a Small Railroad-Brief Overview of Things to Consider.* Washington, DC: Interstate Commerce Commission, 1988.

_____. *Class Exemption – Acq. and Oper. of Railroad Lines under 49USG10901,* ICC2d 810 C (1986).

_____. *Colorado and Southern Railway Abandonment.* 166 ICC 470 (1930).

_____. *Denver Intermountain and Summit Acquisition.* 193 ICC 707 (1933).

_____. Ex Parte No. 274 (Sub-No. 8), *Exemption of Out Service Rail Lines,* November 21, 1986.

_____. *A Guide for Public Participation in Rail Abandonment Cases Under the Interstate Commerce Act.* Washington, DC: Interstate Commerce Commission, December 1986.

_____. *Intercity Bus Industry.* Washington, DC: Interstate Commerce Commission, January 1984.

_____. *The Intercity Bus Industry, A Preliminary Study.* Washington, DC: Interstate Commerce Commission, 1978.

_____. *Railroad Abandonment, 1920–1943.* Washington, DC: Interstate Commerce Commission, 1945.

_____. *Small Community Service Study.* Washington, DC: Interstate Commerce Commission, 1982.

Iowa Department of Transportation. *1983 Iowa Intercity Bus Plan.* Draft. Ames: February 1983.

_____. *1985 Iowa Railroad Analysis Update.* Ames: June 1986.

Iowa Office of Economic Analysis, Department of Transportation. "Results of a Shipper Survey to Determine the Effects of: 1) Federal Deregulation of Motor Carriers Providing Trucking Service to Iowa's Smaller Communities; and 2) The Availability of Designated Highway Routes for Larger Vehicles Used by Motor Carriers Serving Iowa's Smaller Communities." Ames: Iowa Department of Transportation, May 1986.

Isaacs, Randy, Greyhound, Inc., Presentation at the Annual Meeting of the Transportation Research Board, January 1988.

Ivey, Mark, and Pete Engardio. "Commuter Airlines: The Days of Flying Solo Are Over." *Business Week,* August 11, 1986, pp. 75–76.

Jenks, Craig. "Commuter Airlines Face Turbulence." *Journal of Commerce,* April 3, 1987, p. 6A.

Jones, J. Richard. "The Trade-Offs Involved in the Elimination of the Essential Air Service Subsidy." *Proceedings of the Annual Meeting of the Transportation Research Forum,* Vol. 26, No. 1 (1985): pp. 343–49.

Jones, J. Richard, and Sheila I Cocke. "Commuter Airlines Service to Non-Hub Airports." *Proceedings of the Annual Meeting of the Transportation Research Forum,* Vol. 24, No. 1 (1983): pp. 692–99.

_____. "Deregulation and Non-Hub Airports: Discriminant Analysis of Economic, Demographic and Geographic Factors." *Proceedings of the Annual*

Meeting of the Transportation Research Forum, Vol. 25, No. 1 (1984): pp. 251–57.

Keeler, Theodore E. *Railroads, Freight, and Public Policy.* Washington, DC: The Brookings Institution, 1983.

Kidder, Alice E. *Fourth Follow-up Study of Shipper/Receiver Mode Choice in Selected Rural Communities, 1984–1985.* Washington, DC: Department of Transportation, 1985.

_____. *Impact of Regulatory Reform on Shipper/Receiver Freight Service in Selected Rural Communities, 1982: A Second Follow-up Study.* Washington, DC: Department of Transportation, 1983.

_____. *Third Follow-up Study of Shipper/Receiver Mode Choice in Selected Rural Communities, 1982–1983.* Washington, DC: Department of Transportation, 1984.

Klindworth, Keith A. "Impact of the Staggers Rail Act on the Abandonment Process." Mimeo. Washington, DC: U.S. Department of Agriculture, 1984.

Levine, Harvey A. et al., *Small Railroads.* Washington, DC: Association of American Railroads, 1982.

McCaffrey, R. Lawrence, Jr., and Peter A. Gilbertson. *Starting a Short Line.* Fairfax, VA: Virginia Book Distributors, 1983.

McElhiney, Paul. *Motor Common Carrier Freight Rate Study.* Prepared for Federation of Rocky Mountain States, Inc., Denver, May 1975.

Mahoney, John H. *Intermodal Freight Transportation.* Westport, CT: Eno Foundation for Transportation, Inc., 1985.

Markel, S. A. U.S. Congress. Hearings before the House of Representatives Committee on Interstate and Foreign Commerce. 70th Cong., 1st sess. April 1928, on Regulation of Interstate Motor Buses on Public Highways, H.R. 12380.

Mayer, Jonathan D. "Local and Commuter Airlines in the United States." *Traffic Quarterly,* Vol. 31. No. 2 (April 1977): pp. 333–49.

Mergel, Joseph. *An Analysis of the Commuter Airlines Industry under Deregulation.* Staff Study, U.S. Department of Transportation, Research and Special Programs Administration, July 1984.

"Methodology for Calculating Revenues and Costs of Assuming a Short Line Operation." *Wisconsin State Rail Plan.* Madison: Wisconsin Department of Transportation, 1981.

Meyer, John R., Clinton V. Oster, Jr. et al. *Deregulation and the New Airline Entrepreneurs.* Cambridge, MA: The MIT Press, 1984.

Miller, James C., III. "Airport Woes and Trust Fund's Surpluses." *Wall Street Journal,* September 15, 1987, p. 32.

Ming, Dennis, Denver Tolliver, and Daniel Zink. "Effects of Airline Deregulation on North Dakota Fares and Service." *Proceedings of the Annual Meeting of the Transportation Research Forum,* Vol. 25, No. 1 (1984): pp. 265–74.

Molloy, James F., Jr. *The U.S. Commuter Airline Industry: Policy Alternatives.* Lexington, MA: Lexington Books, 1985.

Molloy, James F., Jr., and Ravi Sarathy. "Staying in the Race: Growth and Survival at Commuter Airlines." *Transportation Journal,* Vol. 25, No. 4 (Summer 1986): pp. 31–46.

Moore, Ralph J., Jr., and D. Eugenia Langan. "Short Line and Regional Railroad

Sales: Railway Labor Act Concerns." Paper presented at American Railroad Conference on Small and Regional Railroads, Washington, DC, October 1987.

Morgan, Ivor P. "Government and the Industry's Early Development." In *Airline Deregulation: The Early Experience,* ed. John R. Meyer and Clinton V. Oster. Boston, MA: Auburn House Publishing Company, 1981.

Morrison, Steven, and Clifford Winston. *The Economic Effects of Airline Deregulation.* Washington, DC: The Brookings Institution, 1986.

Motor Carrier Ratemaking Study Commission. *Collective Ratemaking in the Trucking Industry.* Washington, DC: Motor Carrier Ratemaking Commission, June 1, 1983.

_____. *A Report to the President and the Congress of the United States, Part II, Implementation of the Bus Regulatory Reform Act of 1982: The Impact on Older Americans and Effect on Interstate Bus Service.* Washington, DC: Motor Carrier Ratemaking Commission, May 15, 1984.

New Jersey Department of Transportation. *New Jersey State Rail Plan.* Trenton: New Jersey Department of Transportation, 1987.

Notice, *Elimination of Certificates as the Measure of "Holding Out."* Ex Parte No. MC-77 (Sub-3), March 15, 1983.

Oregon Department of Transportation. *Oregon Rail Plan, 1986 Update.* Salem: Oregon Department of Transportation, 1986.

Oster, Clinton, and Kurt Zorn. *The Impacts of Regulatory Reform on Intercity Bus Service.* Washington, DC: University Research Office of the U.S. Department of Transportation, September 1984.

Oster, Clinton V., Jr. "The Impact of Deregulation on Service to Small Communities." *Journal of Contemporary Business,* Vol. 9, No. 2 (Second Quarter 1980): pp. 103–21.

Oster, Clinton V., Jr., and Don H. Pickrell. "Marketing Alliances and Competitive Strategy in the Airline Industry." *The Logistics and Transportation Review,* Vol. 22, No. 4 (1986): pp. 371–87.

Patton, E. P., and C. L. Langley, Jr. *Handbook for Preservation of Local Railroad Service.* National Technical Information Service. Springfield, VA: 1980.

Phillips, Lawrence T. "Structural Change in the Airline Industry: Carrier Concentration at Large Hub Airports and Its Implication for Competitive Behavior." *Transportation Journal,* Vol. 25, No. 2 (Winter 1985): pp. 18–28.

Public Law No. 94–210, The Railroad Revitalization and Regulatory Reform Act of 1976.

Public Law No. 95–163, The Federal Aviation Act of 1977.

Public Law No. 95–504, The Airline Deregulation Act of 1978.

Public Law No. 96–296, The Motor Carrier Act of 1980.

Public Law No. 96–448, The Staggers Rail Act of 1980.

Public Law No. 97–261, The Bus Regulatory Reform Act of 1982.

Pustay, Michael W. "A Comparison of Pre- and Post-Reform Motor Carrier Service to Small Communities." *Growth and Change,* Vol. 16, No. 1 (January 1985): pp. 47–54.

_____. "Regulation of the Intrastate Motor Freight Industry in Ohio." *ICC Practitioners' Journal,* Vol. 50, No. 4 (May-June 1983): pp. 415–32.

Pustay, Michael W., John W. Drake, and James R. Frew. *The Impact of Federal Trucking Regulation on Service to Small Communities.* DOT-OS-70069. Washington, DC: U.S. Department of Transportation, 1979.

Rucker, George, "Section 18: The Last Three Years, Summary Data." Paper presented at the annual meeting of the Transportation Research Board. Washington, DC, January 12, 1988.

Russell's Official National Motor Coach Guide for the U.S., Canada, Mexico, and Central America. Cedar Rapids, IA: Russell's Guide, 1982, 1985, 1986.

Sabo, Martin. "UMTA Charter Regulations—A Fair Compromise." *Passenger Transport,* Vol. 45, No. 44 (November 2, 1987): p. 1.

———. "Short Line Costs in New York State." Albany: New York Department of Transportation, 1974.

Sidhu, Nancy D., Alberta Charney, and John F. Due. "Cost Functions of Class II Railroads and the Viability of Light Traffic Density Railway Lines." *Quarterly Review of Economics and Business,* Vol. 17, No. 3 (Autumn 1977): pp. 7–24.

Sinha, Dipendra. "Some Airports Likely to Lose Commuter Subsidy Pay-outs." *Journal of Commerce,* July 7, 1987, p. 5B.

———. "The Theory of Contestable Markets and U.S. Airline Deregulation: A Survey." *The Logistics and Transportation Review,* Vol. 22, No. 4 (December 1976): pp. 405–19.

Sorensen, Orlo L. "Some Impacts of Rail Regulatory Changes on Grain Industries." *American Journal of Agricultural Economics,* Vol. 66, No. 5 (December 1984): pp. 645–50.

Southard, William. Statement before the Senate Committee on Commerce, Science and Transportation on Oversight of the Motor Carrier Act of 1980, 98th Cong., 1st sess., December 15, 1983.

Stephenson, Frederick J., and Frederick J. Beier. "The Effects of Airline Deregulation on Air Service to Small Communities." *Transportation Journal,* Vol. 20, No. 4 (Summer 1981): pp. 54–62.

Taff, Charles A. *Commercial Motor Transportation.* Centerville, MD: Cornell Maritime Press, Inc., 1980.

Tauchen, Helen, Fred Fravel, and Gorman Gilbert. "Cost Structure of the Intercity Bus Industry." *Journal of Transportation Economics and Policy,* Vol. 17, No. 1 (January 17, 1983): pp. 25–48.

Thompson, W. H., R. D. Voorhees, and K. B. Boberg. "Iowa: A Baseline Laboratory of Motor Carrier Service to Small Communities." *ICC Practitioners' Journal,* Vol. 48, No. 4 (1981): pp. 431–42.

Transportation Policy Associates. *Transportation in America.* 6th ed. Washington, DC: Transportation Policy Associates, 1988.

U.S. Congress. Hearings before a Subcommittee of the Committee on Interstate and Foreign Commerce of the House of Representatives, 74th Cong., 1st sess. February 1935, on Regulation of Interstate Motor Carriers, H.R. 5262, 6016.

U.S. Congress. Hearings before the Committee on Interstate and Foreign Commerce of the House of Representatives, 70th Cong., 1st sess., April 1928, on Regulation of Interstate Motor Buses on Public Highways, H.R. 12380.

U.S. Congress. Hearings before the Committee on Interstate and Foreign Commerce of the House of Representatives, 71st Cong., January 1930, on Regulation of Interstate Motor Buses on Public Highways, H.R. 7954.

U.S. Congress. Hearings before the Subcommittee on Surface Transportation of the Committee on Commerce, Science and Transportation of the U.S. Senate, 97th Cong., 2nd sess., on H.R. 3663, Deregulation of the Intercity Bus Industry, March 8, 1982.

U.S. Congress. Senate. Committee on Commerce, Science and Transportation. *The Impact on Small Communities of Motor Carriage Regulatory Revision.* Committee Print. Washington, DC: U.S. Government Printing Office, June 1978.

U.S. Congressional Budget Office. *The Impact of Trucking Deregulation on Small Communities: A Review of Recent Studies.* February 1980.

U.S. Department of Agriculture. *An Assessment of Impacts on Agriculture of the Staggers Rail Act and Motor Carrier Act of 1980.* Washington, DC: August 1982.

_____. Effects of the Staggers Rail Act on Grain Marketing. Washington, DC: July 1984.

U.S. Department of Agriculture, Office of Transportation. *Final Report on the North Central Regional Symposium on Rural Intercity Passenger Transportation.* Des Moines, IA, December 7–9, 1987.

U.S. Department of Commerce, Bureau of the Census. *General Population Characteristics, Iowa 1980.* Washington, DC: U.S. Government Printing Office, 1982.

U.S. Department of Transportation. *Highway Statistics—1985.* Washington, DC: Department of Transportation, 1985.

_____. *Intercity Bus Service in Small Communities.* Washington, DC: Department of Transportation, 1980.

_____. *Railroad Abandonment and Alternatives.* Washington, DC: U.S. Department of Transportation, 1976.

U.S. Department of Transportation. Urban Mass Transit Administration. *An Inventory of Transportation Services in Places of Less than 10,000 Population Outside of Urbanized Areas.* Prepared by North Carolina A & T State University. Greensboro, 1978.

U.S. Department of Transportation and Interstate Commerce Commission. *The Intercity Bus Terminal Study.* December 1984.

Vellenga, David B., and Benjamin J. Allen. "Airline Deregulation and the Impact on Air Service to Selected Midwestern States." *Proceedings of the Annual Meeting of the Transportation Research Forum,* Vol. 21, No. 1 (1980): pp. 136–146.

Vellenga, David B., and Daniel R. Vellenga. "Essential Airline Service Since Deregulation: Selected States in the Northwestern and Southwestern U.S." *The Logistics and Transportation Review,* Vol. 22, No. 4 (1986): pp. 339–70.

Warren, William D. "Changing Air Transportation Services for Smaller Metropolitan Regions: 1980–1982." *Transportation Quarterly,* Vol. 38, No. 2 (April 1984): pp. 245–66.

Washington State Department of Transportation. *Impacts of Trucks and Railroad Deregulation on Transportation Operations and Economic Activity in the State of Washington.* Olympia: Washington State Department of Transportation, 1982.

Watson, Ripley. "Greyhound Lines Steering New Path to Profit." *Des Moines Register,* April 12, 1985, p. A-3.

Wilbern, J. R., and Associates. *Tennessee Intercity Bus Study.* Vol. 1. Tennessee Department of Transportation, January 1981.

Williams, Martin, and Carol Hall. "Returns to Scale in the United States Intercity Bus Industry." *Regional Science and Urban Economics,* Vol. 11, No. 4 (1981): pp. 573–84.

Williamson, Kenneth C., David J. Bloomberg, and Roger A. Peterson. "Commuter Air Carriers and Federal Equipment Loan Guarantees." *The Logistics and Transportation Review,* Vol. 22, No. 3 (1986): pp. 241–58.

Williamson, Kenneth C., Lawrence F. Cunningham, and Marc G. Singer. "Scheduled Passenger Air Service to Small Communities: A Role for State and Local Governments." *Transportation Journal,* Vol. 21, No. 4 (Summer 1982): pp. 25–34.

Wisconsin Office of the Commissioner of Transportation. *Deregulation of Wisconsin Motor Carriers,* 1983.

Index